# LEADERSHIP LESSONS

## ESSAYS ON HOW TO IMPROVE ORGANISATIONAL PERFORMANCE

JAMES B RIELEY

2

Seraphina
BOOKS

# Introduction

*According to the Oxford dictionary, an essay "is a short piece of non-fiction about a particular topic." The essays in this book are an accumulation of various projects that I have been involved in for more than a dozen years. The term "projects" spans quite a range of subject matter, and purposes for their existance. The reality is that the central focus of all these essays are improving the ability to understand the dynamics at play that are impacting their organisations. The purpose is to help organisations and the people within them to be able to realise their indifividual and collectve potential.*

*Essays are often associated with writing assignments in school. School is where I first came in contact with essays, and upon reflection, I was pretty rubbish at writing them at the time. In most cases, admittedly, the struggles with writing assignment essays was clearly due to a lack of reading the assigned text that was supposed to be the basis for the essay, so no big surprise that I didn't like them. Years later, I discovered that essays are a good way to deal with fundamental issues and challenges facing organisations.*

*Often business-type books require that a reader slogs all the way through until a light-bulb might possibly go on. By writing this book as a series of essays (each barely two pages long), with some luck, readers will be able to read in almost "bite-size" increments, with each essay standing on its own. This makes Leadership Lessons perfect for travel or breaks between meetings.*

*The essays contained in the subsequent pages are printed in more-or-less chronilogically in the order that they were written in, with many of the essays being titled in the form of a question. The reason for the title being in the form of a question is that whilst most any manager in an organisation will be (or should be) looking for answers, it now 2019 and it should be clear that if you don't learn to ask better questions, you will never get the answers you really need.*

*One last point worth mentioning. Years ago, whilst writing a weekly column for the Daily Telegraph, an ex-client sent me a threatening message. The basic drift of the message was that the client thought I was slandering them by alluding to their senior management as contributing to the mess their company was in. My response was that the story wasn't even about their company, and if their senior management was so concerned that the management's decision-making could look less than great to the outside world, perhaps they should put effort into improving it instead of writing threatening emails. Learning lessons is an opportunity for all of us to get better at doing whatever we do. If you think any of the stories contained in these essays "resemble" demonstrated behaviours at your organisation, you might want to do something about it, or work on your CV.*

*James B Rieley*
*Summer, 2019*

# The Lessons

7

# LEADERSHIP LESSONS

## ESSAYS ON HOW TO IMPROVE ORGANISATIONAL PERFORMANCE

JAMES B RIELEY

# Really? More of the Same?

A few weeks ago, after meeting with senior managers at a well-known UK company, I asked several employees about the company. Let me make it clear that the people I asked were front-line employees – they were not the same senior managers that I had come to have a conversation with. And not only were their job positions different, their perceptions of the company were different. Seriously different.

These were some of the comments;
- *'It was a good company in its heyday;'*
- *'It used to be a good company;'*
- *'There is so much acrimony at the staff level;' and,*
- *'It could be good but we aren't told anymore why we are supposed to do the things they tell us to do.'*

These messages were clearly different than those provided by the senior managers. So why was there so much of a disconnect in perceptions?

Too often, there are differences in perceptions of a current reality between what the line employees see and what senior management sees. This can be for a variety of reasons, but the reality is that if the front-line has a different perception of the company than the people at the top, it is not surprising that companies today are delivering the performance that we have seen lately. And this performance gap will not go away by itself. Nor will it go away by just wishing and hoping that it will.

Businesses today (most specifically, the senior management teams of businesses) need to become more aware of the connection between the perceptions of line-workers and performance results. It should not be surprising to figure out that if line-workers are not motivated or don't feel comfortable with a company, productivity will decrease and both the top and bottom lines will be impacted negatively. High performance is being promised to customers every day, but is not achievable in an environment of mistrust or discontent.

Whilst some managers may say that their biggest challenges are availability of capital budgets, product innovation, competition, and regulatory issues, the reality is that if employees have a less-than enthusiastic view of the company, there is little chance that they will deliver the performance that the company needs – regardless of budgets or innovative capability or regulatory environments.

Senior managers need to think and act differently. They need to understand the connection between cause and effect. When an employee says, *'there is too much acrimony at the staff level,'* or *'it could be good but we aren't told anymore why we are supposed to do the things they tell us to do,'* there is something going on that is not good. And that something stems from the belief that senior management is disconnected from what really goes on in the company. It is this 'disconnection' that breeds the belief that the decisions being made by senior management are pretty far removed from the reality of a situation or an environment.

Of course, senior management has access to more and different information than the front line has. That is the way it should be, however, senior management needs to be more open about *why* they are asking employees to do what they do and how it will help the company to thrive and grow over time. Senior management needs to do a better job of connecting declared initiatives to the day-to-day work life of employees. Employees will never become motivated or committed to help the company realise its vision for the future if they don't see how that will impact their day-to-day work activities.

If employees aren't able to really connect to, and become committed to the decisions of senior management, the result will be about the same as we have often seen in the past. And mediocre performance is just not an acceptable option.

Interestingly enough, I sent a note to the senior manager that I had gone to see and thanked him for his time, and then mentioned that I had met some of his employees outside their offices and they told me a completely different story than he had told me. He did write back, but he didn't mention anything about working harder to share the company's vision, or to do a better job building alignment and employee satisfaction. All he said was that he wanted me to tell him the names of the people I had spoken to so "We can deal with these people."

# Are You on the Peter the Great?

A dozen years ago I heard a story on the BBC that said that the Peter the Great, a largest nuclear warship of the Russian navy was being immediately recalled to Murmansk for urgent repairs. The reason was that several days earlier, naval inspectors had been on-board and discovered that *'where the Admirals walked and lived, everything was in good condition, but where they didn't go, the ship was in dire condition and there was a great risk that the problems could destroy the ship itself. And the Admirals were not aware of the problems.'* So is this a metaphor for some of what has been happening in business or what?

Think about what the story that was reported says – not just the words on the surface, but what is behind those words. *'Where the Admirals walked and lived, everything was good.'* Well naturally, the Admirals are the 'senior management' of the organisation, and we know that things are usually nice for them. But according to the inspector's report, where the Admiral's didn't go, *'the ship was in dire condition...and the Admirals were not aware of the problems.'*

So think about some of the organisations you know about. Does the senior management team *really know* what is going on in the company? Are they really in-tune with what it is like to do the real work of the company? Are they aware of the culture of the company and its impact on the company's ability to deliver high performance? Or have they been kept in the dark for some reason?

In most cases, they don't know, but not because they don't want to know. They don't know because so many people are afraid to deliver 'bad news' to senior managers.

First, let's take a look at the whole subject of what bad news even is. I have always thought that there are only two types of news – good news and bad news. Good news is what it says it is – information about success, information about performance increases, information about increasing market share increases, etc. Of course, this is all good news. And it should be. Bad news is usually thought of as the opposite. But the reality is that the only 'bad news' is *not knowing what is going on.* Not knowing is horrendous news, because if you don't know, there is no way you can do something about a problem until it is too late.

So if you accept my definitions of good and bad news, then a worthwhile question to explore might be why are we hesitant to talk about news that is less than exciting? And why do some of us think that *not telling the bosses* will be better than letting them know what is really going on?

Think of what happens when you 'don't know' and then get the 'big surprise?' First, a lot of yelling and screaming goes on – which is not really helpful, nor does it create the environment in which someone would even want to bring you less than good news. Second, reactive thinking tends to kick in – you know, the 'something has to be done right now' thinking. Whilst reactive thinking may seem to be better than no thinking at all, it does tend to just deal with the symptoms of the problems, and not the problems themselves. And third, the really big one in the list of 'what happens when you finally find out,' is that quite often, as we have seen in the media, there is an effort put forth to somehow disguise the bad news so it doesn't look so bad. As if that will change anything. These behaviours only reinforce the belief that 'bad news' is bad and should not be brought to the attention of your superiors. And that my friends, that is a recipe for disaster.

There is a solution, and it is that business leaders need to make it perfectly clear that they would rather know what is *really* going on, than *not know* what is really going on.

Make part of meeting agendas a forum to discuss what is really going on in your company. Get out of the office and see what is really going on. Sit with your employees at coffee breaks and ask them how things are going, ask them what they know that you don't know. Usually, it is the front line employees who are the ones who 'really know,' and in most cases, they will take the opportunity to tell you. But you will have to ask, and to do that; you have to talk with them.

Don't just rely on the information from your direct reports; after all, they are probably the ones who have the greatest fear of telling you what is really going on. But also realise; if your direct reports do have a level of fear of giving you 'bad news,' it is probably because you have created an environment in which that fear has become real. Tell them that you *want to know* 'all' the news, regardless if they think it is good or bad.

If our organisations are to become more effective in consistently delivering high performance, managers need to improve the way in which they make decisions. And to do that, they need to have feedback on their previous decisions, and sometimes, this might mean that they get feedback that is not especially good. The alternative is to make decisions in some fairyland environment in which we think that everything is good. Well, get over it. Knowing both the 'good and the bad' news is better than not knowing. Unless you want a job as one of the Admirals on the Peter the Great ... assuming it makes it back to Murmansk.

## Why Are We So Addicted to Fire-Fighting?

The answer to this question is easy - we are addicted to fire fighting because we like it, we think it can show how good we are at solving problems, and we think that it will help us get ahead in our company. Think about this - who are the people in your company that usually are recognised when it comes time for promotions or bonuses?

In most companies, they are the ones who have demonstrated good skills, including solving problems. Okay, so on the surface that is great. These people love being recognised for their ability to 'fight organisational fires.' But there is something going on here that is not great. Many of the problem solvers in organisations today are people who solve the same problems over and over again, year after year. So if that is the case, are they really 'solving' problems, or only dealing with the symptoms of the problems?

Dealing with the symptoms of problems is different than coming up with fundamental solutions to those problems. Where we get stuck is that we confuse the symptoms with the actual problems. Here are several examples.

In higher education, one of the 'problems' that is faced by almost every college or university is how to avoid all the ups and downs of enrolments. Too often, what is perceived to be the actual problem is non-predictable enrolment rates. This is, however, simply a symptom of the real problem, which is an inability of the institution to consistently understand and meet the needs of students for quality education.

In a manufacturing environment, a perceived ongoing problem is how to produce quality parts and/or products. This is, however, just a symptom of the problem of how to ensure that workers have the appropriate supplies, equipment and motivation to produce quality parts and products. In service organisations a perceived problem is how to keep the pipeline of future business full; but the underlying problem is how to ensure that current and potential customers believe that the company is the right one to do business with.

In all these examples, there is a common theme between the symptoms of the problems and the real problems themselves. The common theme is how decisions are made in organisations. Decisions quite often are not made based on facts, but on beliefs and assumptions that are sometimes not the most accurate. And in today's business climate, the decisions are made in a highly pressurised environment where 'results' are expected quickly. With this type of environment, it should be no surprise that the prevailing way to deal with problems is to throw a 'quick-fix' solution at them.

Quick fixes rarely work over time. It is true that they give the impression of working – after all, the problem does appear to go away, but then comes back again, often with a vengeance. And this is why organisations have people who fight the same fires year after year. Bizarrely, we then reward them for their efforts. Through rewarding them, we send the signal that this behaviour is good, so they become addicted to it, and the addiction becomes a vicious cycle.

Ask your managers how much time they spend on 'problem solving;' and then ask them if the problems they are 'solving' are new or have they seen them before. And if the answer is 'have seen it before,' it is an indication that the cycle of 'quick-fix' thinking will go on and on and on.

There is a way to break this cycle. The first step is to recognise how managers are spending their time, and to be open about the fact that fighting the same fires year on year is not conducive for delivering sustainable performance gains.

Take a look at what the problems that are being attacked are; find out if that same problem has occurred before, and if so, how often. The trick here is to not delude yourself into thinking that just because the problem is 'new' this year, it is a new problem. If the problem has been dealt with in the past and it comes back, you undoubtedly were fighting a symptom and not the problem at all. Help your managers (and other organisational 'fire-fighters') learn how to distinguish the difference between symptoms and underlying problems, and then help them learn how to resolve the problems once and for all.

The second step is to ensure that your 'fire-fighters' have the right skills to put the fires out, and keep them out. In many organisations, one element of training in problem solving that is usually missed is understanding the relationship between cause and effect; i.e. thinking systemically. This is more than just being able to determine the root cause of a problem. Thinking systemically digs deeper and helps identify some of the unintended consequences of the problems, and the solutions. If you don't get to that level, your 'fix' will probably evaporate and the real problem will resurface.

The next step is to stop rewarding quick-fix solutions and instead, reward fundamentally sustainable solutions. By doing this, you will send the signal that 'fire-fighting' is not a behaviour that will be good for the company over time.

There is no doubt that when faced with an organisational 'fire,' it must be put out. But I think that putting it out means it shouldn't come back again.

## Why Can Collaborative Efforts Become Adversarial?

Improving performance is all about changing behaviours. Period. So, having said that, I suppose it is only fair to now get into why changing behaviours can be so difficult. For one thing, too often, we don't even see anything wrong with our behaviours. Take the question of 'why can collaborative efforts become adversarial?'

This is a good question, and as with most good questions, there is a short answer and a long answer to it. To better understand the answers, it might be easier to look a bit closer at the question to understand what it really means.

Collaborative efforts are the result of business (and non-business) environments in which there is more than one business unit and the business units are supposed to work together to get a better result. This is the whole 'synergy thing' in action; combined effective efforts bring higher gains in performance.

So here is how collaborative efforts are supposed to work. You have an organisation that has, on the surface, one or two really big goals that all business units are charged with supporting. The goals are developed as part of an overall strategy, and with the high level goals usually comes departmental goals and departmental budgets to achieve them with. When each department (or division or business unit) achieves its goals, these achievements all add together to support the achievement of the overall company goal. That is how it is supposed to work, and in most cases, it does.

But in some organisations, what actually occurs is that as each individual department puts forth their efforts to achieve its goals, they quite often end up doing activities that can be counterproductive to the efforts of other departments who are just trying to achieve their goals. When this occurs, whilst one department may achieve the gains it seeks, other departments may not be able to do the same. And the effect of this begins to ripple through the overall organisation and can be especially devastating in recently merged companies.

One of the most often seen reactions to this is a drive for additional budget funding, either to acquire additional assets, equipment, or human resources. But all that does is potentially shift the achievements from one department to another, and this sets up a dynamic known as escalation – *you* have more assets than I do, enabling you to do more, so *I* want more assets so I can do more, and then *you* want more, etc. And the end result is a shift from collaborative efforts to ones that are adversarial in nature. It all falls into a competition about who can *look the best*, not how can collaborative efforts can provide leverage so the overall goals can be reached – a win-win situation for you as a manager, for the company, and for your customers.

Intended collaborative efforts that become adversarial can be devastating to companies. They drain resources, they waste time, they sap morale, and they result in a decline in motivation – all contributing to a reduction in performance. Collaborative efforts that do work well drive innovation, creativity, production, and improve motivation and organisational climate; all improving overall the potential for increased performance.

In order to avoid intended collaborative efforts from becoming adversarial, it is important to first recognise that it can and does happen. When goals and budgets are deployed, conversations should accompany them to identify the potential risk for internal adversarial activities, along with ways to identify them *before* they occur and ways to avoid them from happening.

Additionally, it is important to make sure that the goals and accompanying budgets do not *cause* the relationship to become adversarial. This is very important to recognise – quite often, one of the unintended consequences of goal deployment is that the explicit instructions and the implicit meanings can actually *drive* adversarial thinking.

Avoiding this can be done by 'testing' the impact of the goals and budgets prior to their deployment to the various departments. Testing the impact of goals and budgets can and should be done by listening to the people who will be charged with achieving the goals with the budgets they will get. Ask them to confirm that they will be able to 'make it all happen' and if they say yes, then ask them what else might happen as they do it. *'What else might happen'* is a question about potential unintended consequences, and is something that they should be thinking about. If they respond that, 'well, there might be a problem...' then it is time to have a different type of conversation.

This is not to say that simply because attaining goals will be hard work that managers should be cut some slack, but I am saying that the last thing you want to have occur is to set someone up for failure that will shift their thinking into an adversarial mode. This will not help the goals be achieved and additionally, will not help build alignment in collective thinking around success.

Do these conversations take extra effort? Well of course they do, but the real question is, 'do you want to have the goals achieved or not?' If your answer is 'yes,' then you need to do what you can to avoid the potential of adversarial thinking.

Unless you work for an organisation where you can have all the resources you need, anytime you need them, then you will be running the risk that someone else will be after the same pot of money you are after to get their job done. Don't let your team's effort to get the job done become adversarial – this will not help you as a manager; it will not help the company; and it will not help your customers.

# What is the Unintended Cost of Cost-Cutting?

So I can't tell you how often I have heard this situation... a company is in what they perceive to be deep trouble. Their costs are running amuck, their revenues are not what they want them to be, and their profits just aren't hitting the targets they need. So they make decisions to cut costs. This makes all the sense in the world to me. To a point.

First, I do want to clarify something. When a company is haemorrhaging money, it is not a *perceived* problem. It is a serious problem and clearly something has to be done to stop the haemorrhaging. And in most cases, this means cut costs. This applies to any organisation because the logic behind it is quite simple - a company cannot spend more than it brings in for very long before they go out of business. Where I see the problem is the way that the cost-cutting decisions are often made.

The easiest way to cut costs is to reduce your fixed expenses, and in most companies, these fixed costs are employees. Payroll costs, health and other benefit costs, pensions and retirement costs. In most companies, these costs are massive and the savings that they can provide can be tremendously beneficial to improving the bottom line. But although axing jobs reduces costs, something else is lost.

The usual target population of cost cutting through job reduction is the employees who have been there the longest. This too is logical – the employees who have been in a company the longest usually make the most money, and sending them away can save the most, and the exercise does seem to be about saving money. But there is something else that is going on here. Employees who have been in a company the longest are the ones with the most experience aren't they? Aren't they the ones who have usually 'seen it all, tried it all, and know what really works and doesn't work' in the company? And when they are sent away, that experience goes along with them.

Most business leaders would tell you that one of the best assets that they have is employee's experience. This asset unfortunately does not appear in financial statements, nor does it appear in asset valuations. But the reality is that 'experience' is a much sought after asset. And longevity in a job can provide that experience. Experience over time can create wisdom – wisdom quite often can make the difference between making a decision that results in positive outcomes and one that results in disaster.

Experience on the job creates organisational memory, and organisational memory can be extremely powerful in avoiding wasting resources due to trying to 'reinvent the wheel' and forgetting some of the lessons learned that all companies could use to become more effective. And when employees with seniority are dismissed to reduce costs that wisdom, organisational memory, and the lessons learned could disappear with them.
So this can leave a company caught between a rock and a hard place – how to reduce costs through axing jobs of expensive employees whilst at the same time avoiding the potential unintended consequences of that action. As with all business decisions, there is a trade off here. And it is a trade off that needs to be measured carefully before any decision is taken.

Quite often, when faced with excessive spending – either real or perceived – management does work to protect jobs until all other cost-cutting options have been used. But there are other options that should be investigated as well as just the costs that appear on a financial statement.

Most companies suffer from wild variations in processes, and the cost of these variations can be horrendous. Unfortunately, these variations are 'below the waterline' of the expenditure iceberg, and consequently are difficult to see. And to make things even more complicated, the variations in how things are done are quite often the result of previous business decisions about policies and procedures. Reducing the costs associated with variation in processes can yield great savings, but requires that management makes a commitment to route them out, and this requires that they become open to revisiting many of their decisions from the past. And that may not be as easy as just hacking away at jobs.

There is no doubt that when a business is haemorrhaging financially, something must be done to stop the bleeding. But without being open to exploring all avenues of cost reduction before looking at job cutting, management may be setting itself up for bigger problems further down the road.

# Why Is It So Difficult to Get to the Finish Line?

Several years ago, I had been asked to sit in on the senior management meeting of an organisation that makes automobiles. Not your typical automobiles – their entire annual production is three cars. This company manufactures and races grand prix racers, and whilst they have done well in the past, they were suffering – and the reason was the same reason that most manufacturing companies suffer.

When the meeting began, the managing director gave an overview of where the company was this year, and his message was not too soothing. Lots of despair; lots of finger pointing; lots of recriminations; lots of silence in the room. I couldn't resist the opportunity, so I asked the MD exactly what the problem was. His response was typical – *'the problem is that we are not winning this year.'* Well, I knew that they weren't winning, but I also knew that not winning was a *symptom* of the real problem, and not the problem itself. *'Yes, I know you are not winning, but what is the underlying problem,'* I asked again. *'The problem is that we don't have the number of people or the financial resources of the winning teams,'* I was told.

Okay, so now were getting someplace, but something didn't add up. Several years previously, the company had done considerably better so I decided to push a bit for clarification. *'So several years ago, when you had a better season, was that when you had more people and more resources?'* The room full of highly paid senior managers became even more quiet, largely because everyone there knew that when they had a better season several years before, they had even less people and less financial resources than they did now. Clearly, something else was wrong. And it wasn't until after the meeting that things began to become clear.

The managers in the meeting represented all the main functions of a company that makes and races grand prix cars – human resources, finance, design, engine, aerodynamics, chassis, drive train, etc. When the 'formal' meeting was over, 'real meetings' began. The concept of the 'meeting after the meeting' is very typical on management teams. Issues are talked about at the 'formal' meeting, but some of the biggest decisions are made at the 'meeting after the meeting,' usually conducted with either massive lobbying or lack of dissenting viewpoints. Isn't decision-making fun?

At one of these 'meetings after the meeting,' two interesting things surfaced. The first was that the meeting that just had occurred was one of three that had taken place in the previous year with all senior managers present – each senior manager represented an integral part of the company. The second thing was that in the previous three months, the engine guys had been able to deliver 20 more horsepower for their efforts. Now in the case of grand-prix cars, an extra 20 horsepower can make a major difference, so that was good news I thought. And even more good news came from the aerodynamic guys – they, in the past months, had been able to make the car a percentage 'more slippery.' Okay, so lets figure this out...the engine has more horsepower and the aerodynamics are improved; but the overall performance didn't improve. And the reason the performance didn't improve was that the car actually went slower. Slow is not good for a grand-prix car. I couldn't resist and asked how this could possibly be, but the answer was pretty obvious. The engine guys and the aerodynamic guys were located in different parts of the facility grounds and didn't talk to each other. I don't mean didn't talk to each other daily; I mean they only talked to each other at these senior management meetings, and by now, it was clear that they didn't happen too often. No wonder that they team was delivering crap performance – the communications internally just wasn't happening.

Here you had a complex organisation, producing a complex 'product,' and all the various departments were working their tails off to do the right thing. And because they didn't talk to each other, the fruits of their efforts were not necessarily helpful overall. What had happened was that, whilst the engine guys were desperately trying to squeeze more power out of their engine, the additional power they derived resulted in required changes in other parts of the vehicle. And at the same time, the aerodynamic guys were doing the same thing – working their tails off to make the car more slippery at speed, which they did. But the combination of the additional horsepower and the improved aerodynamics didn't 'work' together. And the car went slower. And they didn't win.

What was happening in this example is not unique. Companies from all sectors suffer from the same malady – an inability (or unwillingness) to communicate effectively in order to ensure that departmental efforts do not become counter-productive, or even worse, adversarial. All of this can happen quite innocently. In the office of the CEO or MD or whoever is the most senior person in your organisation, the company goals are usually quite clear. But as the goals are deployed downward, they tend to become 'segmented' – each unit of the business is supposed to improve what they do, with the intent being the overall product or service is better. Keeping close contact with individual improvement efforts is key to avoiding the problems that this company was having – extra horsepower is great, but if it causes other design challenges that no one knows about, it is pretty hard to see how the extra power will help.

Your company may not make grand prix cars, but the same dynamics apply - if there is little or no communications between the organisation's various functions and departments, improvements (which is what the functions are supposed to continually deliver) may not deliver their promise. And then the company and its management can't deliver its promise to shareholders either. And then there is no way you will ever get to the finish line.


## What is Wrong with This Picture?

On a recent flight to London, I found myself reading one of those airline magazines, and in it, I found an advert for Michael Porter - the Harvard professor who has done well selling books on strategy. The advert was designed to almost make Porter look like a Clark Kent just before he transformed himself into Superman. And cartoon-like speech bubble that is coming out of Porter's mouth said, 'when operational effectiveness is no longer enough, you need to make time for strategy.' Cute, but it made me think; 'is he implying that if you aren't effective, having a strategy will make any difference?'


Clearly, every organisation needs to have an idea of where it is going, and how it is going to get there. That is what strategy is all about. But a strategy without being effective about making it happen is like having a roadmap to your favourite holiday spot, without a car to take you there. And equally clearly, Porter makes his money by getting people to buy into his views on strategy, so this is the direction that his adverts would go. But the fact that managers will most probably flock to his one-day seminar to listen to those views sends a message that many managers today are still locked into the 'flavour of the month' reactive thinking.

I tend to think that Porter's strategy views are good, but what concerns me is that at some point, managers are going to have to come to grips with the realisation that what is really needed today is something that seems to have been lost along the way in business. What has been lost is the ability to test all decisions against one criterion – is this decision common sense? Not a difficult test, but for some reason, we seem to have lost sight of it.

Here are some examples of the implications of common sense in decision-making.

- Does your organisation have a clear vision of where it is going? If not, how do you expect that managers and employees will how to help you get there?
- Does anyone in your organisation measure the company culture and climate? If you don't know how managers and employees feel about the way the company is run, how can you expect that they will be as committed as they need to be to achieve the vision?
- Is there an explicit strategy of how to achieve the vision? If your managers and employees can't see what needs to be done, how can anyone expect them to contribute to success?
- Does your strategy address how to deal with the level of variation in processes and systems within the organisation? If not, the ability to even be effective will be severely diminished. Excessive variation is a plague in businesses.
- Do your managers keep pressing for efficiency, or do they work to become more effective? Efficiency is wonderful, but at the end of the day, nothing can equal being effective. If your organisation (and its managers) is effective, they will make better decisions; and efficiency will happen without extra effort.
- Is there a serious commitment to on-going learning in the organisation? If training is cut because things get tight – which they always do at times – then your ability to innovate and stay competitive will be lost. The speed and effectiveness with which an organisation learns is a key differentiator in today's business world.
- Are your employees committed to organisational goals and initiatives, or are they just compliant? High levels of compliance are great, but if managers and employees are simply compliant, it will mean that you need to keep them under control. If they are committed, the biggest thing you need to do is just stay out of their way as they keep achieving and surpassing goals.

- Do your company's managers spend excessive time fighting long-standing problems? If they do, you are wasting resources, time, energy, and negatively impacting the belief in the company (and with shareholders) that the management team is right team to manage.
- Is the strategy focused on just hitting the numbers, or focused on ensuring that the organisation (and its people) can realise its potential? Any half-competent set of managers can hit the numbers; but it takes solid leadership to enable the company to realise its potential. And being able to focus a company on realising potential is the only path to a sustainable organisation over time.

There is no doubt that any organisation needs to have a roadmap to follow. But it is also clear that without using common sense as the ultimate 'test' for any decision, the chances that you will get to where you want to go are slim to none.


## What Can We Do About Our Baggage?

Ever think about what happens when the company decides to sack someone because they are just not getting the job done, and then they bring in someone else to do it? On the surface, a decision like this makes sense – if the job is not getting done, get someone else to do it – but with it comes a risk.

Each of us comes to a new job with baggage; the ways of doing things that we learned in a previous job, mental models about how a job should be done, and multiple tools that we have learned over time to get the job done. All this baggage can be good for a new employer, after all, it could bring in the veritable 'breath of fresh air' to a company. But quite often, the 'new ways,' new mental models, and new tools can create a different set of problems for the employer.

Here are an example: I know of someone who was hired as a very senior manager by a long-standing service company with the charge being to 'shake things up' as well as 'get the job done.' He had been hired to replace someone who had grown up with the company, but for some reason, 'had lost the plot' according to the CEO. So the new guy was hired and although welcomed by the entire management team and the employees he met with, he quickly began to run afoul with the CEO. In his effort to introduce new ways of getting things done, he ran up against 'the company way' of doing things. The 'company way' is a cultural thing, and is present in many companies today. The new guy had had the audacity to suggest that 'there might be an easier way' to get from point A to point B, and his easier way (which was easier I might add), if used, would cause employees to question if 'the company way' was in fact, the best way. And this was complicated by the fact that 'the company way' had been designed by the CEO when he started the company years before. The new guy lasted about three years before becoming so disenchanted that he left.

Dealing with our 'baggage' and being able to deliver upon the promise of getting things done is a major challenge that most organisations face today. And as with most challenges, this one is in reality an opportunity.

The opportunity lies in how performance appraisals are used. There are three ways to look at performance – through the organisational hierarchy lens, through the organisational value-chain lens, and through an additional lens he calls 'effectiveness areas.' The hierarchy lens looks at the actual performance of achievement, based on the employees level within a company; the value-chain lens looks at achievements based on how they contribute to the success of the company. Both of these lenses are relatively common in business, but the effectiveness area lens is different. Effectiveness areas are a combination of 'what managers are good at, what needs to be done, and what managers like to do.' By incorporating an effectiveness area lens in a performance appraisal, the employer has a better chance of getting what it wants (and needs), and the manager has a better chance of being able to successfully utilise the competencies, skills, and tools (the baggage) that he or she brings to the job.

The baggage we bring to a new job is not good or bad, it is just baggage. It is a compilation of what we have learned over time, and if it can be incorporated into the expectations of a new employer, the chances that our baggage will not become to heavy to carry will be greatly improved.

# Drinking the Kool-Aid?

Years ago, there was a group of people in Guyana who, blindly following the instructions of their leader, consumed a concoction of a liquid, and all perished. Now this might seem like a stretch for a business metaphor, but a fair question is, how often are we prepared to blindly follow? The reality is, too often.

I have been working with a senior management team. The group, comprised of members from Europe, America, and the Far East, are all pretty smart guys. Actually, very smart. And whilst in a non-formal meeting environment, they proffer their views on just about anything relating to their business, once they are in a structured meeting, they tend to lose this sense of bravado.

At a recent meeting of the group, an interesting thing occurred. One of the team actually pushed back at the CEO on an initiative. Whilst I wouldn't have given him too many points for his style, he did get high marks just for pushing back.

The ability, and more importantly, willingness to push back is critical in business today. You read the papers; how often have we read about an organisation that woke up one morning mired in the most ridiculous situation. And quite often the reason is that no one bothered to express concerns about what was going on; what direction the company was going; or how they were going to make investments in the future. And when that happens, it is too late for anything other than fixing blame. The reality should be that anyone who was aware of a relatively 'stupid move' on the part of management and doesn't speak up *is* guilty.

I am not advocating that everyone needs to feel like a whistle-blower. Not at all. But I am advocating that if, when in a meeting, you hear something that doesn't make sense, you need to stand up and say, 'hey, this doesn't make sense.' One of several things might happen.

First, the person you say this to might become extremely defensive. Okay, so they are defensive. Then let them explain it more clearly so there is the chance that it *will* make sense. And if it still seems like a daft idea, just maybe it is. And if you decide to go along with an idea that is daft, then you deserve to be held partially responsible for the outcomes.

The person might yell at you for sounding like an obstructionist, or even worse, might accuse you of not being a 'company guy.' Does going along blindly with anything that is said make you a 'company guy?' Or does having the best interests in the company make you a company guy?' I tend to think the latter is far better. In our lives, we have seen many examples of people who just 'went along' with blatantly disastrous ideas (think Enron; think Global Crossing and more).

Remember the story I was mentioning earlier? Well, during the meeting, the CEO and the VP went back and forth for several minutes, with neither of them being won over. It was agreed to revisit the concern at the next meeting. After the meeting was over, I was talking to the CEO about the incident and he said that he sure wasn't too thrilled to have had that happen during the meeting. But – and this is very important – his level of respect for the VP 'increased dramatically, because he wasn't afraid to push back.' And it caused the CEO to wonder why no one else had ever pushed back in the past. Surely, some of his ideas weren't Nobel Prize quality, but no one ever would push back. 'Why do you suppose that is?' he asked me.

Pushing back, especially to a CEO can appear to be a career-limiting action. But if it is done appropriately the risks can be mitigated - 'Do we know what the unintended consequences of this might be?' or 'Can you provide us with the rationale for this?' or 'Isn't there another way to accomplish the same end?' By not pushing back when things don't seem right, we may seem like team-players, but we risk our companies doing something that could negatively impact supplier and customer relations; lose money; losing credibility; and eventually, going out of business. The objective of pushing back is to make sure that clear thinking is behind initiatives, not blind obedience.

Pushing back appropriately may involve taking a risk; not pushing back almost guarantees the escalation of risk. Like the CEO said, he may not agree with what was said, but he respected the VP for taking the risk. You decide which one is best one to take.


## Why Do We Allow Gaming the System to Continue?

Several years ago, I met some managers in a federal agency of the United States government. They had been charged with reducing the overall costs of purchasing some weapons systems, and to make sure that they did this, they had been offered a set of incentives – get the vendors to reduce the costs to the government, and you, as a purchasing manager, would get a monetary bonus. Not a bad deal. Except for the fact that the vendors wanted no part in reducing their very nice revenue streams. After two years of this activity, an audit showed that a considerable amount of bonus money had been paid out, but the overall cost of the weapons had actually increased. So what do you think was going on here?

The answer was simple. The purchasing people had figured out how to 'game the system.' And what was even more amazing, they were quite open about it. Here is a synopsis of what they had figured out. According to one of the senior procurement people, when they were told that they would be expected to convince the vendors they dealt with to lower their prices – something vendors don't like to do – they approached the challenge in a different way. They asked their vendors to work with them and together they came up with a way to 'shift' some of the costs away from the direct purchase price to another category of expenses, in this case, they went for long-term maintenance contracts. The end result was the overall cost of 'purchasing' the systems went down, but the overall costs actually increased. But the metric by which the procurement people would be measured was 'purchase price,' so, as they had done this, they received their bonuses.

Here is another example of how gaming the system circumvents the intent of managements drive to reduce costs. A mid-sized global company was being hit with massive costs due to its employees flying around Europe and America in business class. The head of finance decided to require that everyone should fly economy as a cost-reduction initiative, and sent the word out in the form of a policy decision – from that day forward, flights that were internal in Europe or America would be only authorised if they were based on the lowest possible airfare. It really didn't take some of the employees too long to figure out that if they booked their tickets at the last possible minute (last minute in airfares is usually the day before travel), the cost of business class would be the same as a fully flexible economy ticket.

The intent of this policy decision was sound, but the implementation of it had faltered, and whilst many employees followed the policy and booked economy, quite a few others hid behind the specific words of the policy – lowest possible airfare – and continued to rack up higher than necessary expenses.

It is pretty apparent that gaming the system is alive and well in many organisations (which of course is not good). The question is, 'how can it be stopped?'

First, it is important to make sure that initiatives, and the way that they are presented, are clear, both in implementation and in intent. This is easier in an organisation that has high levels of commitment and a positive work climate. Organisations that have less than desired commitment and work climate are ripe for gaming.

Second, prior to an initiative being rolled out, it is very helpful to 'test' it for potential unintended consequences – will this initiative bring the results it is intended to, or will it result in some employees spending time figuring out ways to get around it?

Third, make sure that the initiative is based on sound thinking – is this the only way to accomplish the goal it is intended to, or is there another way to do the same thing?

Fourth, engage employees in coming up with ways to achieve the intended goal. Front line employees are smart, they have seen it all, and they usually know how to really get things done. If they feel that they are part of solving problems, i.e. part of the solution instead of being accused of being the problem, they will help. The overall result will be a lessening of gaming the system, and an improved organisational climate.

The good news is that gaming the system actually is recognised as a serious problem for business; the bad news is that it is still out there.

## Searching for the Horizon?

In business, there is little that is as important as having a clear vision to follow. Without a vision, it is difficult to understand how any business can do much besides wander around aimlessly. When I learned to sail sixteen years ago, the whole concept of vision became quite clear to me.

I used to keep my boat on the island of Mallorca in the Mediterranean. From Mallorca, I could sail due west to Valencia Spain, or north to the Spanish-French frontier, or northeast to Monte Carlo or San Remo Italy. I could sail due east to Sardinia, or southeast to Tunisia, or south to Algeria, or even southwest through the Straits of Gibraltar and into the Atlantic. And whilst each of these places has their own special attractions, I noticed that whenever I took the boat out of the harbour, I always pointed it in the same direction. As a matter of fact, ever since I began to sail, I always pointed my boat in the same direction. I headed toward the horizon.

For me, sailing was all about...well, sailing. Stopping in marvellous ports along the way was great, but the real attraction for me was to be on the boat sailing toward the horizon. It was my vision of what sailing is all about.

Several weeks ago, I was meeting with a senior management team of a large organisation, and I told that story. Not just because I like the story, but because some of the members of the team were visibly restless because they felt they had lost their way to *their* vision. The real reason was that they probably never had a clear picture of their vision to begin with. They had been focussing on just the financial aspects of their vision; what their revenues would be, what their stock price would be, and what their profits would be. Most certainly, these are elements of a vision, but not the real essence of what a corporate vision is all about.

What they were looking at was akin to the tip of an iceberg. Easy to recognise and measure, but the tip of an iceberg doesn't provide a complete picture of what is out there. To understand an iceberg – why it moves the way it does – you need to be able to see what is below the surface, because that area is where the real strength of an iceberg lies.
It is the same with a corporate vision – you need to look below the surface of the obvious 'numbers' to see what it will take to make the numbers happen.

You need to identify what policies and procedures you will have to have solidly in place to successfully achieve the results you want. You have to have a clear understanding of what mental models managers and employees will need to have to be motivated enough to achieve high performance. And you will have to have the right people in the right jobs for the right reasons, all demonstrating real leadership. Because if you don't, you company will be like a sailing boat without a rudder, easily swept off course when the wind picks up or when the waves begin to build. And just like in sailing, the winds and waves that businesses face can wreak havoc on a journey toward your vision.

Without a clear vision and the right structures, mental models and support, a company will not be able to achieve its vision. And don't think that this only is applicable to large companies. A good example of a 30-person organisation just was in the news.

Ellen MacArthur, a 28-year-old English woman, just set the record for the fastest time around the world in a sailboat single-handed. Yes, she had incredible support from weather, health, nutrition, and navigation experts, as well as the best technology available, but she managed to break the world's record for single-handed sailing around the world. She was described as having commitment, tenacity, and a thirst for success by the media.

When she arrived back in Falmouth amidst thousands of cheering fans, someone from the BBC interviewed her, and it became apparent to me that her vision is so clear to her. She was asked what she wanted to do next – she had just stepped off her boat after 71 days and over 27,000 miles – and she said, '*I just want to go sailing again soon.*' I think that senior management teams could learn a real lesson from her – it isn't just getting there that is important…it is how we are *going there.*

## When Is "Doing Enough," Not Enough?

The short answer to the question is to do more. Yes, this does seem so simple; if you haven't do enough, just do more. But *'do more'* is not really an answer. *Do more what? Do more when? Do more how?* As with most questions, the quick answer usually only brings forth a new set questions.

The first question that surfaces is probably, *'why wasn't the effort that was put forth 'enough?'* This question begins to explore issues around knowing what the real expectations were. I say the 'real' expectations, because in many cases, expectations are not made clear or only touch on pieces of the larger puzzle of what an organisation is trying to accomplish.

The second question that comes to mind is, *'do our people have the appropriate skills and competencies to deliver on our expectations?'* Or more simply put, *'did we try to do something that we couldn't do in the first place?'* In many organisations, there is an assumption that managers and employees *do have* the right skills to get the job done. And in most cases, that is right; but only if you consider technical or mechanical skills. There are not that many organisations who put equal effort into providing technical or mechanical skills *and* interpersonal and communications skills. And it stands to reason that if managers and employees are somehow lacking in those skill areas, their ability to get commitment from others and build alignment around what needs to be done will suffer.

The third question that should come up is, *'why should we even consider that we have done enough?'* Doing enough implies that the most important thing is to achieve a specific goal or set of goals. Well that is fine – after all, goals are there to be met, aren't they? But the reality in today's business world is that just doing enough, is not enough at all.

Think about it this way. What do you suppose is the most important thing to an Olympic athlete; becoming better or just winning? If you talk to most of them, they will tell you that it is getting better, and better, and better. Winning (achieving the goal) is only a momentary place in time. And when the athlete wins, what do you suppose his or her competition is doing? They are working their bums off practising more and more so that they can be better. Yes, winning is important, but winning is only temporary.

Hitting a specific business goal is only gratifying for a moment – or should be. Business success is something that is measured over time, and specific goals are in reality, only milestones along the larger journey.

This situation is typified by organisations that are trying to grow. The questions that should be raised when considering organisational growth include; why are we trying to grow? How much do we want to grow? What else is going to happen along the chosen growth pattern? And what will we do when we get there?

Too many organisations – or more appropriately, too many senior decision-makers in these organisations – avoid answering these questions. Actually, I don't think that they even consider them; especially the ones about *'what else is going to happen,'* and *'what do we do when we get to where we want to be?'* The reason for this is usually because they believe they are too busy pushing for results that they don't have the time. This is a typical example of the short-term, reactive thinking that is present in businesses today. Managers are under pressure to *'hit the numbers'* and, unfortunately, understanding some of the unintended consequences of growth and understanding a longer-term future than months is deemed not important. I do know managers who claim that these are both very important issues to consider, but when they are asked then why they don't make the time to think about them, the answer given most often is, *'we just don't have the time.'*

This is nothing more than an abdication of responsibility. Doing *'just enough'* is rarely *'enough.'*

## And On the Third Day....?

Running a business is not easy work. Antoine de Saint-Exupery once said, *'perfection is attained, not when there is nothing left to add, but when there is nothing left to remove.'* This statement certainly applies to management, but unfortunately, we rarely see things this way.

Business today is interesting. Most everyone agrees that costs can be trimmed, but few agree how it can be, or should be done. So the cost-cutting method of choice seems to be slash and burn, and in most cases, the easiest places to begin are training and development. Forget all the pronouncements about the importance of improving the hard and soft skills of your people; forget all the commitments that have been made about giving the employees the ability to realise their potential – just cut, cut, cut. Next, go after other programmes that are run by people who do not have the political clout to stave off the cost-cutters. Keep cutting until there isn't much left to cut. Well, except for those favourite programmes and initiatives that the front office likes – those sacred cows do tend to remain. And what is even worse, when the pressure to cut costs is almost over, most everything begins to creep back in, as if things won't be good again until all the fat is back. Of course, it comes back with new names so we don't realise what has happened. Apparently, those lads in the posh offices think that we are all pretty stupid, and that we don't understand what is happening.

For some reason, there are many managers out there who don't *feel complete* unless they have more and more to manage. We love to keep adding. Figure out how the system works, then because of the climate we live in, slice and dice it into something that gives the appearance that we are fiscally responsible, then work like crazy to make it more complex and unsustainable again.

I am a huge believer in the need to create environments in which people can realise their potential, and in most cases, this means that better decisions need to be made. And if you can have an environment where the decisions are better, you will find that the decisions will focus on the right things, for the right reasons, and at the right time. In the case of cost-cutting initiatives, this probably means
programmes that support the long-term success of the company need to stay, and spending that is not in alignment with strategic goals and initiatives should go. Right about now, there are managers out there who are working out how to *prove* that their pet programmes *do* support the strategy, but the reality is that most of them are off the mark. And in many cases I have seen, miss the mark by miles.

There is one good test to see if programmes mesh effectively with strategic direction: *if we spend money on this initiative, will it get us closer to where our strategy is trying to take us?* Now let's not be foolish about this; almost anyone can make a case that damn near everything a company does should get it closer to where it wants to go. But the reality is that many of them don't, and the things that don't move you closer need to disappear. If management put half as much effort into this type of exercise as they put into the due diligence put forth when trying to acquire something, we might find a different situation that many companies are in today.

If management does ask this question, then the next thing to do is to figure out which of the remaining programmes provide the greatest leverage. It doesn't make sense to do more and more things to make the strategy work, but it does make sense to focus on the vital few things that can really make a difference.

In most organisations, these vital few things include 1) improving the decision-making process; 2) ensuring that your people have the skills and competencies they need for today and for tomorrow; 3) ensuring that the people have the resources needed to accomplish what needs to be accomplished; 4) focus on improving effectiveness instead of efficiency; and 5) having a set of processes, systems, and structures that allow these things to happen. Anything else is probably irrelevant and won't add value. Do the programmes that your company spends money on directly meet these criteria?

We need to stop the *cut then restore* mindset of business today if our companies are going cease going through non-valued added cycles.

And if you can sort this all out, you just might be able to resurrect your company so it can realise its potential.

## Stay Hungry; Stay Foolish

Before he passed away, Steve Jobs had given a commencement address at Stanford, and in it he gave some pretty heady advice to the graduates. Jobs spoke about some of the key lessons he has learned over the years, and one of the lessons stuck in my mind. He said, at the end of his talk, that if the students were to be able to realise their potential, they should 'stay hungry and stay foolish.'

When you think about it, many of us, when we were just beginning our business careers, were far hungrier than we are now. Many of us have become quite risk adverse over the years in business. So what do you suppose causes this shift in behaviours?

It seems, from talking to many senior managers over the years that as we become 'settled' in our positions, our need to be hungry diminishes. We are where we are, and we have accomplished what we have accomplished, and we may not feel the need to put those gains at risk. This doesn't happen to everyone, but it does appear that some of us are more concerned with making our mark on an organisation than we are with stretching ourselves into places we have never been before. And the same holds with taking risks. Many senior business leaders I have spoken to offer consistent lip service to the concept that without some level of risk-taking, many of the business successes we have seen over the years would not have occurred. But at the same time, the signals are pretty clear that risk-taking, even within parameters, can be extremely risky to one's career. The bottom line is that we know intuitively that in order for managers and employees to contribute to the achievement of greatness for their companies, they need to be willing to constantly challenge themselves and to take risks. And this is where the problem lies – if senior management teams don't begin to demonstrate the behaviours that we know intuitively to be right, many companies will continue to muddle through, delivering sporadic results that no one is keen to see.

I do need to be clear about what this means. I am not advocating managers and employees becoming hungry to the point that they will choose personal success over everything. One of the downsides to promoting 'hungry' behaviour is that without a clear picture of what 'hungry' might mean in a corporate structure, adversarial relationships can arise with people striving to get access to desperately scarce resources; and an organisation that has adversarial relationships occurring within its structure will never realise its potential.

A good model of what hungry could look like can be found in some of the entrants into the corporate world that we have seen dazzle employees and the markets alike. It means surrounding yourself with people who are not only competent, but who have bought into and are incredibly committed to the future vision for the company. Hiring the 'best' people means more than scavenging through the ranks of valedictorians from the big business schools of the world. Quite often, the 'best' people are the ones who do have the right skills, but even more importantly, share in the collective hunger to build a great company.

The same can be said for being 'foolish.' Being 'foolish' does not mean that you should allow people to take actions that have little resemblance to acceptable business risk-taking. Encouraging risk-taking in business means that first the senior management has to be clear on what risk-taking means in their respective environments. At the end of the day, nothing is guaranteed in business, and consequently, all actions have some level of risk-taking associated with them; but taking risks that do not fall within specific parameters can spell doom. Risk-taking parameters will vary from organisation to organisation, but in most cases, some of the parameters would include; 1) actionable decisions should be made, or at very minimum, validated collectively; 2) decision-makers need to explore some of the potential unintended consequences of actions before the decisions are made; and 3) the lessons learned from the process must be part of the knowledge sharing process within the company.

Staying hungry and staying foolish may be difficult for many managers, and the level of willingness to challenge oneself and take risks can vary from person to person. But if our organisations are to be able to realise their potential over time, it does seem that Mr. Jobs has just reminded us that it won't happen without our managers demonstrating behaviours that we have seen in the past. It is a lesson for all of us.

## Mr. Sawyer's Solution?

Mark Twain's **Tom Sawyer** is a great story...a great story of how to influence others to do the work you are supposed to get done. Yes, the metaphor of *getting someone else to paint your fence* is one of life's dreams in business – how to influence others to get things done. And with all the business schools cranking out MBA-laden graduates, and managers over-burdened with work, you would think that it would be a hot topic. But for some reason, we don't hear too much about it, other than the traditional, 'I am the boss; now get out there and work harder.'

Influencing is a key competence for all managers. It is, to quote a dictionary, *'causing something without any direct or apparent effort, and, 'a cognitive factor that tends to have an effect on what you do.'* Okay, so that is a definition, but the big question that I keep hearing is, *'how do I do it better?'*

In order to really influence your employees, you can either revert to the stick method or the carrot method. I tend to think the carrot method works best. This is because once you begin to use the stick, you need to continue to use the stick; and that simply leads to a disgruntled, pressured workforce that costs you more (because you need to hire people to wield the sticks). The carrot method works better, but only if you understand what motivates your people. Yes, money is a big motivator, but in today's world where every company on the block is cutting costs, that probably isn't a viable option. That only leaves one thing: connect with your people.

Employees are motivated when they feel that being motivated is worth the effort. Getting up each day and getting all fired up about going to work does require effort, whether you are a front-line employee or a senior manager. Just knowing that today could be a crap day trying to fix all the problems that you didn't have time to fix yesterday isn't exactly an exciting prospect. Especially if you don't feel that your boss values you and your effort. However, if you get up each day knowing that the company (and your boss) values you and your work, it can be very motivating. Connecting with your people – understanding what their issues are; understanding what they need to actually get their work cleared out each night; and understanding what you can do to assist them can make a world of difference to an employee; regardless of what level of the hierarchy they reside on. Talk to the people who report to you. Ask them what you can do to make their work lives easier. Yes, you may encounter some pretty angry people, but if you listen to what they say, and then try to do something about it, you will be on your way to seeing a motivated workforce. This is all part of influencing them to do what is needed to be done.

The next part of being a good influencer is being able to help your people truly understand why you have asked them to do whatever you have asked them. This means that, first; you understand the situation they are in. Asking employees to do more (I never hear about managers asking employees to do less anymore) will probably cause them to think, *'why should I have to do more?'* You had better be able to respond with something other than, *'because I said so,'* or, *'because my boss told me to tell you to.'* These are all lame signals that you don't get it yourself, and your influencing days will be over faster than you can imagine. Helping the employee see how his or her contributions will actually make a difference is a good response to the 'why' question. But clearly, to do this, you will have to believe it first. Employees who contribute *do* make a difference. These are the employees who you want to value, and treat accordingly. Not just through lip service, but through actual recognition. Be willing to celebrate personal and team contributions. You don't have to give them a financial bonus necessarily, but it is always nice to have your boss meet you at the pub for a couple of pints to talk over how the effort went. Cut your employees some slack when the pressure is not on; let them know that you *do understand* that they have put forth extra effort and you appreciate it.

And the best part of being a good influencer is when you ask for employees input on how to make the initiative (or process or whatever) work better. Talk about how the effort could be done better next time. Give them the respect that they long for by asking them for help, instead of telling them over and over again to do it your way. I know quite a few managers who shudder at the thought of even hinting that they don't have all the answers, but the reality is that they don't. By asking for input, you send a signal that their contributions are valued, which is a strong
motivator, and gives you the opportunity to influence outcomes.

I know a manager who was saddled with a tremendous task that he could not accomplish single-handedly. He wanted to influence others (the team that reported to him) that they should roll their shirtsleeves up and help get it done. But no matter what he tried, they balked...until he said that he would be out there with them. And he did. The task took three days of non-stop effort, but he was there on the front-line the entire time. His people saw his commitment and joined in. This was a great example of how to influence a situation to achieve superior outcomes; the task was done, the employees gained respect for their manager; the manager gained respect for the team members; and his ability to influence was increased dramatically.

Now if you don't like that idea, just start telling everyone else to work harder. But be aware; one day you may wake up to find out that you will have to paint your fence all alone.

## Measure Twice, Cut Once

A good friend of mine was relating a story to me recently of when he was younger, and in school. He was taking a woodworking course, and the instructor kept telling everyone in the class to measure twice, and then you only had to cut once. A sound lesson, and one that metaphorically applies to every decision-making process in organisations - make sure that you are making the right decision, for the right reasons, at the right time; and the chances are that you won't have to make another decision because the first one didn't do what you wanted.

There are many reasons for rushing the decision-making process in organisations today. Whether it is the perception that something has to be done now because of competition, or externally driven pressures, or just massive problems, the self-driven pressure to make quick decisions is a curse that is plaguing organisations from all sectors, and of all sizes.

I use the term 'self-driven' on purpose, because for the life of me, I cannot believe that any Board or shareholders would condone making management decisions foolishly. And yet, decisions that are made without enough thought are just that. The excuse given by management is, of course, 'we can't afford to take extra time to make the decision.' This excuse – and that is all it is – is actually, inexcusable.

Decision-makers are there to make decisions about the choices that an organisation makes. But inherent in this – ask any Board or shareholders – is that the decision will be well thought out. That is why we pay management decision-makers what we do.

The whole concept of 'not having enough time' should fall on deaf ears, because when decisions are not well thought out, the amount of time (and resources) that is wasted far in excess of what it could have been. Several years ago, I saw a study that had been commissioned to determine overall elapsed time from idea conception to actual effective implementation. The process went something like this: 1: decide what to do; 2: test the validity of the decision; 3: do a pilot of the implementation; 4: make any revisions necessary; and 5: deploy the decision. The overall elapsed time (in the study) was found to be 10 – 40% longer when step 2 was neglected. And regardless of specific situations, 10 – 40% more time equates to additional costs that need not be incurred.

Now I don't know all the specifics of every organisation on this planet, but I do think that I understand that shareholders would not be happy if they knew that because of managerial ineptitude, resources were being wasted for no good reason – resources that could be used far more effectively to helping an organisation realise its potential.

Here are a few things that decision-makers need to consider:

1. Is this decision the most appropriate one at this point in time?
2. Will this decision, if implemented effectively, move the organisation closer to achieving its desired future?
3. What will some of the unintended consequences be if the decision is implemented (examine both the positive and negative unintended consequences)?
4. What resources will be needed if the decision is implemented?
5. What resources are currently available?
6. How many people will we need to get onboard with the decision to make it work the way we need it to?
7. How will we best communicate the decision, and why we are making it?
8. What don't we know?

If decision-makers take the time to run through this short check-list (and believe it or not, the time needed to do this is nothing compared to what will be needed to fix the problems incurred with a bad decision), they will find that their jobs will become easier. If the decision-makers jobs become easier, it will mean that they are becoming more effective.

And lets be clear...I am by no means saying that decision-makers should become paralysed with fear that they might do the wrong thing. I am saying that they need to conscious of the decisions they are making, and the ramifications of them. And at the end of the day, it is effective decision-making that can make or break a company. Measure twice, cut once...sound advice for all decision-makers.

## How Many Options Do You Need?

I saw it again this weekend. Another published report about a CEO whose company wasn't delivering the profits that he had projected. What I saw was the comment that the CEO (and what just about every other CEO in this situation says), he *was determined to stem the declines.*

I thought it might be nice to point out what some of the options for stemming profit declines seem to be, based on what I have seen being done in many similar situations.

Option A: Get your key people together – these are usually your direct reports – and yell at them. Make sure they clearly understand that quite obviously, because they haven't done what they were supposed to do about keeping the profits up, they are worthless slackers that should all be sacked. It is helpful to make sure that you do a lot of pointing of fingers at these no-good, incompetent specimens of managers, whilst at the same time, ensure that your voice is punching out some seriously high decibel ratings. A nice touch, employed to make sure they understand your displeasure at the situation, is to get the veins in your forehead to rise up and start throbbing.

Option B: Call a press conference – this should be easy, as business media reporters are always looking for a good story – and explain that the shortfall in projected earnings really isn't your fault. Because there are so many ways to use this option, you can easily blame 1) Global Warming; 2) Those pesky countries that are unfairly using their cheaper labour to do what your more expensive labour should be doing; 3) Unions – note, this excuse is usually used in conjunction with excuse number 2); 4) Those completely inappropriate government regulations; 5) Inflation; and 6) the old stand-by, OPEC. If some idiot reporter tries to ask you why you didn't anticipate any or all of the excuses you use, just say, *'you obviously don't understand business, do you. Next question?'* Do not – I repeat, do not – let your marketing guys handle this press conference. It is good for you to show what a great leader you are by doing this by yourself. Oh yes, finish the press conference with some veiled reference to a cunning plan you will soon come up with to resolve the mess that isn't your fault.

Option C: Get your strategy people together, and after whacking them with some of the first option for coming up with a lame strategy to begin with. Tell them they had better get a new strategy, and get it ready by the time you get back from the golf course tomorrow afternoon. This shouldn't be too much of a problem for them, as all they have to do is dredge up an old strategy and put a new cover on it. Make sure they understand that the new strategy must be printed in colour and have a shiny cover on the folder.

Option D: Take responsibility for the decisions that contributed to the profit shortfall and resign. (*Right, like that is something that a many CEO's would actually do.*)

Option E: Figure out what is occurring. Be careful with this option, because it will take some time and require serious listening on your part. Get out of the office and go meet with customers – old customers, and people you thought would be potential customers – and find out why they aren't buying your products or services. Stay out of your office and go meet with some of the people who do the real work in your organisation. No, you can't do this at your club – you need to go where they are, when they are doing the real work. Ask them what they see the problem is. Taking notes is a good thing to do here, because they will probably give you an earful and you won't be able to remember it all. Meet with your managers and find out if they are getting all the resources that you probably promised they would get to have the job done.

With all these groups (I know it seems like a lot of work, but they probably think this is what you are supposed to be doing anyway), after they tell you whatever they tell you, say, *'let me tell you what I am hearing,'* and then say it back to them. This is a good way to make sure you really understand what they have told you – yes, you can use the notes you have taken. Call a meeting of your senior team, and with all this information, do something differently than you have been doing previously. You really don't have too much to lose, after all, the previous things weren't working anyway, were they?

Option F: Tell the shareholders and the Board to go piss off. Caution: This, along with Options A, B, and C, may not be the smartest thing to do. And seeing as how few CEO's seem to be keen on Option D, I would suggest you settle for Option E…this is, after all, what you get paid to do, isn't it?

## Divining Success?

I was talking to a good friend the other night, and the subject of 'divining' came up – you know, using some mystical way to find something. But instead of talking about finding water in the desert, the question that was raised was, *'are companies flexible enough to find opportunity in this market (without sacrificing the mission/vision)?'* The answer is, *'they can be.'*

Finding opportunity is a function of both understanding what you do, and what you *can* do. Too often, however, many key decision-makers become locked into a mental model that *'this is what we do, because this is what we have always done.'* A fair mental model, but it does reflect a rather myopic view of what it takes to be successful in today's business climate. In order to increase the potential for organisational success, it is important to view *'what you do'* from a different perspective.

Several years ago, I was working with someone who had a clear vision of what her organisation should become in the future. Over a series of meetings, I kept pressing for reasons of why that vision was so important, and eventually was able to determine that the vision was important, because it *always had* been important. Not exactly the best reason to try to steer an organisation in a certain direction I thought.

I asked the CEO what she would have if her company were able to achieve her vision, and her response was predictable. *'If we achieve our vision, we will be the best in our market.'* A good, but still myopic response. *'If you achieve your vision, will part of what you will have will be that your company will have realised its potential?'* I asked. *'I hope so,'* was all she could say. This, unfortunately, is just not good enough, especially in today's marketplace. The challenge she faced was not just realising her company's vision, but to make sure that the vision wasn't too restrictive. A restrictive vision (or mission) is one of the biggest impediments to finding opportunities that can help an organisation grow.

CEO-types (and other key decision-makers) need to begin to ask themselves a series of questions, and whilst these questions might be painful, they are critical.

1) What is the vision for the future of the organisation?
2) Why is this vision so important?
3) If we attain the vision, what will we really have achieved?
4) What else will we have achieved?
5) Are there other ways we could achieve the same things?
6) Are the potential scenarios that our organisation may encounter in the future going to help us or hinder our ability to achieve the vision?
7) How will we deal with these scenarios?
8) If opportunities arise along the way, will we be flexible enough to take advantage of them?
9) How will it be able to do this?

Now whilst all the questions are important, it is the last two questions that will really tell the story about whether or not the organisation will be flexible enough to take advantage of opportunities to realise its potential.

Organisations need to understand what their processes and systems really do, and what their employee's capabilities really are. In most cases, this information is currently not available, largely because the answers are found in typical 'check-sheets' that reside in a filing cabinet in someone's office – *we have this or that system, we use these processes, and our people have these skills.* Nice information to have, and it does look great in an annual report, but with this type of thinking, it will be pretty difficult for an organisation to capture opportunities (or create them).

To really understand systems, processes, and capabilities, what needs to be done is determine *'what else'* the systems *can* do, *'what else'* the processes *can* do, and *'what else'* the employee's capabilities are *able* to accomplish.

With this information, the perspective of what a company does, and how it does it can change. And if the perspective can change, the ability to seek out, and take advantage of, opportunities increases dramatically.

The ability to be flexible can be a key differentiator for business success, and like most things in business, being more flexible is a choice.

## Ikean Lessons

Ikea is an organisation that has been able to achieve high levels of success through a simple formula: provide inexpensive products of relatively high consistent quality that you can put together yourself. One of the keys to their formula is that most of their products are packed in flat containers – easy to store, easy to ship, and easy to sell. Of course, you do need to put all the bits together so it looks just like the fab design you saw in their catalogue.

On the surface, it is the same with many of the strategic plans that companies come up with today. The plan looks great on paper, and you are told that you have all the bits you need, but when it comes to putting it all together, you quite often end up highly frustrated because the results aren't as you wanted.

The reason that this occurs so often is that, whilst the plan looks good on paper, the people who are charged with making it happen are not able to actually do what is needed, much less 'sell' it to the organisation. There are several reasons for this.

The principle reason that strategies don't result in the gains they promise is that managers and employees do not see how they fit into them. This is a crucial issue regarding strategy implementation: if managers and employees don't see how their contributions directly impact the success of a strategy, they will not actively work to make it happen. Senior management, when communicating a new strategy (whether it be a new strategic direction, or simply an evolution of an existing strategic direction), need to incorporate a clear picture of managers and employees contributions, why they are important, and what they need to be. And then go out and test to make sure that the managers and employees really do understand.

The next problem area is that many strategies do not provide a realistic framework for ensuring success in an anticipated future scenario. This is either because senior management hasn't done its scenario homework – they aren't aware of what scenarios the organisation might find itself it – or because the strategy is not realistic based on what the anticipated scenarios are. A strategy that does not take into consideration what the future might bring is a strategy that will not work. And a strategy that is developed without an understanding of what that future might be is nothing more than a reflection of incompetence on the part of management.

The issue of making sure that a strategy direction incorporates the human, financial, and skill resources is another inhibitor of success. Too often, strategies are assembled without enough effort being put into taking into consideration what it will take to make it happen. Managers who are charged with specific strategic efforts are caught between potentially conflicting goals: focus on the strategic implementation or do the day job, and, consequently, neither responsibility is done well. This is complicated when the assignment of appropriate financial resources to enable the strategy to work are not available, and the same holds true when the people assigned to implement a strategy do not have an appropriate level of skills that will be needed. And unfortunately, too many organisations believe that what we foolishly call 'soft-skills' are not critical, when in reality, the ability to think effectively about the challenges an organisation faces; the ability to influence others to accept those challenges; and the ability to demonstrate leadership are the skills that can make or break a strategic implementation.

A good strategy is one that clearly articulates how important managerial and employee growth and learning is in the organisation. It has been often said that one of the most impactful differentiators for organisational success is how fast an organisational population can learn. And yet, most strategies either pass this point over, or simply relegate it to something that is just an HR department problem.

If an organisational strategic effort does ensure that managers and employees see how they 'fit' into the strategy and how their activities directly contribute to it, if it ensure that it can work in an anticipated future, if it ensures that the organisation will have the resources and skills that will be needed to make it happen are available; then the organisation just may have a chance of creating its own future. If not, a strategy won't be worth the high-gloss, multi-colour paper it is printed on. The lessons are clear; before trying to 'sell' anything, make sure that what your customers expect is what they will get.

## Event Dear Boy, Events

When he was Prime Minister of the United Kingdom, Harold Macmillan was asked by a young journalist after a long dinner what can most easily steer a government off course, he answered "*Events dear boy, events*". In short, politics can be unpredictable. And based on many of the results we have been seeing in the business pages, the same holds true for business. Unfortunately, however, in business, it is not the results that are unpredictable; it is the way in which management plans (or doesn't plan) for events, or the way in which they react to them.

Not that many years after America On-Line began to make headway in the US market, someone in their organisation came up with the ultimate marketing plan: send out CD-ROMS with a free download programme for the AOL online service to virtually everyone in America. On the surface, this was a relatively brilliant plan – make installation and enrolment in AOL's online service painless so that the company would be able to see a dramatic increase in their customer base. But events took over and the plan turned into a near disaster. The events that took over were the millions of people who actually accepted the offer and after installing AOL onto their computers, they all went online. The mass influx of customer activity overtaxed the AOL system and suddenly, they were risking alienating many of the existing and new customers, putting the overall plan at risk. Could this have been anticipated? Probably, but the point is that no one apparently did.

British Airways had been suffering from bad press due to unhappy customers that had suffered through delays and cancelled flights due to work stoppages. So the lads at BA put together a plan to reverse the bad image and get more people in their seats again. But as with the experience that AOL had, events mucked up BA's plans. Gate Gourmet, one of the largest sub-contractors that BA uses, was under serious pressure from the airline to reduce costs, and as part of the food supplier's solution was to cut back on their workforce. But when the news broke, the Gate Gourmet workforce at Heathrow Airport decided to respond with a work stoppage. And the work stoppage spread to the baggage handler's that BA uses, and the airlines arrivals and departures at the airport ground to a halt. Their plan to recover from bad press suddenly was destroyed as the work stoppage, and subsequent queues of people whose flights were cancelled, and once again, BA was in the news for not meeting customer's needs.

Diageo, the drinks maker, has been for the past year, on a roller coaster, but overall, the stock price had increased quite a bit in the past twelve months. Things were looking up, and then the virtual parade of hurricanes went marching through the south eastern United States, chopping away at demand, and consequently, sales. And whilst some might say that hurricanes are not exactly predictable, the very fact that they can occur means that there should have been a contingency for short-term drops in sales. Another 'event' that has played havoc with Diageo, and quite a few other companies has been the dramatic increase in the price of oil.

Whilst these examples of events that have created problems for companies may seem to have been out of the realm of anticipating them, the real point is that most organisations are not the best at planning for contingencies, regardless of how obscure they seem at the time.

Planning for contingencies is not all that difficult, but the first step is to be aware of what *might* occur. To do this requires a shift in the traditional thinking processes. Encourage your people to not only come up with the intuitive events that might occur, but to also think counter-intuitively. Quite often, this can be done by making a list of the very worst things that could happen to your organisation, and then work backwards to figure out what events might possibly cause them.

Next, identify what you can do to either *prevent* the events from happening, or to *mitigate* the negative effects that may accompany them. Follow this with a plan of what you will do if you find yourself in the middle of something you won't like.

Or, there is another option. Just spend some time standing in front of a mirror practising saying to your shareholders, *'Poor performance? Well, it is because of events dear shareholder, events.'* And then spend some time getting your CV up to date, because you just may need it.

## The Downside to "Stepping In"

In many companies, the process used to deploy initiatives is to delegate the tasks to teams. On the surface, the process is quite clear and sound: explain to the team what needs to be done, give them the resources needed, and wait for the results to appear. However, quite often, the planned initiative deployment process fails for one reason or another. And often, when this occurs, a manager will step in to drive the deployment himself. The rationale for this decision to 'step in' is based on the belief that it is the manager who has the responsibility to ensure that things do get done, and if something falters, it is the manager who should be held accountable.

Whilst this may ensure that the initiative is does get implemented (assuming the manager is competent to do so), several unintended consequences may occur. Three of the unintended consequences are that,

1) the team will never acquire the experience needed to do this effectively in the future,
2) the manager will never give them the opportunity to learn, and
3) this managerial intervention may generate the expectation that the manager will intervene again in the future.

This can negate the willingness of the team members to put forth appropriate effort, whilst at the same time, setting the manager up for failure due to over extending himself. All unintended consequences can create fundamentally systemic long-term problems relating to the growth potential of the organisation; and short-term problems in the form of the willingness of employees to be committed to achieving organisational goals.

By looking at the potential unintended consequences of actions before they are taken, it is possible to see if the action makes sense.

The real issue here is *'how to ensure that teams can do what is expected of them,'* not getting the job done. If managers feel the need to step in, they need to understand what the underlying problem is, and in most situations like this, the problems are that team members either do not have the skills they need to do the job, they aren't clear on what needs to be done and why, or there are roadblocks in their way that they are unable to clear away. And if a manager decides that regardless of the underlying problem, that he or she should save the day instead of solving the problem, the resulting dynamic will pre-empt the team member's future ability to do what is needed. Bad for the team members, and even worse for the organisation.

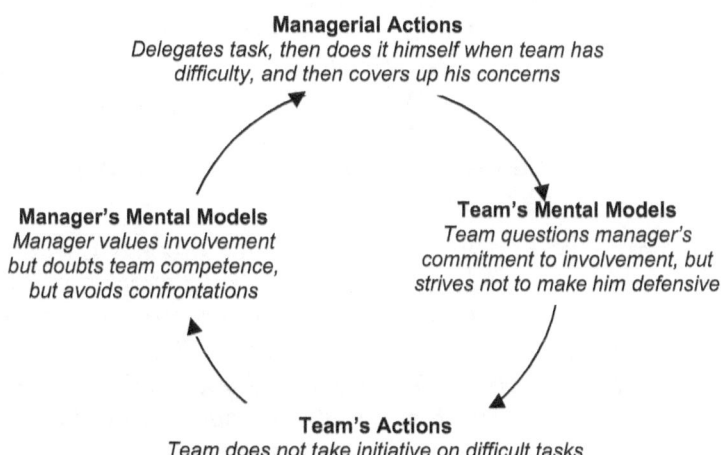

**Managerial Actions**
*Delegates task, then does it himself when team has difficulty, and then covers up his concerns*

**Manager's Mental Models**
*Manager values involvement but doubts team competence, but avoids confrontations*

**Team's Mental Models**
*Team questions manager's commitment to involvement, but strives not to make him defensive*

**Team's Actions**
*Team does not take initiative on difficult tasks*

Whist stepping in to save the day does feel good – we all like to be the organisational saviour at times – it will only reinforce the beliefs of both team members and management. Prior to a team being charged with accomplishing a task or initiative, it is important to first:

- Ensure that team's charged with initiatives have an appropriate level of skills and resources to get the job done on time, in full.
- Ensure that the team members have a full understanding of what needs to be done, by when, what the measures of success will be, and why the initiative is important; i.e. how the initiative connects to the vision of the organisation.
- Ensure that potential roadblocks to success are removed before they are encountered.

Wanting to help out is a good thing, especially when things aren't going exactly as we wanted them to go, but sometimes for managers, stepping in can result in more long-term on-going problems that it solves.

## Blinded by Our Own Beliefs

It is pretty commonly held that most of us make decisions based on our beliefs. Peter Senge, author of *The Fifth Discipline*, once said, '*do we believe what we see or do we see what we believe?*' I think that Peter is right – we don't just believe what we see; we tend to see what we believe, especially in business. People have the ability to take their beliefs and craft them into truths about what an organisation is doing, for what reasons, and if it even makes sense. And then, it can be these mental models that cause us to filter out the true reality of a given situation.

A good example of how this happens was recently given to me by a retired CEO from Australia. Whilst talking about how managers make decisions, Kelvin Hack asked me, '*If you are hovering over Los Angeles California in a helicopter, and wanted to travel to Reno in Nevada, which direction would you go?*' He also asked me '*what would be the first country I would encounter if I was in Detroit Michigan and went directly south?*' Having spent many years in America, I felt quite confident that I knew the answers, only to be surprised that my answers were not correct. Mr. Hack's questions caused me to reflect on how often we make decisions based on what we believe without taking the time to find out if what we believe has any semblance to the reality of the situation.

Humans live in one of those 'good news-bad news' environments. We posses the capacity to make decisions based on accumulated knowledge – that is the good news. The bad news is that quite often, our accumulated knowledge is stilted by our beliefs and assumptions, and in many cases, it is these beliefs and assumptions that cause us to make decisions that in hindsight look quite daft. This dynamic is a plague in the world of business.

I know of several CEO's and MD's who are extremely bright guys, but too often, they are so caught up in their own beliefs that are quite removed from the reality of a specific situation that the decisions they make get them into trouble over time. Case in point: I recently met an MD who really believed that his workforce was aligned and thought he was the best person to lead the company into the future. I asked how he knew this, and he told me that he had asked some of his direct reports and they all told him that he was. Okay, fair enough, but when I asked him if he was confident that their answers reflected the reality of the environment, his reply was that it was, and if I didn't believe it, I could ask the employees myself. So I did, and what I found was startling. Whilst all of the MD's direct reports did confirm the information, front line workers (the ones who actually do the real work of the company) had a different view.

The level of alignment (support for senior management decisions) was perilously low. Almost 25% of the employees I spoke with said that it didn't make a difference who was the MD – the company would just keep ticking along, and over 50% said that the MD was 'out of touch' or 'less than qualified' to lead. *(I have cleaned up their actual responses quite a bit)* When I reported this to the MD, his two main concerns were *'who said that?'* and *'they don't know what they are talking about.'* His beliefs – reinforced by information that was provided to him by people who were less-than-objective – didn't allow him to even consider the possibility that his view might be incorrect. And because of this, he was making decisions about employees that were distorted.

Too often, managers find themselves trapped into accepting their existing mental models about situations because they are convinced that their mental models reflect reality. In short, they only 'see' what they have already deemed to be what they should be looking for. And this can result in devastating problems over time – problems about what goals are worth striving for; problems about what it will take to achieve the goals; problems about what else might happen as activities designed to achieve goals are implemented; and problems about how to sustain the gains achieved.

If managers wish to become more effective at what they do, they need to be willing to examine their own beliefs and assumptions, and if they are shown to be less than accurate, change them. If not, they risk making decisions that may plague them long into the future.

*Oh, I almost forgot. The correct answers to Mr. Hack's questions are 'Northwest' and 'Canada.'*

## Have You Tied Your Own Hands?

I met with a good friend who had recently taken a position as communications director for a large European company, and he related to me one of the challenges that many companies face, and then what his company was doing about it.

His remit was quite specific – to develop a sound internal communications methodology. The company had been showing incredible growth and its senior managers recognised the need to improve internal communications. And whilst he did identify and map out a successful way forward, he also encountered some serious unintended consequences of the solution.

The plan was to figure out a way to get the message out about the company's strategic direction, but it didn't take long for him to see that the infrastructure to do this didn't support the goal. There were inconsistencies from department to department; some managers had a solid sense of the strategy and did share that view; but whilst others had a view, they had been less-than-effective in sharing it; and some departmental managers didn't even see the entire strategic picture.

The challenge my friend faced was complicated by the very success of the company. As the company had grown, quite naturally, the workload for many managers and employees increased, and this increase in workload had begun to sap morale and over time, employee retention had become an issue. An increasing turnover in employee and managerial ranks made keeping the strategic message clear had become even more problematic. So senior management ensured that budget managers were given funds targeted to improving communications and learning, but the growth of the business meant that time to communicate and learn was surpassed by the need to keep the growth engine accelerating. My friend's path of choice was to engage managers and employees.

Engaging a workforce can be challenging, but the rewards from doing this can pay huge dividends. Initially, the challenge is to find out exactly who knows what in the organisation. This can be done through surveys, but the end product too often resembles what employees think that managers want to see. A more effective way to determine the real depth of knowledge about where a company is going, why it is going in that direction, and how it will get there, is to hold small meeting conversations. Assemble small cross-sectional groups of the organisational population, and ask them how the company functions. This will yield a series of organisational 'variables' – elements of the business that can either improve or decline over time. By linking them together with arrows, it is possible to illuminate how that group of people see the business operating. And by doing this with multiple cross-sectional groups, it is relatively easy to gain an understanding of the similarities or variances in workforce understanding of where the company is, and where it is going. And additional benefit of these conversations is that the people in each individual group begin to 'see' other managerial and employee views on the situation. This type of learning, *peer-to-peer learning*, is far more effective than simply trying to 'tell' people what you want them to know.

Once you have an understanding of the collective view of the organisational situation, you can then plan specific events targeted to expand that understanding across the business.

In situation, the director had put together a combination of events; specific strategy days – meetings targeted on deploying a common vision of the organisational strategy; and 'company away days ' – meetings targeted to combining shared learning and build additional alignment on where the company was going, and how it would get there.

One of the keys to ensuring that a company can realise its potential is to ensure that managers and employees alike have a shared understanding of what the organisational strategy is. And the first step to do this is to determine what and how much they know about it.

Unfortunately, if you don't engage the workforce, this can be brutally difficult to do. But by letting them share their views of how the business really works, and then building a programme around that baseline, it is possible to not only engage the workforce in the process, but to engage them in a way that they accept the strategic challenge and make it theirs. This makes far more sense than letting an existing communications infrastructure keep your hands tied.

## Happy Salmon Day

Yes, for many managers in today's 'interesting' business world, many days may seem like Salmon Day. You know, the day in which we have the distinct feeling that we are demonstrating behaviours similar to those of salmon.

We work like crazy, fighting our way upstream against the current of the business that keeps trying to throw us backwards; over rock-like obstacles; being pummelled against the flow. And if we make it over the top, we get to die. Isn't work life grand? After speaking to quite a few managers of various organisations recently at a evening programme, I found out what a typical 'Salmon Day' looked (and felt) like to a few of them.

1) *"Oh, it is interesting. The new matrix reporting system sure looked good on paper, but trying to stay on top of which boss wants what on any given day is becoming increasingly difficult. The lines keep becoming more and more blurred, and with all the new initiatives flying about, I am convinced that the clarity we used to have is probably only visible on E-Bay's collectibles page."*

2) *"If I wasn't already hair-challenged, I am sure I would be soon. I was just put in-charge of the new effort, but then was told that the budget I had been told I would have would be a bit less, and delayed. Then later I was told it would have to be cut even further. All this whilst having it pounded into my head that this was one of the most important efforts the company had ever undertaken, and wasn't I lucky to be the one to drive it. Right."*

3) *"The new guy that was brought in to fill my boss' vacancy was touted as being the perfect fit for the company. Then we found out that one of the big reasons he had been hired was that he had no previous experience in our sector and the Board thought that this 'different perspective' would be a good thing to have. Of course, no one told us – we read about this in the media. So much for building a team effort. And to top it all off, all he talks about is his 'new way of doing things' and has made it pretty clear that if we don't get onboard, we may not have a place here. If it weren't for the salary to cover the new house, I am pretty sure I would just fall on the sword and have it over with. It can't possibly be any worse."*

Notice anything common in the little stories I heard? Okay, other than they were all told by three managers who didn't seem that chuffed about their jobs? What struck me about them was that in each of the stories, it was as if there were so many structural roadblocks to high performance and high job satisfaction. I say artificial because in each of the stories, the problems were a combination of both real and perceived structural issues that suddenly had become bigger than the actual problems themselves.

The underlying fundamental problem in story number 1 is really all about the organisations' decision-making processes and how they are communicated. Story 2 is all about decision-making and communications. And story 3 is all about decision-making and communications. Notice the recurrence of certain themes here?

Most problems in organisations, whether real or perceived, usually relate to either the way in which decisions are made or the way in which the decisions are communicated. It isn't *what* decisions were made, but *how* they were made and communicated. And because of this, employees can begin to question the decision-making ability of senior management, as well as their willingness to communicate at all.

These underlying fundamental organisational problems can make every day seem like Salmon Day to those who are charged with doing what needs to be done, and unfortunately, because of the problems, what needs to be done actually rarely gets done.

Managers need to think of what needs to be communicated, and to whom it should be communicated. They need to make sure that the messages that are sent are complete, understandable, and provide all the information needed to make sure that the recipients can use the information to deliver high organisational performance. And to make sure that the messages are received in the way that they were meant to be received, managers need to find out how the information was interpreted, and if necessary, clarify them. Because if they don't, those on the receiving end will continue to think they are in an endless upstream swim over obstacles that need not be in the way.

## The Wisdom of Marx

The cardinal rule of business is that, if you want to stay in business, you need to take in more money than you put out.     Groucho Marx, not exactly the world's best-known business guru, summed this rule up with his quote, *"A child of five would understand this. Send someone to fetch a child of five."*  Perhaps some of the managers of the companies we read about should follow this advice.

One of the behaviours that we are seeing quite a bit of in the business world is the lemming-like drive to keep costs down. There is no doubt that keeping costs low is important, but it does seem to boggle the mind that, if we all recognise this, why is it that so many companies seem to have to drive cost-cutting initiatives over and over again?  I can only assume that the answer must be found in one of three reasons.

1) The initial cost-cutting effort wasn't done well.  Of course, this would call into question the competence of those that led the effort, and in many cases, these are the same people that have been asked to do it again.  Will they get it right this time, or is this part of their job descriptions – run a cost-cutting initiative every couple of years.

2) New cost pressures have surfaced and management needs to once again do some trimming.  Of course, this may call into question the ability of senior managers to do what they are paid to do – keep the company out of trouble.  Aren't they paying attention to industry, consumer, and competitive trends, or do their job descriptions only talk about fighting old, recurring problems instead of avoiding them?

3) After the previous cost-cutting adventure, costs have crept back in, resulting in the same problem all over again. Of course, this may call into question why decision-makers let the costs creep back, which would call into question their ability to manage at all. Doesn't the term 'keep costs under control' focus on the word 'keep?'

From many conversations I have had with managers, it seems that the third reason is quite prevalent – they cut costs hard and fast, but over time, the costs just seem to creep back in. And when I enquire as to why this happens, or even more appropriately, why they let it happen, they just shrug their heads and say that this is what happens. Not exactly a sound reason I would think.

Clearly, even after a cost-cutting initiative, there can be (allegedly) sound reasons to incur costs; new initiatives, acquisitions, capital equipment requirements, and training people to use the new equipment or follow new procedures. All this makes sense to me, but what I don't get is why management allows expenses for line items that were cut rise back to previous levels. If the expense was previously too high, what changed that now is causing it to resume?

Whilst previously deemed excessive costs creeping back up is one problem; the message that this sends to employees can be even a bigger problem over time. Employees look to management to make sound business decisions, and in most cases, these decisions are measured by the employees (and shareholders) by a simple test: do these decisions appear to be in the best interests of the business? An even easier test is, 'do these decisions have any resemblance to common sense?'

Let's look at the problem again. Costs are too high, so a cost-cutting initiative is implemented. But over time, the costs creep up to, or near to, previous levels. Perhaps Groucho was right, a child of five would understand this. But most of the employees and shareholders I talk to are not five, and they just don't get it. And how then do you think that they view the competence of management?

Management has (or should have) a set of serious responsibilities, one of which is to keep costs under control. When costs exceed prescribed levels, it is fair to assume they should be cut. But it is equally fair to assume that they should not be allowed to creep back unless there is a sound reason. Because if they do creep back, it is also fair to assume that either a) they were actually needed in the first place, or b) the managers that allowed them to creep back should be the next thing for the organisation to get rid of.

## When the Truth May Not Be the Truth

We all believe in something, and pretty much, one of the things we believe is that what we know the truth. Yes boys and girls, we know our beliefs are as true as 2 + 2 = 4. Of course, there are others who do not believe us but clearly, they are wrong...or so we choose to believe. In business also, sad to say, our beliefs are only *our version* of the truth and quite often the gap between what we believe and what others believe can get us and our organisations' into trouble.

Here is the way the whole 'truth' thing works. There are some universally held truths: the afore-mentioned 2 + 2 = 4; *the earth is round*; and *companies are in business to make money*. Few would disagree because these statements are largely self-evident (although it pays to remember, it wasn't that long ago that the prevailing belief was that the earth was flat). But then there are other types of truths, such as: *I am not paid what I am worth*; *we are the best company in our market segment*; and *our company's management team is competent to lead us into the future*. These are perceived truths which some people may (or may not) believe. But that does not make them universally accepted.

The problem with perceived truth in business arises when the perceptions somehow take on a life of their own, and we press the point to ensure that they are taken as read. And the problem is aggravated when those who we want to convince already believe that what they are being told is not the truth at all. This can lead to both believing that everything put forward is not the truth, as well as reinforcing the belief that the person trying to do the convincing is either incompetent or unethical. Either way, the problem of getting people to buy into this or that initiative is diminished.

Several years ago, just after a meeting with senior executives of a major international airline (a meeting in which I was told that the level of employee satisfaction was high and becoming higher), I had a chance meeting with quite a few employees standing at the company transport area waiting for the shuttle that would take them to the employee car park. I asked them about employee satisfaction and was told that the senior managers were; a) over their heads; b) incompetent; c) not capable to lead the company into the future; d) a group of liars who were only focused on ensuring their pensions would be 'fat.' I was also told that, in most cases of top-down communications, the line workers just kept doing what they knew what needed to be done and disregarded all the 'gung-ho' rhetoric that was always laced throughout the messages. This demonstrates a clear gap in the perceptions of truth that was preventing the company from realising its potential.

Earlier this year, whilst sitting in on a senior management meeting, I heard a regional MD explain away the fact that his people were not competent to deliver the required performance. And yet talking to some of the on-site people, I was told that their requests for more effective equipment and training had been disregarded as 'not necessary.' Both sides firmly believed that their versions of the situation were *the truth*. And yet they were different and this difference was causing serious problems for the company.

The question in both examples shouldn't be '*which version of the truth is correct*,' but instead should be '*how can we avoid this truth gap in the future in our organisation?*'

The answer is to listen. Listen to what people say, and then even more importantly, listen to what is behind what they say. By listening to what is behind what people say, it is possible to understand why they believe what they believe. Our beliefs are the basis for our own versions of the truth. If you are standing on the edge of the sea in Land's End and can't see New York doesn't mean that the world is flat and has an edge, just as telling yourself that you are a great manager doesn't actually mean you are one.

Unless we have incontrovertible evidence of something, it is our beliefs that tell us if it is *the* truth or not. All managers in organisations need to be willing to find out if their version of the truth matches up with others versions. Because if they don't, the truth gap will continue to grow and lead to problems that they haven't even thought of yet. And that is *the truth*.

Do you know the story about Coleman's Mustard? I was talking to a business friend the other day, and after a while, the conversation lead to the advantages of using technology at every opportunity. And then I recalled hearing about how adapting technology, for the sake of doing it, can sometimes result in precarious unintended consequences.

The story, as I was told it, was about how Coleman's made so much money. Years ago, when the company passed from one generation to another, the new head decided to do something a tad radical. Instead of just selling mustard in those jars that everyone had become so familiar with, he wanted to expand the business by selling his trademark product in squeezable containers and individual serving packets. A great way to expand their market share the company's decision-makers thought. So using the latest available technology (this did occur years ago), they began to offer product to the marketplace and in a relatively short period of time, sales were booming...and profits were falling. As the story goes, the son went to his father to ask for some sound advise; and was told the following; in the old container (the jar), consumers would spoon out a dollop of mustard onto their plate and then apply it to their food. The 20% of the dollop that actually made it onto the food covered our operating costs, and the 80% that was left on the plate and eventually washed away when the dishes were cleaned was our profit.'

This story, whether true or just some urban legend that has taken on a life of its own, can hold seriously important lessons for company decision-makers who are in love with the latest and greatest technology. There is no doubt that technology (whatever you might take that to mean) has made our lives easier, and has enabled us to accomplish more with the time we have. But, and this is a big but, this doesn't mean that we should all go zooming down the technology motorway like a herd of lemmings running to the cliff-edge.

Just going out and buying into whatever new technology you can find can be good, but the only way you can really realise the potential of such investments is to realise that the technology is not the real answer. In an article in the summer 2006 issue of the Sloan Management Review, research showed that there were two central lessons about implementing technology. First, realising the potential of an IT investment requires 'heavy investment in a wide range of complementary assets to support the technology – along with the patience to wait for these investments to pay off.' Second, using the technological advances really pays off when new structures and processes are developed to utilise the technology more effectively.

If you are keen to go deeper down the technology route – in most cases, this would mean information technology – then you need to consider four different, but interconnected elements of your organisation. These four elements are Vision, Technology, People, and organisational Structure. The elements all complement each other with the Vision piece giving the organisation direction – what you want your organisation to look like in the future; the Technology piece being the vehicle to simplify and accelerate how the systems and processes can work; the People piece being the way work actually gets done; and the organisational Structural piece being the way the decisions are made.

The key to these four elements is how they impact the real bottom line of business – how you make money. Without a clear vision of where the organisation is going in the future, profits can be made, but not sustained. Understanding what that future may bring can be the make or break factor in ensuring profits can be sustained over time. By effectively utilising technology to simplify and accelerate how systems and processes work can reduce your costs and, consequently, increase your profits. If you understand how the work in your organisation really gets done – the people piece – you can ensure that resources are made available in the right places, for the right reasons, and at the right times. And by understanding the organisational structure, you can leverage decision-making, ensuring that managers are focused on the right areas.

Whilst all this may seem like extra work, it is really just the common sense part of running an effective organisation and ensuring that the wisdom of your organisational version of Mr. Coleman is not washed away.

# Ensuring All the Pieces Fit Together

One of the big challenges that senior business leaders face is trying to ensure that everyone in their respective organisations see the same basic puzzle, and that decision-makers are not distracted by the 'cool and sexy' business opportunities that they may become enamoured with as they try to grow their businesses. This challenge should not be underestimated.

A good example of how this challenge can become a problem was facing the CEO of a global manufacturer recently. He had managed to take his company from what most analysts described as 'dire straights' to a solidly growing business with many opportunities in front of it. And whilst this all sounds like a good news story, the problem he was facing was that decision-makers, for several years being told to not spend any non-necessary money, were now being told to look for growth and acquisition opportunities to keep the current success pattern moving forward. As some of the managers with budget responsibilities were putting forth capital expenditure requests, the CEO noticed that many of the requests didn't seem to fit with the current direction of the company. The last thing he wanted to have happen was to be the head of an organisation that, after a rather heroic battle to get the company on track, was losing its way once again.

There is no doubt that becoming distracted by 'cool and sexy' opportunities is both easy and fun to do. And whilst the CEO didn't want to dampen the enthusiasm on the part of some of his managers for growing the business, he was concerned that unless growth acquisitions were in alignment with the direction of the company, it would be too easy for all the gains to wither away. When the managers were queried on the validity of a potential investment, the responses were largely in the category of 'this is a great opportunity, and if we don't move on it, the competition will.' That type of reasoning wasn't exactly what the CEO was looking for. Yes, clearly some of the opportunities were 'great,' and the CEO was sure that the competition might be also looking at them, but the bottom line was that if an opportunity didn't fit with where the company was going, and the way it was going to get there, it wasn't worth investing in.

The solution that made the most sense to the CEO was that when participating in cap-ex meetings, which he did quite often, he facilitate a conversation about the company's operating model. The vehicle he used to do this with was a system dynamics diagram that identified the key drivers of the organisation, along with how all the drivers interacted with each other. Initially, managers who were touting the latest 'hot' opportunity not only didn't understand the purpose of the conversation; they also struggled with the diagram, as it looked like a large plate of spaghetti, according to one of them, with arrows going all over the paper. But the CEO was confident that by using this type of vehicle to frame the conversation, he would be able to help the managers either shed more clarity on why an investment was sound, or come to the realisation that it was daft. Either way, the company would win, as the managers would have a greater understanding of how all the pieces fit together in the organisational growth puzzle.

The diagram listed the key variables that impacted organisational success. These variables included application of technology, research and development, quality of service, image, customer satisfaction, customer retention, number of customers, and competition. It also included the variables of employee satisfaction, motivation, commitment, employee turnover, training, skills, and company growth. The variables were connected to each other with 'causal' arrows, which showed how, if done effectively, employee satisfaction leads to additional motivation; and how quality of service leads to customer satisfaction and then to customer retention.

By using a diagram that showed how the organisation operated, the CEO was able to lead the conversation by listening to the proposals for acquisition, and then asking the question, 'if we make this acquisition, what will the impact be on our operating model?' The manager who was making the proposal was then asked to show the impact on the diagram.

Whilst an expected answer was that an acquisition would support the company's growth, but as was seen in one example, an unintended consequences of it would be that the quality of service could fall, due to the fact that the acquisition would result in a fractionalisation of priorities and service delivery due to the fact that it would take currently focused resources and shift them to the assimilation of the new company. Implicit in this would be a high risk of commitment falling within the organisation because an acquisition that was not immediately supportive of the current organisational direction would send the signal that the management decision-making process was not cohesive. One of the reasons that the company had been successful was that the level of commitment to organisational initiatives had been so high, and the risk of losing even some of that commitment was problematic. After a short conversation weighing the intended and unintended consequences of the acquisition, the proposal was withdrawn.

By using a system dynamics picture of the organisational operating model as the basis for discussion the CEO was able to achieve several things;
- Managerial alignment around how the organisation actually delivered its products and services globally was increased.
- The managerial thinking process about what potential acquisitions actually made sense prior to the proposals being submitted was improved dramatically.
- The managerial ability to justify rational acquisitions was increased, as they now had a way to explain how all the growth puzzle pieces fit together.
- Managers were better able to build alignment within their own operating units because their reports were able to see how their activities fit into, and supported, the overall organisation.

Ensuring that managers are able to make effective decisions is crucial to long-term organisational success. In order to do this, it can be very beneficial to help managers understand how their decisions will impact the organisation's ability to realise its potential. Making decisions in today's complex business world can be like putting together a jigsaw puzzle, and the ability to make sure all the pieces fit together appropriately can be the make or break difference in achieving sustainable success.

## The Onset of Creep

So here is the picture...your company was stuck a bit. The numbers weren't being hit; the level of overall efficiency was slipping downward; fire fighting was rampant; and the prospects for the future were as dim as a 10-watt bulb. So you and your fellow managers were told to turn the place around, and after a while (and a massive effort), it happened. You were back on track again. Things were on track, the numbers began to be hit, and life was looking better. But over time, all the key indicators of success began to creep backwards again. How could that happen? You had done what had needed to be done, and yet, all the indicators showed that soon you would be back where you started. Creep had set in.

Downward creep is not out of the ordinary. As a matter of fact, downward creep is the norm after turnaround efforts, and this is why. Most turnaround efforts, whilst strong in intent, end up being exercises in myopic reactive thinking. Think about the reasons for the pressure to turn the business around – the numbers weren't being hit; efficiency was slipping; fire fighting was rampant; and the future was looking dismal. In most organisations, when faced with these indicators, managers begin to crank up the pressure to improve and deliver better performance. Fair enough; but the way it is traditionally done is the problem.

In most situations that we have examined, the turn around effort focuses on figuring out where the gaps are between the performance results that are currently being produced, and the desired performance. This is all fine, except for one thing: the performance that is usually being looked at is solely financial performance. Now clearly, financial performance is the most often used measure of company health. Improving rapidly falling financial performance can be done by slashing and burning – the ultimate in quick fixes for business. Get rid of all the variable expenses you can, including cutting payrolls, chopping out all training, exorcise research and development, and otherwise cut spend to the bare bones. And if you do this well, you will most certainly improve the bottom line of the company. But if follow this method to regain financial stability, in most cases, in the near future, the problems can begin to reappear. It is the onset of creep.

Cutting payrolls can generate massive savings, but it can also result in the loss of organisational memory, followed by activities that are akin to reinventing the wheel. Not good. Chopping out training saves money, but it also means that your people will not have the skills and knowledge that your competitors will have. Not good. Exorcising research and development saves money, but will most certainly put you behind your competitors and their ability to innovate. Again, not good. All these activities will result in a better bottom line, but only in the short term.

If you want to seriously (and sustainably) turn the business's performance around you need to look deeper than the obvious. The phrase 'there is more going on that meets the eye' explains it all. 'Bad' numbers, low efficiency, fire fighting, and poor future prospects are all symptoms of an organisation that has excessive variation in its processes and systems; a human resource architecture that doesn't match with what the organisation is attempting to achieve; lack of commitment to ongoing learning within the company; and a distinct lack of leadership. The company may have some great managers, but managers are not the same as leaders; and managing an inappropriate structure won't deliver sustainable performance results.

If you want to avoid the onset of creep, you need to ensure that at least some of your managers are equipped to lead, and that they keep their focus on building a *sustainable* future for the organisation. This means that they think in terms of what it will take to deliver acceptable financial results *every quarter,* not just next quarter; they have the ability to influence others to see this same picture; when working to achieve goals and targets, they understand the potential unintended consequences of initiatives and activities; and they demonstrate that they are worthy of the title of 'leader.' They are able to make the hard decisions that need to be made, but at the same time, communicate them so that your people understand why they are being made. They need to do the right things, for the right reasons, at the right time, in the right way. They cannot fall back on the same reactive management thinking mode, because if they do, the onset of creep will lead your organisation right back toward oblivion. Which, by the way, is not good.

## It's All About Perspective

There are many organisations today that are at the fabled '*fork in the road.*' Whilst most managers queried would come up with similar answers when asked the question, '*what do we need to do to achieve our company's vision;*' it is clear that there are many different views about how to do it.

For senior management, this fact can be a bit mystifying. Strategic plans that are deployed throughout organisations tend to have a singular message; a message that focuses on what needs to be done. But quite often, the methods used to achieve the strategic initiatives are left open to interpretation. This is why so few companies actually do realise the potential of their strategic plans.

The problem of differing perspectives on 'how to do what needs to be done' results in fractionalised efforts, wasted time and resources, a can result in a demoralised workforce. Clearly, these results are not good for business.

One of the management techniques to deal with this problem is to press harder for results, which can actually work, but it is a solution that is not sustainable, and using it causes more problems over time. The only real solution is to ensure that managers and employees have a clear picture of what needs to be done, how it should be done, and the rationale behind why it is important. The reason is that in order to ensure that a strategy can actually be achieved; it is crucial to remove as much ambiguity from the decision-making process as possible.

In order to remove this ambiguity, senior management needs to do several things.

1) Be sure that the organisational strategy, if implemented effectively, will lead directly toward the desired future vision for the company. A strategy that does not mark out the path toward the desired future and at the same time, identify the ways to go down that path is just a waste of good paper.

2) Ensure that strategy identifies the few, vital activities that provide the greatest leverage in making forward progress. A strategic plan that identifies *all* the things (organisational-wide activities) that will need to be accomplished will do nothing but increase confusion and promote multiple perspectives on what is really most important to focus on. Use a prioritisation tool to sort through the myriad of *possible important activities* to get the list down to the *three or four important activities* that will provide the greatest leverage.

3) Ensure that a clear process is identified that mid-managers and employees can follow that will allow them to identify and develop the next tier of activities. The process should follow a pattern of

sub-activities, when done effectively, will contribute to the successful completion of the vital few activities. A clear process to follow begins to eliminate ambiguity around how to decide what employees should focus their efforts on so that what needs to be accomplished *can* be accomplished.

4) Be careful to ensure that the strategy picture you want to communicate covers all the various dimensions of the strategy. A sound strategy covers not only the financial and business growth aspects of what needs to be accomplished, but also the cultural aspects that are key to hitting those targets. Neglecting to cover the organisational cultural aspects of a strategy will only lead to a reduced ability to achieve the goals.

5) Test to make sure that the picture that you *want* your people to see is the picture they *actually see*. This is not to say that the picture must be perfectly identical – having diversity in perspectives is important in order to make sure that something stupid doesn't occur, but there is a big difference between perfect alignment, and alignment that ensures that the company gets to where it needs to go. Alignment in organisational initiatives and goals means alignment within parameters. It is akin to driving down the M4 (assuming you are there on a day when traffic actually moves). You may be headed out of the city toward Heathrow, but it doesn't mean that everyone has to be in the same lane, going the exact same speed, driving the exact same car, listening to the exact same music on the radio. Everyone on the motorway that day is headed in the same direction, but with some variation on the actual means to get there.

Having multiple perspectives in organisations is good. But it is only good if the perspectives are on the same goal, for the same reasons; and removing much of the ambiguity around what needs to be done, and for what reasons, can only help you get to where you want to go.

## Not Seeing the Signals?

We have seen this happen over and over again: senior business managers make strong commitments to learning and personal skill improvement, but when something runs amiss with projected profits, all the promises and commitments disappear faster than lemmings rushing to the cliff edge. These behaviours send several signals to managers and employees...and the signals can be devastating over time.

I have interviewed quite a few managers at companies that have seen this happen – MD's pledge that learning and training is the most important thing a company can do to ensure a long-term future (which is true), but when profits fall, training is the first thing to be hacked away; and when training disappears, most learning opportunities disappear with it. Reactions by employees and shareholders seem to fall into several categories of statements.

- *The long-term future of the company is not really important apparently.* This reaction - when employees are told that the only way to ensure long-term success is to learn faster than the competition, but training is cut as soon as things are tough - the conclusion that management is only focused on the short-term seems pretty logical. Cancelling training programmes will undoubtedly save companies money, but it is just a demonstration of reactive thinking on the part of the senior decision-makers. When profits fall, or don't meet expectations, cuts probably do need to be made, but cutting training is like amputating your child's legs if he falls of his bicycle. Sure, he won't fall anymore, but he also will never be able to ride again.

- *The senior guys just don't get it, and are not worth us putting in all the extra effort they ask us to do.* When training programmes are cut, some organisational senior managers just expect that employees will continue to learn on their own. Well, fair enough. If employees recognise the need for life-long learning, it stands to reason that they would continue to seek learning opportunities on their own. However, the problem is that self-directed learning can stray from what employees need to learn to be more effective in their jobs. Organisations need to invest in training their people, especially new employees, in how the company does what it does. They need to train employees, especially long-time employees, in change and how best to deal with it. They need to train all employees, especially management, in how to communicate more effectively. If the company doesn't sponsor this training, the chances that the employees will learn it are slim.

- *Senior management cannot be trusted to keep their word.* This might be the scariest of the signals that employees glean when training is stopped. If the senior managers can break a promise to train people – so that they can help ensure that the company will remain competitive and not be subject to profit shortfalls - what other promises will they break is a common question; a question that is asked just before employee commitment begins to plummet. Any organisation that does not have employees that are committed to the company direction and the team that is leading the strategic initiatives that should achieve a company vision is doomed to ongoing fluctuations in ability.

Cutting programmes designed to ensure long-term company stability and success is nothing more than short-term, reactive thinking. When some research has shown that the single most powerful differentiator for corporate success is the speed with which a company's employees can learn, this type of cost-cutting represents thinking that is myopic at best, and more appropriately, corporate lunacy.

Most certainly, when times are tough, costs must be monitored very closely, and excessive costs must be cut away. But just because training is one of the most obviously visible costs that are available to go after, it doesn't mean that management needs to take the easy way out. In most cases, this is a result of a lack of real leadership in organisations. Leaders are different than managers; management is all about keeping things within control, but leadership is all about creating environments in which organisations can realise their potential.

If your organisation is suffering from unacceptable profit levels, think twice before you fall into the management trap of just whacking away at easily visible costs, especially when cutting them may result in serious unintended negative consequences that few organisations can recover from. Or, if you think that short-term, myopic reactive thinking is the way to go, then just don't be surprised when the long-term future of your company simply disappears over time.

# The Observor's Paradox

I recently was in a meeting in which the MD of a medium-sized service organisation wanted to find out how well he was doing in leading his company into the future. An admirable effort on the surface to learn what was going on, but the way in which he went about it was abysmal. He found himself in what is known as the observer's paradox.

The paradox occurs when the observation or measurement itself affects an outcome, so that it can never be known what the outcome would have been if it were not observed. In the case of the managing director, he began by asking his direct reports how things were going, and just what do you think they told him? Most of them were quite complementary about the MD's leadership, with only one person expressing some mild concern that the company would not be able to achieve the rather ambitious plans for the future the MD had set out. So the MD aggressively pressed for details of what the manager was seeing and within seconds, the manager waffled, eventually saying that there were some naysayer's in the company, but he certainly wasn't one of them. Everyone left the meeting feeling good...well at least the MD felt good.

At the meeting after the meeting – the one that usually occurs at some coffee machine – more doubts surfaced. But critically, there weren't any conversations about why no one said anything in the formal meeting. Having sat in on quite a few meetings like this for clients, it was pretty clear that one reason that no one said anything was that it was a well-known fact that less-than-complimentary comments to the MD could be a risky move in the company.

Sadly, this dynamic occurs in too many organisations today. There are many MD's who send out verbal messages that they, in fact, do want to know if there are potential problems looming on the horizon. But parallel to these verbal messages are somewhat subtle signals sent out that problems with a strategy could lead the Board to believe that its choice to lead the company may not be the best one, potentially putting an MD at risk.

The question is, *'if you are an MD, how do you ensure that you will be told if there are problems looming in the future, whilst at the same time, not being made to look incompetent?'* And if you are a manager, *'how can you provide open honest feedback to your superiors without then feeling the need to update your CV?'*

The answer to both questions is to understand what might happen before it actually happens. Unfortunately, too often the 'what else might happen' only looks at potential situations through rose-coloured glasses.

Managers who are seriously interested in knowing how the people they supervise view their skills, style, and leadership abilities need to do several things.

1. Create a feedback process in which the feedback is sent to someone other than yourself. This will help ensure that the feedback will be honest and open. Ensure that whomever is sent the feedback will not tell you who said what.
2. Ask for feedback on several key elements of organisational progress. These include; A) Are we really on track with our strategy? B) Are we susceptible to problems with our implementation process? C) Am I doing everything I should be doing to enable our people to do what needs to be done? D) What can I do better to create an environment in which we can realise our organisational potential?' E) Am I demonstrating the leadership behaviours that we will need for our company to succeed? The key to the last question is to find out what behaviours you have been demonstrating. If your people cannot 'see' you demonstrating the behaviours that they believe are important for your company to succeed and are congruent with your organisational values, then you aren't doing them well enough.
3. Ask what your employees and peers would like to see you do more, and what they would like to see you do less.
4. Be open about the fact that you want to create an environment in which you, your employees, and your peers can all become better at how they do what they do. Inform employees and peers about the feedback you have received, and what you are doing to learn from it. Share with them what you will do more of and less of in the future, and ask them to tell you if they aren't seeing the changes.

There are risks with doing all this. You may hear feedback that is not especially complimentary, you may find out that there are some potential problems looming that no one had seen before, and you may find that you need to change the way your behaviours are demonstrated. But if your objective is to create a better functioning organisation, this is the best way to begin.

# Trying to Stay Dry?

During the 2005 elections in Germany, Norbert Walter, the chief economist for Deutsche Bank, was quoted as saying "There's the old German saying, *'Wash my fur, but don't get me wet.'*" He may have been talking about the fear of change on the part of Germans, but the statement applies to employees of most businesses today…all over the world.

We all know that change is the only constant in business, or by now we should know this. I can't think of the last time I heard that change is not something that employees will be subject to. But at the same time, whilst we may accept that change is here to stay in our organisations, we sure don't like it when we are the ones who are asked to do the changing.

Being in an organisation that is moving in a direction you don't like is like being on a plane that is flying from London to Reykjavik – if, when you realise what the destination is, you decide you don't want to go there, your choices are to either A) get off the plane (a hazardous thing to do at 12,000 metres); B) close your eyes and hold your breath thinking that the pilot will somehow sense your feelings and reroute the plane to Palma (as if that would happen just for you); or to C) get with the programme and understand why going to Reykjavik could be a valuable experience.

There are several problems with the way that organisations introduce change to their people.

1. *If no real case for change is given, there will be little chance that the employees will buy into the effort.* A case in point can be found in the global energy companies around the world today.  Most cases for change involve lack of necessary profits, but in the case of the oil companies, there seems to be no end to the current gusher of profits that the companies are experiencing due to the price of crude oil.  All the talk we used to hear about incompetence in decision-making has disappeared and instead, managers are just reeling in the glory of how smart they must be to be generating all this money (which of course, is not the reason they are flush with money.  They are profitable because of external forces that have driven the price of oil to unheard of limits, resulting in massive profits for them).  This is what we

call, being at the right place at the right time; and one can only wonder if they will take this opportunity to make the changes that should be made so as to not waste the profits. Examine your case for change, and if it is difficult to find, look at some of the systemic ramifications of continuing to do business as it is being done today.

2. Too often, *employees do not see the benefits from the change effort* – benefits that they should experience directly and indirectly. If employees cannot see 'what is in it for them,' the chances that they will ever buy in will be almost non-existent. Employees are not stupid, and they, for the most part, will believe that change is taking place for the sake of change unless you can help them see the benefits that will come to them. And in most cases, this does not just mean more money. Employees are keen to know if the change effort will help them learn and grow, help create an environment in which they could become more motivated, and increase the chances that the company will become more sustainable (and consequently, they might be able to keep their jobs). Help employees see what is in it for them if they buy into, and become committed to the change effort.

3. *In many cases, change is perceived to be just another corporate programme*, and not an underlying parameter that all organisations need to deal with. Programmes come and go, and if the employees believe that change is just another one of those, many of them will develop a bunker mentality and try to wait it out. The defence mechanisms that they use to keep change at bay are complex, but usually effective. This results in depressed employee morale, wasted time and resources, and falling performance. By having a consistent message that everyday, change will need to be occurring in the organisation, employees will be able to shift their mental models to accept change for what it really is...a way to improve an organisation's ability to survive, to grow, and to prosper.

Dealing with organisational change is much like what Franklin Roosevelt said years ago; *'the only thing we have to fear is fear itself.'* It is the responsibility of senior management to make sure that organisational change and fear do not have to be used in the same context. This, however, will require a change in mindsets on the part of management as well as those of employees.

76

Unfortunately, it is apparent that many senior managers in organisations today in the UK must have been raised to believe that Norbert Waller's statement about Germans is right, and they don't want to get wet either.

## An Oncoming Train?

When organisations plan for the future, one of the questions that should come up is, 'is our plan going to achieve what we need for a sustainable future?' This question is critical, especially in light of a study commissioned by the Institute of Directors that said that sixty-nine percent of the respondents to the question, 'what factors inhibit future thinking in your organisation' stated that they were 'too busy.' Too busy to figure out what they future might bring? Wake up lads; the light at the end of the tunnel just may be an oncoming train.

According to the IOD report, thirty percent of the respondents mentioned that they had 'a lack of in-house expertise,' and another thirty-one percent sited 'inadequate resources' as the reason that their ability to see into the future was inhibited. These responses raise a very serious question – *how can organisations expect to survive into the future when no one is trying to determine what that future might bring?*

Yes, managers today are probably busier than ever, but busy doing what? Most of the managers I speak with seem to have their diaries filled with ongoing, recurring problems that have never been really solved. They are inundated with assignments and responsibilities that feed the addiction to reactive thinking and fire fighting. Just look at the stories in the media: budget airlines that don't seem to care if they alienate customers because they assume that other customers will fill the seats; energy company managers that are so busy patting themselves on the back for high profits that they forget that it wasn't their decision-making excellence that generated them, but instead the global demand for oil; and senior managers who quick to say their heads are on the line, but then shun the responsibility for organisational performance. It might be time for shareholders to press for more accountability for the future of business.

The ability, or in many cases willingness, to look to the future can be a make or break competency for companies. Behaviours and skills that were acceptable a dozen years ago just don't cut it in 2005. Being 'too busy' to try to put clarity on potential scenarios that a business may face is akin to driving your car at high speed day and night, just to rack up as many miles as possible. Sure, you may see your odometer climb quickly, but if you don't stop once in a while to check the engine or put petrol in, you will end up on the side of the road sitting watching your competitor cruise past. To put it plainly, there simply is no excuse for not trying to understand what the future might bring, unless of course, you don't care. And in some companies I know, that is the case.

The average tenure in a senior organisational position today is declining. CEO's seem to last as long as summer in England, and when the new one arrives, the first piece of business appears to be how to make his mark on the company. That behaviour is almost understandable; they are given high-paying jobs with lots of responsibility and are under pressure to deliver the performance results the last guy in the position apparently wasn't able to deliver. But seldom do we see new leaders begin by focusing on ensuring that the business will survive long after they have retired. Instead, the focus is on driving short-term results that distract from the larger issue of sustainability.

Over 30 years ago, the people at Royal Dutch Shell did planning based not only on what they needed to accomplish, but also on *what might happen in the future.* They were the only energy company who had plans ready to deal with what we know as OPEC. And these plans enabled them to be prepared when the price of crude oil skyrocketed. They were thinking in terms far longer than the literal tomorrow. Unfortunately, this ability within Shell has disappeared, as now they, as we have seen, seem to have had a focus on managing the market expectations through number manipulation. The story of GEC-Marconi is another prime example. When Lord Weinstock was the head of GEC, the company kept thinking about what the future might bring. No, it wasn't sexy and cool to do that, but the company was profitable and stable and positioned for the future. And then Weinstock was sent away and new people came in who were blinded by some cool and sexy investment opportunities that they thought could improve their immediate future. And as shareholders of Marconi can attest to, the once proud company is just a shadow of its previous self, and probably lucky to be in business at all.

Does Ryanair really think that they will always have enough customers with their apparent policy of 'do it our way or go find another carrier?' Are the decision-makers at BP that sure that the price of oil will never again go down? Do the senior people at BA think that just because they use to be the best airline, they will always be good enough to remain in business? What are these companies going to do if they are wrong? Come on lads, let's use some common sense and realise that the future is not guaranteed.

Senior management needs to re-think some of their priorities. Planning for the future is just as important as planning for next quarter, and not having people looking long-term as well as short-term is inexcusable in today's business world. This applies to all organisations, of all sizes, and from all sectors. If the light at the end of the tunnel is really an incoming train…is too late.

## None of the Above?

You have seen this happen before. As a matter of fact, you may have actually experienced it. You are faced with several options when making a critical decision and whilst you realise that neither of the options are all that good. None-the-less, the expectation is that you make a choice, and the options that have been identified are all that are available. What do you do? Most respondents to this question say that they would opt-out for one of the available options, with the reasoning being that these are the only choices. Perhaps.

Many decision-makers end up taking one of the available choices because either they don't want to slow down the decision-making process, or, they don't want to risk alienating a superior by being perceived to be 'not with the programme.' The reality is that both of these are simply excuses for not fulfilling managerial responsibilities.

Managers are paid to make the right decisions, at the right time, for the right reasons; and to do that, they need to ensure that several things should be considered.

- Decisions should be based on hard data. The term 'hard data' should include items such as fiscal impact on the organisation, the level of potential commitment to the decision, and if it makes sound business sense. In organisations where 'intuition' is an acceptable rationale for decision-making, it is too easy for decision-makers to become distracted by trendy and sexy opportunities that may surface, which intuitively feel 'right' at the time. Check out the data to make sure that the decision is right; and if you can't find supporting data, then re-think the decision.

- Prior to decisions being made, the consequences of them should be considered. One of the reasons to make a decision is because of the intended consequences; but often, it is the unintended consequences that are overlooked. If these are overlooked, a decision that looks good today may, in the future, look like a disaster. Identify *all* the intended and unintended consequences prior to committing to the decision.

- The ability to implement the decision – whatever it is – should be part of the decision-making process. A decision that cannot be implemented effectively is not a good decision. In this context, 'ability' means having the appropriate level of financial and human resources available; having a commitment from senior management to keep the resources available; and ensuring that there is enough alignment around the challenge the decision holds.

- Test out the decision before it is made. The challenge of testing the decision is not as complicated or time consuming as it might sound, and the time spent making sure that it is *right* is always far less than the time it may take to recover from a less-than-effective decision. Find out if the decision makes sense by asking those it will impact, and in many cases, that means front-line employees and managers. In some organisations, this may seem counter-intuitive, as these people aren't the ones who are pad to make the decisions. However, these are the people who will have to deal with decision outcomes, and the probability that they will know if the decision makes sense is high.

- Ensure that decision-makers have the option, and are encouraged, to express concerns about options that, even after all these steps are taken, still do not make sense. Organisations that do not allow dissenting opinions to be raised are organisations that will be doomed to fail over time. The challenge of course is to not simply hear people say that they don't like this or that decision, but instead have the opportunity to explain why the decision doesn't make sense; and then if possible, come up with other options that could be explored.

The whole purpose of having a sound decision-making process is to ensure that good decisions are being made. Good decisions are the ones based on data, with unintended consequences being considered, that can be implemented effectively, and that have been tested to make sure that they are the right decisions, at the right time, for the right reasons. Anything else is simply unacceptable in today's business world.

## Being on the Edge

The "edge" carries many connotations in business, and some of them are rather interesting. "He is on the edge" can imply that the subject is over-stressed, working past his capacity, and about to do something that may cause the organisation serious problems. But it can also imply that the subject is positioned to have a unique perspective on what is taking place in the organisation, and why. The first explanation should be cause for some type of human resources or training intervention. The second explanation should cause some senior people to sit down and hear the story that the subject may have to tell.

In business, perspective is crucial. Being able to see both the detail complexity that is occurring, whilst at the same time, being able to see the dynamic complexity can provide a perspective that can yield important information that can help an organisation realise its potential. Most managers are, because of their positions and responsibilities, are saddled with detail complexity; production or service delivery statistics, revenue projections, and reports on just about everything. All these are important, and having people focused on detail complexity is not a bad thing. However, unless some people are also focused on the dynamic complexity within the organisation, all the planning and efforts will not yield sustainable desired results.

Being able to see and understand dynamic complexity means that you not only see what needs to be done, you also understand why those choices are the most appropriate. Dynamic complexity is all about the inter-relationships between the "what" and the "why" of business decision-making, and being able to see and understand the dynamic complexity that is present often requires that the observer views it from "the edge."

An example of how this works can be found through the example of a forest. The observer of detail complexity is someone who is standing directly in front of a tall tree. He is able to see the bark of the tree, and might be able to identify which type of tree it is, what its girth and height are, and how close it is to the adjacent trees. If asked to tell the story of the forest, his perspective (standing immediately in front of a tree) will prevent him from giving an effective (and accurate) representation of what is going on. However, if the observer is standing on the edge a plane flying overhead, he is able to describe not only the entire forest, but also see why the forest is growing in the way it is, as well as what threats the forest may be facing in the future. The first observer sees only the detail complexity of one of the trees in the forest, but the second observer sees the dynamic complexity of the forest and what is going on around it.

In the case of business, a line manager sees the detail complexity that surrounds his or her department or business unit; however, an "on the edge" observer of dynamic complexity can see and understand the inter-relationships of why the organisation performs as it does, and why managers demonstrate the behaviours they do. The ability to see and understand dynamic complexity is crucial when an organisation is facing competitive pressures, for organisations trying to sustain rapid growth, and for organisations that are involved in trying to integrate multiple cultures due to a merger.

The task is to be able to see the right mix of detail and dynamic complexity so that an organisation can realise its potential. Because most organisations are awash with detail complexity and continually reward managers for focussing on it, the challenge for senior management is to see that other alternate perspectives can and will surface.

One of the best ways to accomplish this is to require managers to examine how efforts to achieve their goals will impact other areas of their organisation. The ability to see how individual or departmental efforts impact other areas of an organisation is a technique that elevates the perspective of managers. By looking at both the intended and unintended consequences of activities can provide new insights as to the dynamic complexity that is present in all companies. Not only does this help managers better understand the implications of their activities; it also helps to close the gap that is usually present between the real complexity and the perceived complexity in an organisation.

As more managers are able to shift their perspectives of how the organisation actually works by viewing it from "the edge," the ability of the organisation to realise its potential is increased.

## Right in Front of You

When is the last time that the obvious stared you right in the face, but that others on your team weren't able to see it? This happens more than we would like to believe; and in most of these cases, the fact that others can't see the obvious can lead to mis-placed efforts, mis-appropriated budgets, and other forms of wasted resources. A good question might be, *'why is it that they can't see what I see?'* But a better question might be, *'how can I help others expand the way they view opportunities, challenges, and looming problems?'*

Many managers who experience this dynamic – you see something others don't – assume that one of the reasons is that the other people are incompetent or don't have the same brilliant set of skills you do. In some organisations, this might be true; but a more likely explanation is that everyone else is so pre-occupied with those things that they perceive to be urgent instead of those that are crucially important.

The ability to distinguish between urgent and important can be critical in business today. Yes, situations that need to be addressed immediately to avoid problems can increase the 'urgent' inbox on your desk, but in most cases, if the things that are in reality 'important' are addressed, the number of urgent crises is diminished.

Another problem that can negatively impact manager's ability to see what is important is that most managers have been taught to think in a linear fashion; 'A' leads to 'B,' which leads to 'C' and then to 'D.' This is fine, except in any system – organisations are, after all, just systems – there is feedback. The ability to see this feedback – 'A' leads to 'B,' which leads to 'C' and then to 'D' but at the same time, when 'C' changes, it also causes 'A' to change – can make the difference in making good decisions or not-so-good decisions.

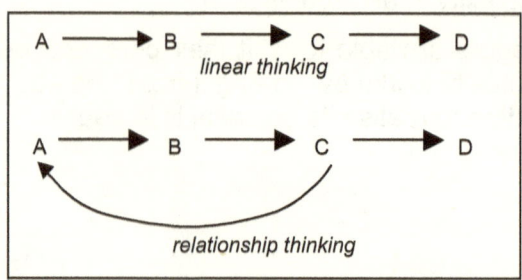

By understanding the feedback loop – the interrelationship between variables in the system – it is possible to better see how decisions impact actions. This is accomplished by understanding that the more you do one thing (for example action 'B'), whilst it will result in 'C,' it will also reinforce (or aggravate) 'A.' With this understanding, you can make a more informed decision about the need to re-think action 'B.'

Managers and decision-makers who are able to understand the interrelationships between system variables tend to see what others do not see. It can also explain why some managers are more effective than others, and why some organisations that do not utilise systemic relationship thinking are not able to realise their potential.

If you want others to see more, there are several things you can do.

1. Begin to hold conversations about what is important and what is urgent in your organisation. Make a list of all the challenges that need to be addressed, and then classify them into one of the two groups. If your lists make it look like everything is both important and urgent, establish criteria to make the distinction between the two. Typical criteria include 'available time to address challenges,' 'challenges that will move the organisation toward its vision,' 'problems that have arisen in the past,' and, 'things that can be delegated.' Once these criteria have been applied, it will be easier to see what is

crucially important (challenges that will move you closer to the organisational vision) and what is simply urgent (problems that have arisen). If your lists still have overlaps, do it again. If you spend all your time on the 'urgent,' you will never be able to address what is really 'important' for your organisation.

2. When you are talking to other decision-makers about what needs to be done and why, ask if any of the options will have side effects. These can be intentional or unintentional, as well as being good or bad. This new 'view' may look more complex, but that is because organisational systems are complex, but by being able to actually see the complexity (and its implications in decision-making), managers are better able to make the right choices, at the right times, for the right reasons. By beginning to look at the consequences of actions – especially the ones that are not easily visible – it is possible for other decision-makers to expand their view of what needs to be done, and why.

If others in the organisation still aren't able to see and understand what you see, you need to either re-think how you communicate, or re-think if they are the right people to have involved in helping chart the future or your organisation.

## A Business "Bad-Hair" Day

The term 'bad-hair day,' in the context of business, could mean days when things are unmanageable or when everything seems to go awry. If you work for an organisation, and you are breathing, you have experienced these. And, as you probably will again experience them again, this could be a good opportunity to review your options.

Option 1: Put the blame on someone. This option is often used and perhaps has the greatest number of sub-options; competition, incompetent staff, lack of resources, and governmental regulations to name just a few. With so many 'reasons' that could have contributed to the mess you have found yourself in, this option can be easily used.

Option 2: Go home early and pray that tomorrow things will sort themselves out. Several stiff drinks on the way home usually accompany this option, along with the chance to vent your frustration with the chaos to the barkeep. If you are lucky, by the time you get home you won't remember a thing.

Option 3: Deal with the problems and move on. This option, whilst it may not be as much fun as the other two, is the only rational way to deal with days like this. If you decide that this option makes the most sense, here are some things you can do to assist you.

1. **Find out what are the root causes of the problems**. This is not as difficult as it can appear. First, make a list of what could be causing the problem. Second, sort out which items on your list are 'symptoms' of the problem and which are actual items that have caused the problem to occur. The trick here is to understand that quite often, the real causes are several steps removed from what you are experiencing, and because of this, you may need to keep 'going back' several steps to find the cause. It is also important to realise that your problems may not be the result of any one thing, and it can be very helpful to look at the relationships between several causes to determine how things have become so mucked up.

2. **Come up with choices of how to get through the current situation before things get out of hand.** Once you have sorted out what the real cause (or causes) is, you can make a list of what can be done. You can do this yourself, or, if you are really interested in clearing up the mess, ask for input as to what others see as ways forward. I know quite a few senior managers who have great distain for asking for help, but these are the same people whose intuition can often mislead them. Make a list and get someone else to see if the list makes sense.

3. **Determine which of these choices will minimise the effects of the problem and which will prevent it from occurring.** This step may seem a bit over the top, but the reality is that unless you know what the results of any actions will be, you may find yourself reliving the same problems over and over again.

4. **Prioritise your choices based on sound criteria.** Your criteria might include: available resources, available time, available support, and ability to overcome internal political problems that can sabotage your efforts, but regardless of what they might be, use some criteria to make sure that what you decide to do, you can actually accomplish.

5. **Explain to those affected by the problem what you are going to do, and why.** One of the biggest reasons that things

run amuck in business today is the lack of effective communications. Not only is it important to ensure that your team knows what you are going to do, but also it is also important that they understand the rational behind your decision. If they don't understand either or both of these things, there is a high possibility that you won't get the support you need.

6. **Actively work to surface organisational 'undiscussables' that may prevent you from achieving what your organisation needs to achieve.** The impact of 'undiscussables' should not be underestimated, as they often represent the issues that can either make or break the ability of an organisation to be effective. By getting these out into the open and talking about them, it is possible to defuse defence mechanisms that managers and employees use as a way to resist changing the way they do what they do.

Whilst this all may seem to be 'extra work,' and you may believe that you don't have the time to do them, the reality is that if you don't, your organisation will continue to suffer from the mediocrity that is an outcome of business 'bad-hair days.'

## Plastics

No, this isn't about the plastics industry, nor is it about recycling problems. It is about what we remember, and why we remember it. We all seem to be able to remember certain quotes from movies: *'Plastics'* – the Graduate; *'Frankly my dear, I don't give a damn'* – Gone with the Wind; *'May the force be with you'* – Star Wars; and *'I love the smell of napalm in the morning'* – Apocalypse Now. These are all things we remember from movies for one reason or another. Whilst we may remember these phrases, it is interesting that we rarely remember much of what our organisational leaders tell us during those allegedly inspirational speeches that we sit through.

There are three main reasons that this can happen. Reason 1: the person giving the speech is not inspirational; reason 2: the message isn't inspirational; reason 3: a combination of 1 and 2. And if those reasons are not enough, there is something else that causes many of those allegedly inspirational messages to fail. The key rule that anyone who is trying to communicate needs to remember is; *the ability to communicate effectively depends on what the audience hears, not solely on what is said.*

The ability of people to actually hear what you say can depend on several communications lessons.

1. **People learn from stories**. Many presenters that I have witnessed seem to think that a speech accompanied by a plethora of PowerPoint slides that are littered with data is the best way to get a point across. There is no doubt that presenting data is important in today's pressure-laden business world. But the reality is that few people actually are able to remember all the data that is shown, assuming that they can even read it on a slide. We learn from what we remember, and, if you think back to when you were young, you weren't provided data; you were told stories. We remember and learn from stories, and because of this, using stories to communicate a point is a good method to use. If you believe that your organisation doesn't have a 'story,' then you need to think back to what a story actually is.
2. **Data is rarely inspirational**. What is inspirational is a presentation that provides the listener with a way to understand that the future of the organisation will be better than its current reality. By setting up a creative tension between the desired future and the current reality, it is possible to create in the minds of your listeners a vision for why your organisation needs to move toward that future.
3. **You need to connect**. Over the years, I have found two types of organisational presenters. One type is able to read a prepared speech very well, often, without appearing to be actually reading a prepared text. This is fine, but often, it comes off as just what it is – a recitation of words that are devoid of any passion. The other type of presenter is recognised because he (or she) is able to connect with the audience. This ability to connect is key to a good presentation. When individual members of an audience can each believe that the presenter is speaking directly with them – as opposed to just talking at the entire audience – the potential for the audience members to actually listen to what is said is increased dramatically.

The key to all this is making sure that what you, as a presenter, say is actually the same thing that audience members hear. The gap between what is said and what is heard should not be underestimated.

The absolute worse thing that can happen during a presentation is for the audience to mis-interpret what your message actually is. This does not mean that they necessarily don't hear the words – it means that they attach different meanings to the words than you intend.

In order to counteract this dynamic, only use data sparingly and when it is needed. Instead, explain what you want to explain in a story or metaphorical format. And avoid appearing to be simply reading some pre-prepared speech; let the audience know that you are passionate about the messages you are communicating. If you find these presentation lessons to be 'not your style,' then you run the risk that what will be remembered is your style (or lack of it) instead of the message you want to share. As with most management actions, it isn't 'what' that is done that makes a difference; it is 'how' it is done.

## Rosebud

It was in the Orson Wells movie classic, "Citizen Kane," where 'rosebud' was mentioned. Whilst the real-life personalities that the main characters in the movie were modelled after were quite obvious, viewers walked out of cinemas wondering what 'rosebud' actually meant. You know, kind of like being in a management meeting when some senior leader says something that no one really understands. In most cases, we all sit there and bob our heads in agreement, but we aren't exactly sure what he or she really meant. We have all seen this happen, and often, we are the ones who are left wondering.

The impact of the need to be clear about messages in business should not be underestimated. Examples of this can be found in messages around:
- An organisational vision – if managers and employees are not sure where an organisation is going, their ability to help it get there will be more difficult than it needs to be.
- An organisational strategy – if decision-makers are not clear about what activities they need to do to achieve a strategy, their

efforts will be dis-jointed, mis-aligned, and often times, result in wasted time and resources.

- Specific organisational initiatives – if there is not clarity around the rationale behind initiatives (often this occurs in change initiatives), the chances that alignment and commitment behind those initiatives will be mitigated dramatically, virtually ensuring failure.
- Feedback on organisational and individual performance – if performance feedback is not clear and specific, managers and employees will not know where to focus to improve.

In all of these examples, the lack of clarity around a message or messages can result in problems that can easily be avoided.

Recently, whilst talking with an MD of a global company about this issue, his response was that his *people are extremely competent and they should know what I mean.'* Perhaps. This assumption is one that many senior leaders hold, but the reality is, in many cases, quite different. During an informal survey on the subject of clarity of communications, it became clear that many messages are clouded in ambiguity.

This was evident by some of the comments offered. *"When I ask for specific direction about which priority is the highest, I am told to just get on with it.'* This response, whilst perhaps sending the signal that the expectation is that the recipient is competent enough to decide, also is wide open with interpretation options; which can be fraught with potential problems over time.

Another respondent mentioned that when he has asked his MD if he agrees with the way an initiative is progressing, the response he hears is, *'I am okay with it.'* Being 'okay' with an initiative is not the same thing as acknowledging that it as a good thing to do, nor is it the same thing as approving its implementation.

There are several key issues around making sure that the messages we hear are the ones that are intended.

1. When asked a direct, closed question, it is best to respond with either a yes or no response. Too often, managers tend to respond with painfully vague answers or explanations about the complexity of the issue, when all the person who asked wants is a yes or no. Anything but a direct answer to a direct question will only result in confusion. **Take the ambiguity out of**

**answers to questions.**

2. When doing team, group, or organisational communications, make sure they are clear and concise. Messages that are vague or open to multiple interpretation do nothing other than send the signal that management is not sure what needs to be done, and the natural assumption that follows that is that they may not be competent to lead. **Do not assume that people understand what you mean, make sure your messages are clear and understandable.**

3. Communications need to include answers the questions that managers and employees need to have answered. In many situations, what is communicated does not address the issues that are on managers and employees minds. **Ensure that you understand what your people need to know, and give them the direction that they need to deliver consistent high performance.**

4. Don't assume that people understand your message; ask for feedback on what you said, and what they think it means. **Receiving real feedback is the only way to ensure that what you have communicated is being 'heard' in the way it needs to be heard.**

Vague messages and communications are open to multiple interpretations, and in the business world of today, that can only lead to long-term problems that can be easily avoided. Unless of course, you want your people waste time and opportunities wondering what you meant instead of doing what needs to be done so your company can realise its potential.

## A Shark in Formaldehyde

Too often, organisations under pressure to change suffer from additional dilemmas. Who in the organisation is competent to lead the change effort? How do we ensure that all the effort really accomplishes something? How will we know when we are done? These are all fair questions, but unfortunately, there is no singular answer that is always correct to any of them. Instead they set up a new Damien Hirst-like question. Several years ago, the Tate museum in London shocked the world by exhibiting Hirst's latest work – a shark suspended in a box filled with formaldehyde. And in the art world, it stimulated the question, *'is is art?'* A similar question arises from most change programmes. *When is a change effort really creating a new environment and not simply as effective as re-arranging the deck chairs on the Titanic?*

Last week, I received a letter from a business manager who was concerned that the people who were leading the change effort in his company were not really competent to do so. His question was *'how can I show them what they really need to do if they don't see it themselves?'* My experience is that you can't. About the only way to ensure that people decide to do something differently is to help them see the gap between what they do now, and what they need to do in the future. All the talking in the world about shifting behaviours will not carry an iota of weight as compared to managers and employees discovering the gap themselves. But, if you can help them see the gaps that might be present between where they want to go (and why), and where they are now; and what skills they need to have to drive change, and what skills they have now; the potential that they will want to have those gaps close is highly increased.

To see the gap between where you want to go and where you are, assemble a small group of managers and articulate *all* the dimensions of what the future organisation they want (or need) are. This is an important point; ALL the dimensions mean a picture that looks at more than just the financial aspects of the desired future. The reason for this is two-fold; first, the *numbers* are just outcomes of the newly changed organisation. What you want to be able to see are the dimensions of the organisation that will drive those outcomes. You should do this with more than one group – different managers have different perspectives, and it is always best to see if there is alignment in how the challenge is seen.

Second, if numbers are all that is important, just save your time and go out and buy a few hundred whips and force everyone to work harder until the numbers are achieved. This is lame, old thinking that it is clearly not sustainable, in today's business world.

The dimensions you are after are answered by questions like 'what systems and processes will be needed in the future?' what reward structures will be needed? What mental models will be required? What levels of alignment in thinking? What competencies will be needed? When you get some consensus as to this picture of the desired future, then identify what the *current* organisational dimensions are. Rest assured, there will be a gap, and in some organisations I have seen, the gap is rather intimidating. But because your competition is closing their gaps, you have to.

Next, sit down with the managers who will be charged with making the change programme successful and show them the outputs from the previous exercise, and then ask them what they are prepared to do differently *beginning tomorrow* to close the gaps. But if you really want this effort to succeed, ask them what they will do differently in four specific managerial competency areas; how they think, how they influence, how they achieve, and how they lead. After they have done this, they need to do a peer and subordinate review. Do their responses make sense? Will these new demonstrated behaviours in thinking, influencing, achieving and leading, be able to close the gaps between where the organisation wants to be and where it is? Historically, when doing this review, managers discover, and come to the self-realisation, that what they have done in the past will just not be good enough in the future.

Yes, you may experience push-back or at very minimum, looks of bewilderment, but managers need to realise that the organisation is the way it is because of the decisions that had been made up to that point in time, and *the way they acted those decisions out*. If the organisation is to change; i.e. become a sustainably high performing organisation; then managers need to realise that the only way it will happen is if they do things differently. All the memo's from the home office; all the veiled threats from analysts; all the yelling and whinging from employees and customers alike will not change behaviours unless managers can see for themselves what needs to be done. And the only effective way for them to do this is to see it themselves.

If your managers decide that they don't want to do this, or think that they are too busy or important to do this, then you may want to just ring up Damien Hirst and see if he can put them in formaldehyde too. Who knows, they then might be more valuable than they are now.

# The Play's the Thing

You might have thought that William Shakespeare was writing about some managerial behaviours when, in Hamlet, he wrote, *"The play's the thing."* Based on what some companies are experiencing today, he was spot on.

Shakespeare could have been writing about how some senior managers in organisations game the system by appearing to demonstrate aligned behaviours, but are in fact, walking a very fine line between incompetence and insubordination. Here is how this all works.

You have a managerial team that is supposed to deliver a set of goals or targets, and the team's leader identifies what needs to be done. The leader has also made it quite clear that there is a way in which to accomplish these goals or targets that are congruent with the values of the organisation. The team members go off to do what needs to be done, but when the results begin to be clear, the emphasis of some of the managers has been put on the achievement of the goals, but not the way in which they were achieved. This signals to the team that what is most important is getting things done, and how they are done are of a lesser importance. When managers see these 'signals,' it is no surprise that their efforts become focused on the 'what' and not the 'how.' Yes, this probably will mean that there is an increased chance that goals will be achieved in the short-term, but it also means that in the long-term, the company will lose its ability to achieve any sense of sustainability in its goal-achievement efforts.

In today's business world, where short-term thinking, driven by a misplaced sense of the need for overnight success, seems to reign supreme, there is a belief that organisational values are nice to have on paper and nice to banter about. This belief accompanies the belief that behaving in accordance with the values is only advisory. Sadly, when this happens, others see this behaviour in the organisation and they too begin to believe that getting the job done at any cost is the most important challenge they face. This is an open invitation to an organisational population to game the system, whenever and wherever they choose. The proliferation of this behaviour is a key indicator that the ability to continually hit key strategic targets will be short-lived.

There is a way to curb this behaviour, but to do it,
senior decision-makers first need to make a choice
between having their people hit the targets at an cost, or hit the targets whilst working within the framework of organisational values.

Assuming that most key decision-makers do want to enable a positive future based on organisational values, i.e. acceptable behaviours, what needs to be done include:

1. Organisational values, when identified, need to have clear demonstrable behaviours identified so that managers and employees alike will be able to see 'how' things should done. Whilst some organisations struggle with matching up sought-after behaviours with values, this is not that difficult to do, if the organisation is seriously interested in having its values be something other than just another set of advertising slogans.
2. Whenever responsibilities are assigned for the achievement of goals or targets, the message needs to be sent that the achievement efforts need to be in alignment with organisational values. The message needs to be made perfectly clear: the achievement of the goals is important; the achievement of the goals within the framework of organisational values is critical.
3. When performance reviews are held, any deviance from organisational values needs to be discussed openly. Operating within a values framework is quite often an organisational undiscussable, and if deviances from a values framework are not talked about, the behaviour will continue and eventually sink deeper and deeper into an organisation. Non-compliance with operating within a values framework needs to be punished by a reduction or elimination of performance bonuses, or in some cases of repetitive abuses of stated values, termination.

In a time when achieving and sustaining organisational growth is one of the main topics of conversation in businesses (which it always seems to be), the ability and willingness to do so within a values framework is key to sustaining the gains achieved. If your managers do not believe this to be the case, then perhaps you need to find new managers, because if you don't, your ability to achieve what your Board and shareholders expect over time will be as dead as the author of Hamlet.

# Are We Asking the "Right" Questions?

Sitting in on management meetings can be both interesting and enlightening. Most of the meetings I am asked to sit in on focus on the challenges facing an organisation, and how to resolve them; all of which is good. The technique that most management teams use to find out which solutions are best is by asking questions. Logical, right? But judging from the difficulty in many organisations to achieve sustainable results, something must be wrong. The problem is that in many situations I have seen, no one seems to be asking the right questions.

Asking questions in meetings is an excellent way to find out what you need to know, but there are several issues that sometimes result in the information being interesting, but of little value in the overall decision-making process. The most important questions should focus on the key issues that will impact an organisations ability to deliver sustainable success, and not just the things that are easy to measure.

Quite often, questions seem to be focused on how much progress is being made during an implementation process. This may be for a specific initiative, a venture into a new market area, or even about the tactics involved in an overall strategy. Yes, progress reports are important, but rarely is the question asked of, *'how will this bring us closer to our overall company desired future?'* Without this question being asked, it is possible (and happens quite often) that the answers received can become mired in the minutia of detail complexity, and lead to the respondent believing that the minutia is what is most important.

The same holds true when new initiatives are proposed. Too often, the questions that are asked relate to specific details about the proposed initiative, and whilst these questions are indeed important, unless the central question of 'how will this help the company overall' is asked, the detail can overwhelm the central issue.

We all would like to believe that most organisational managers are making decisions based on data, and because of that, they collect data on just about every detail that you can imagine, and that could be part of the problem. We have so much data that we are drowning in it, and much of the data only focuses on the detail complexity within our organisations.

In business, detail complexity can surface when specific processes and results are measured. Whilst these measures are important, they really don't address the key levers that drive business success. What they do show are the results of how things get done, and by solely looking at the results – an 'after-the-fact' measurement – all that can be done is react to results that are not what you want them to be.

By looking at the dynamic complexity within an organisation – examining the cause and effect relationships between various organisational processes and their structure – it is possible to understand the potential results before they are visible by exploring the patterns of behaviour and the systemic relationships.

Detail complexity may include measures like *'productivity levels,'* *'market share,'* *'profits,'* and *'voluntary turnover,'* whilst dynamic complexity is represented by such things as *'organisational climate,'* *'ability to grow,'* *'ability to deliver sustainable performance,'* and *'belief and commitment to management's direction.'* Measuring the details only tells you what the results are; by understanding the underlying dynamics behind the details, it is possible to understand what the unintended consequences of organisational efforts might be. This is the information that is needed to put structures, processes, and systems in place that will ensure the outcomes you are after. These are the things that should be the focus of questions.

To make this even clearer, given the choice, would you rather know how well you have been doing, or how well you will be able to do? Asking questions that will result in answers of how well you are doing, which are in reality, questions about events that have already occurred; are fine if all you want to do is tick boxes. Ticking boxes can be a nice activity, but all it does is let you feel good (or bad) about what has happened in the past. If you want to know how well you will do - enquiring about the things that will really make a difference - then you should be focussing your conversation on the dynamic complexity in your organisation.

The next time you are in a meeting, the first question you should be asking is, *'are we asking the right questions?'*

# What We Plant is What We Get

Most of us understand this quite well. If you plant tomatoes in your garden, what you eventually get is tomatoes. If you plant wheat, you get wheat. The same holds true with the mental models we plant in our minds. If you believe that one of your managers is a high performer, what you will look for is the evidence that supports your belief that he or she is a high performer. If your mental model is that a different manager is incapable of delivering consistent high performance, that is what you will look for, and that is undoubtedly what you will see.

Because of these mental models, and the corresponding expectations that accompany them, we tend to base our actions on what we assume, as opposed to what could be.

These actions manifest themselves in ways that support your mental models. In the case of someone whom you believe is, or will be, a high performer; support is provided in terms of budget and rewards. You provide budgetary support so the person can continue to deliver the performance that you expect. You deliver reward support (either in words or financially) so that the person will continue to be motivated. In the case of perceived non-performers, budgets are often reduced. Your mental models tells you that, if they are not delivering the performance you need, why waste any more money on them; and verbal or financial rewards become non-existent. Whilst these actions are almost logical, there is a potential flaw with the thinking, and the flaw is, *'what if the reason that the person is not demonstrating performance is that he or she is not receiving the support that would enable him (or her) to deliver upon your expectations?'* If this is the situation, then your mental models may become self-fulfilling prophecies – you think that they are not performing so you treat them as if they are not capable of performing, and then they don't demonstrate performance. This dynamic has been documented many times, and the result of the decisions can be devastating.

In 1968, Rosenthal and Jacobsen published research (Pygmalion in the Classroom) in which they explained how student performance was driven by the expectations of teachers. The study focused on a class of students that were about to move on to the next grade level. The researchers put together an arbitrary set of student evaluations and passed them on to the teachers of the next grade. The evaluations showed that some of the students were high performers, and some were consistently low performers. At the end of the next term, the student's results matched exactly with the evaluations. Sadly, the evaluations were arbitrary and not based on reality. When teachers had been told that some students would perform better than others, they treated the students in a way that ensured that they would demonstrate high performance. The students who were identified as low performers did indeed perform at a lower level.

If that example isn't enough to understand the impact of mental models, look at the picture below.

What do you see in the picture? When this has been shown to many managers, the first comment is something like, '*I see three red-Pac-Man-like figures.*' A fair enough answer. But some managers reply that they see a white triangle. Another fair answer. The managers who saw the white triangle were asked to provide the definition of a triangle, and most respond with, '*a three-sided geometric shape, whose combined angles total 180 degrees.*' A spot-on definition of a triangle, but in the picture, there are no sides, just the *illusion* of sides. The managers were able to *see* what they *thought* they were shown, even though what they thought didn't match up with reality. The same thing happens to many managers when faced with difficult decisions.

Quite often, the mental models of decision-makers take precedence over the reality of a situation, and the results can be disastrous. The key is to find out if your mental models do resemble the reality of a given situation. This holds true whether the situation deals with people, investments, strategic direction, or the potential impact of competition. The ability to validate your mental models can be a strong differentiator between achieving sustainable success or just being relegated to the compost heap of business.

# Total and Complete Rectitude

The online definition of *'rectitude'* includes *"rightness of principle or practice; exact conformity to truth, or to the rules prescribed for moral conduct."* Whilst an organisational leader might be making decisions in this manner, it doesn't preclude the fact that direct subordinates of the leader may not be.

Organisational behaviours in senior management teams, or more appropriately, *demonstrated* organisational behaviours are the signals that mid-managers and employees use to guide their behaviours. The fact that an organisation may have a stated set of values that are designed to guide the decision-making process and the way that interactions are supposed to take place are nice; but if mid-managers and employees see a disconnect between what is said and what is acted out, they will usually follow the behaviours that they see.

When this occurs, there only are a couple of options available to the head of a company. He (or she) can either; A) whip his people into shape so that they behave in the prescribed way when making decisions and/or when interacting with others. B) sack those people who are not demonstrating the organisational values; or, C) provide the people with coaching and at the same time, put in place a hard-core leadership educational programme for high potential employees who may one day be needed to become the new senior team.

Option A, whilst the intuitive choice for many leaders, can be more than an uphill slog. The problem is that personal and collective behaviours are not developed overnight, and because of that, they cannot be changed overnight. This is complicated even further because some senior managers believe that their behaviours have been the path to their current success, and with that belief being the mental model in action, there is no rational reason that they can see to change. A further complication is that in order to get managers to change often means that they need to realise that they could lose performance bonuses. This 'stick' can be difficult to use, especially if the manager is still delivering the financial results that are part of their goals.

Option B could be used, but this option brings with it complications as well. When managers are sacked, they are almost always replaced. The hiring process can be deep and broad, but the reality is that managers are hired usually based on their ability to deliver results, and if given the choice between hiring someone that can 'hit the numbers' and 'demonstrate the values,' usually the ability to hit the numbers wins out. So whilst getting rid of someone who doesn't demonstrate organisational values may seem like a good idea, just be conscious that the replacement person may come with baggage that doesn't fit either, regardless of how good they are at delivering on goals

Then there is Option C. This option is only applicable in organisations where the leader is dead serious about ensuring that he and his people will be able to realise their potential and, consequently, that of the company. Providing coaching for senior managers whose behaviours do not match up with organisational values is one critical in the short-term. Where this often misses the mark is those in the organisation who take it upon themselves – most usually because they have been told to do so – are woefully incompetent to provide the level and impact of coaching that is required. This can be due to the fact that they have come from the existing culture and cannot gain the respect of the person(s) being coached or because they are just not able to do what is needed.

The second element of option C is to implement a hard-core leadership programme. This could mean chucking managers off to one of the trendy B-schools, but even that usually doesn't provide the leverage needed. Most internally driven management development programmes, whilst designed with the best of intent, also rarely create an environment in which managers can hone the skills and competencies they will need to be effective *whilst doing so in the framework of organisational values.*

A better option would be to put together the equivalent of a 'tutoring' programme for senior managers that you believe could be the future of your organisation. This can be a bit tricky, as you do not want to raise the expectation of those in the programme that they will be promoted instantly, but instead, use the programme as a way to find out who might be able to be promoted when the time is ready.

The challenge for senior leaders is clear: operating with rectitude is important; making sure your people do the same is critical for sustaining success.

# Team-Building Folly

The term 'team building' has taken on many connotations in the past decade. In many organisations, a 'team building' session ends up being an exercise in which participants are trudged around tree-tops and walking across perilously-appearing rope bridges. In many cases, if you are lucky (read this as serious sarcasm), you can even have the chance to fall off some tree branch into the waiting arms of your fellow team members. Sounds like a fun time? Whilst these type activities usually do result in some pretty interesting stories, the actual increase in 'team' is quite low. When you match up the actual results plus the cost of these events, especially for senior management team members, the result can best be described as folly.

I do understand the purpose of team building. In today's organisational structures, regardless of being hierarchical or matrix oriented, it is crucial that everyone on a team functions like a real team, not just a group of well meaning people who, with the best of intentions, never seem to realise their collective potential. To me, team building is all about ensuring that the 'team' acts as a team. This means supporting each other's efforts to ensure that the organisation delivers what it has promised to it shareholders, customers, and other employees.

Now if you think you can accomplish this by slogging through some forest or up a mountain, good on you. But if you have tried that and still aren't seeing your people function like a real team, then you may want to adjust your mental model about how to achieve team thinking, and team behaviours. The key elements of building a serious high performing team fall into several categories.

## Understanding organisational parameters
In many organisations, teams mis-understand, or simply don't know what the parameters are that they are required to work within. This can result in disastrous results when planning strategic initiatives, with many of the outcomes being a loss of motivation and commitment. I have witnessed seeing very subtle parameters that do not surface until a team has put huge amounts of effort into planning, and when they do surface and the team discovers that all their work was for nothing, the 'revised' plan is weak and probably won't do what needs to be done. Find out what the parameters are before teams are set loose to come up with solutions to problems.

## The impact of dynamic v. detail complexity

For some reason, managers still are locked into the mindset that looking at details is more important than looking at the interrelationships of those details. This is what dynamic complexity is all about; understanding what causes the 'detail's to be what they are. By shifting away from the myopic detail view, it is possible to teams to come up with fundamental solutions to long-standing problems instead of falling into the trap of reactive, non-systemic thinking.

## Surfacing team and organisational undiscussables

This one can be a bit tricky, just by definition. It can be difficult to begin to talk about undiscussables, largely due to the fact that they hide underlying issues in organisations that are either politically driven or a function of less-than-effective managerial behaviours. Having said that, unless undiscussables are brought out and talked about, they will continue to fester and prevent the team (or organisation) from ever realising its potential.

## Managing expectations

By now, we should all know the 'rule' that states that 'behaviours get worse before they get better.' This is an important key to setting expectations, but it does not reflect the complete reality of coming up with new ways to do things. The reality is that just about the time that employees learn a new way to do something, they also need to learn why this change has been made. This double-dip in behaviours may prolong the time before new performance behaviours can be actually seen, but without understanding that this will happen, employees, shareholders, and management can become disenchanted with progress.

## The need to demonstrate sought-after behaviours

In an environment in which just about every organisation on this planet has a set of stated values, unless managerial team members actually demonstrate that their behaviours match up with the values, there is little chance that employees will become committed to follow team derived initiatives, or for that matter, respect team members at all.

So here is your choice: the next time you set up a senior management team building event, you can either sit in some room and actually try to create an environment in which your team can act like a team; or hope that as you fall out of a tree in the woods somewhere, there will be someone there to catch you. Of course, if your team doesn't act like a team and demonstrate that you are worthy of being leaders, this fall could just be the first of many.

## The Pigeon or the Statue?

We all have choices in the way we do our jobs. No, we don't necessarily have the option to not *do* the job that our job description prescribes, but we do quite often have the option of *how we do* our job. And sadly, I have met too many people who believe the number of options we have can be counted on two fingers; and they seem to believe that the options are to be the pigeon or the statue.

We all recognise what these two options entail – to either be the one who dumps on others, or the one who is dumped upon. But there is a third option: to do the right thing, for the right reasons. But for some bizarre reason, this option, whilst it is quite often bantered about as *the* thing to do, rarely what we feel is a truly viable choice available to us.

I used to know a senior manager who was a highly skilled 'pigeon.' Highly skilled, in this context means that he was adept at swooping in to see how one of his teams was doing; berating them for not getting things done on time and in full; then flitting off to dump on another team that reported to him. His teams all felt as if they were statues; statues covered in the residue of his 'visits.' Was this the best way to help his team's become more effective? Well, apparently, he felt so, after all, his performance was being measured on his ability to get results from multiple teams, which he was doing. The fact that the teams were not delivering the performance they could have been delivering he could shrug off to incompetence on the team member's part.

I knew another manager who was also brilliant at acting out pigeon behaviours. He too would appear on the scene, only to trash his people for not doing what needed to be done, only to then rush off to beat up another team that reported to him. His rationale for this behaviour was that he had so many people to manage that he had little or no time to help them achieve higher performance.

Then there was a third manager who, after being put in charge of multiple teams, did begin to exhibit pigeon-like managerial behaviours, largely because her peer managers all told her that this was the only way to ensure that she would be able to keep in touch with all her people. But soon she began to break with this behaviour and started to check in with her teams with a simple question; *'what can I do to help you achieve the goals the company has set for the team?'* The first team she tried this on was gobsmacked. *'What could she do to actually help them?'* They were so used to being beaten up that their response was a collective silence. Her reasoning was that she was aware that there only are four types of people in organisations: those who are committed to achieve corporate and departmental goals; those who don't understand what may need to be done or why; those who don't have the appropriate skills to do what needs to be done; and those who choose to be resistant. As her team's performance wasn't what was needed, she believed that the team members fell into one or more of the last three groups. Whilst this was her *belief*, she knew that the only way she could find out for sure was to ask.

When you observe organisational managers, it is pretty easy to recognise repetitive patterns of behaviour, and acting like a pigeon is one of them. Some of them might be partially hidden away behind management promises that are interspersed with excuses, but by looking a bit deeper, it is not that difficult to see.

Most senior managers are quite keen to profess both an understanding that ensuring that mid-managers and employees need to have high levels of skills, and an equally impressive set of statements about their commitment to ensure that ongoing learning for these employees is crucial to long-term organisational success. But for every senior manager who claims to be supportive of these two statements and does something about them, there is one that talks a good story but then does nothing. Well, to be fair, 'doing nothing' is not exactly accurate – what they do is come up with a myriad of excuses why 'this is not the right time.' This is pure bollocks.

Whilst being a pigeon may seem like a bit of fun and a clear demonstration of power, the reality is that over time, this will not accomplish what they might expect it to.

The only sound path forward for managers is to develop an understanding of what needs to be done, who are the most appropriate people to do it, and then help them see why the challenge is important, how their contributions will help the organisation move forward, and give them the resources to get it done. No pigeons, no statues, only motivated workforce that is committed to achievement of goals.

## Mirror Mirror, On the Wall

Whilst it is known that using metaphors to build commitment in organisations can be a powerful tool, it can be, at times, a bit tricky to achieve the desired results. Recently, I had spent time with an organisation where the story shed light on some of the difficulties in doing this.

The organisation has a history and reputation for being able to deliver results for its customers. But at the same time, the organisation's leadership has been living in an almost fairy tale-based world, that whilst they are good at what they do, their mental models might be not reflective of reality. This has been complicated by the fact that they are in an industry that seems to operate in feast or famine environments. These factors have all contributed to the story that was articulated in interviews with current and past employees.

The story as metaphor that surfaced in conversations with employees was based on an excerpt from Snow White. In the Brothers Grimm fairy tale, one of the characters was the Queen, who had *'dark powers and knowledge'*. She also had a magic mirror that she continually asked *'who is the fairest of them all?'* The mirror always responded that *'she was.'* And then one day, the mirror said she wasn't, which sent the Queen on...well, you probably know the rest of the story.

When the story began to surface through employee interviews, the logical question was *'why this story?'* The reasons that were provided all seemed to focus on one central issue – the issue of leadership.

The head of the company, who was also its founder, was, by all accounts, quite brilliant at what he did. He was highly skilled; was an extremely competent manager, but having these two characteristics does not always mean that the person will be a brilliant leader. It was apparent from the level of talent that he had assembled in his company that he was able to create a compelling vision. However, it was also apparent from the interviews that his vision of being able to consistently compete with the industry leaders was relatively unobtainable. And this is where the story as metaphor really begins to take shape.

In the Brothers Grimm story, the Queen (the leader of the population) spends an inordinate amount of time checking to see if she really was as good as she thought she was. The CEO of the company (the leader of the organisational population) consistently talked about how good his company was and how they were as good as his steepest competition. The mental model of the Queen in the fairy tale was reinforced repeatedly by the mirror. The mental model of the CEO was reinforced repeatedly by the company's successes and by his senior team. One day, the mirror told the Queen that she wasn't the best, and she went into a rage and caused all sorts of mayhem in the land. After finding his company in the famine part of the cycle, the CEO went into 'reorganisation' mode sacking key managers and haranguing those that remained to 'work harder;' with the resultant mayhem being devastating to the company. This dynamic happened whenever revenues sank in the company, which only reinforced the metaphor in the minds of employees (and caused many additional key employees to leave).

It was extremely telling that the story as metaphor that surfaced didn't focus on organisation's successes, but instead on the demonstrated behaviours of the CEO.

The lessons of story as metaphor from this example are quite important. Too often, there are beliefs and assumptions of managers and employees that are un-discussable; and in this case, it was the demonstrated behaviours of the CEO. Surfacing and talking about these undiscussables can be key to overcoming organisational obstacles, but the fact that they cannot be talked about for 'political' reasons means that the obstacles will remain. Often the knowledge that there are organisational undiscussables can be de-motivating and hamper efforts for an organisation to realise its potential. By surfacing the undiscussables through stories as metaphors can reduce or eliminate the risk of talking about them openly. This can create an opportunity for the organisation to address, and with some effort, actually remove the obstacles.

In other organisations, where the metaphorical story is positive, it can help motivate and excite managers and employees to put continue to put forth additional effort to meet the challenges ahead.

Either way, simply understanding an organisation and the dynamics that are present within it does not mean that employees will increase their level of commitment to organisational initiatives unless they can see that there is a reason to do so. Using a story as metaphor for the organisation can provide that reason.

## Athenium Wisdom

Through the years, we have all heard some pretty powerful wisdom about business. And in many cases, the wisdom didn't directly apply to business when it was first said. Such is the case with a bit of wisdom from Aristotle. His quote, something that all organisations should live by, is, *"We are what we repeatedly do. Excellence, then, is not an act, but a habit."*

If you dissect this quote, you can see two clear elements. First, *'We are what we repeatedly do.'* I can only imagine what prompted Aristotle to write this, but the message for business, and more importantly, business leaders, is that what is most important is demonstrated behaviours.

Managers and employees look to their senior leadership to know what they should do. These 'instructions' often come in the form of directives, strategies, and messages. But they also come in the form of demonstrated behaviours. It is fine to know 'what' to do, but the real message of 'how to do it' is most often a reflection of the behaviours that are demonstrated by the senior people. If your senior people talk about the importance of working within a values framework, then you look to see if they are doing the same. If they are, then you probably will follow suit. But if they aren't demonstrating the values they talk about, then most likely, you won't either. The whole issue of demonstrated behaviours should not be dismissed lightly – if you want your people to do the right thing, at the right time, for the right reasons; then you need to do the same.

The second element, *"Excellence, then, is not an act, but a habit,"* also directly applies to organisations today. In the world of business, there are a plethora of types of 'excellence' certifications. There is a collection of ISO certifications; national quality awards, and other types of recognition that are supposed to proved that your organisation provides excellence in the products or services it delivers. Often, decision-makers determine that having one of these certifications would be good for business. If the decision is based on the fact that the discipline required in getting the certification will be good for the organisation, then it is a good decision. If, however, the decision is based on a perceived need to just obtain the certification for marketing or public relations purposes, then any lessons learned in the process will be washed away faster than a receding tide.

The bottom line, as well spotted by Aristotle, is that you cannot 'act' out excellence whenever you feel like it. Sure, you can do what you need to do to obtain the certification, but the reality is that these certifications mean that you actually 'do' what you say you are doing; every day; every month…all the time.

If you talk to organisations that have achieved an excellence certification, what you hear is that the real benefit of the effort isn't the award itself, but the habits that are a result of effort that was put forth to achieve the certification.

Experience tells us that there are two types of learning. We can memorise what to do for a test, as we often do in school; or we can learn what we need to do in order to apply the learning. Simply passing the test – getting the certificate of excellence – isn't really learning. Learning takes place when *how we do what we do actually changes*.

Learning how to achieve excellence isn't without its pitfalls. It is like learning to walk, or learning to ride a bicycle. No one learns from doing things right the first time; we learn to walk and to ride a bicycle by falling down. We make an attempt and fail, but we try again, and again, and again. We learn through practise, and when we begin to excel at whatever we have learnt, doing it becomes a habit.

If you and your organisation seek to achieve excellence – and I do mean sustainable excellence – the wisdom of Aristotle is an appropriate guide to follow. First, make sure that everyone understands what the level of excellence you are after. Second, make sure that you demonstrate the excellence you expect from others. Third, help your managers and employees be able to learn how to demonstrate excellence. And fourth, practise what you, and they, have learnt.

There is another option, of course. You could just change all your internal and external marketing communications so that they have the word 'excellence' featured prominently...and then sit back in your office and hope someone believes it.


## Waiting for the Dot?

Remember the early days of television? Remember what would happen when programming would end at night? The picture would suddenly disappear into a small white dot on the screen. Sort of like what has been happening in business. Big initiatives are announced with a flourish; people rush about as if they were scampering down the steps at the South Kensington tube station; and after a while, all that is left of the initiative is a small burning memory.

The issue of how to help an organisation deal effectively with change is one that plagues companies from all sectors, and of all sizes. Too often, we are deluded into thinking that change initiatives are just that – initiatives. But the reality is that organisational change occurs every minute, of every day.

Simply put, organisational change does not start when someone gets a bright idea to redo the way work is done; organisational change is about the only constant left in business today. Our problem is that, because most changes are small and barely visible, they are not recognised as *change*.

We all change, every minute of every day. And yet, because the changes that we experience are incremental, we hardly notice them. But when something big happens to us, we recognise it instantly. It is the same with organisations – the day by day changes that we experience in our organisations slip by easily, but when someone announces that 'we will now change…' we quite often are struck with the horror that the changes will impact us; what we do, how we do it, and when we will do it.

I have experienced this with the heads of large organisations – they are all for clear, distinct organisational change…until they are told that they need to change first. 'No, I don't need to change what I am doing; I am the CEO.' But the reality is that if they don't change, then it will be very difficult to get others to both see why they have to change, and then demonstrate different behaviours. There are, however, ways to ensure that 'change' is not as difficult as we believe it to be.

First, make it perfectly clear that change is an ongoing process in all organisations, not just another initiative that will come and go (until the next time). Too often, employees view highly visible 'change programmes' as just that, a programme that has a start and an end. We need to help employees (and managers alike) to realise that change is just an ongoing parameter of business.

Second, ensure that the CEO is onboard, and willing to be the first to demonstrate different behaviours. The example I gave earlier occurs too often – CEO's who accept that change must occur, but aren't willing to do it themselves. Senior managers must be willing to ask managers and employee if they can see them changing. Simply saying you are changing is not enough – if your people can't see the changes, it doesn't count.

Third, help managers and employees see the impact of their current behaviours impact organisational performance. We all tend to emulate the behaviours of those who in control, regardless of if they are parents or managers. If your boss yells and harangues employees about performance, you will do the same; and verbal violence is not the way to get employees to commit to performance improvement.

Fourth, make it perfectly clear what the organisation is trying to accomplish, and then give the managers and employees the opportunity to identify ways in which they could evolve their behaviours into something more conducive for attaining this new working environment. Employees need to believe that they are valued, and the best way to do this is to ask them for their input...and then make it very clear that you are really listening to them.

Fifth, don't assume that someone else is going to do all these things. Taking responsibility for change is everyone's responsibility, but that doesn't mean that everyone will step up to the challenge. The next time you are in a meeting, make sure that change is on the agenda, but ensure that the main topic of conversation is what *you* can do to help others understand that change is not just another flavour-of-the-day programme.

If you don't do these things, your performance improvement efforts will become fading dreams; and at the end of the day, you will find yourself watching positive organisational change becoming a disappearing dot.

## Business Brownian Motion

If you could look through the windows of many organisations, what you would see is people scurrying around, rushing from one task to another. But what you wouldn't see is with all the rushing about, few tasks are actually accomplished to the level they need to be. What is being demonstrated is similar to Brownian motion; a term used to describe why pollen particles seem to 'bounce' around when put on the surface of water. Named after botanist Robert Brown, Brownian motion explains how the ever-moving molecules of water bump into the pollen particle repeatedly and randomly, causing it to be in constant movement. This motion – people being pushed many directions at once - is present in many organisations.

Most organisations today are under pressure. Their managers are feeling pressure to stave off competitive threats, drive new initiatives, deal with regulatory demands, build alignment within an organisational population, and make strong contributions to the organisation's bottom line. Because of this, they often take on more challenges (or are given more challenges) than they can do effectively. This can cause them to bounce from one challenge to another, desperately trying to deliver on the expectations, regardless of whether they are self-imposed or not. Just as they really focus on one challenge, with the best of intentions, another one comes along and sends the manager off in a new direction.

The effects of this 'Brownian motion' on organisational performance can be devastating. Efforts to address challenges often do not reach closure. Managers suffer from burn-out, which leads to mistakes. Employees see these behaviours and begin to believe that confusion or even incompetence is commonplace in managerial ranks. Organisational effectiveness is relegated to becoming a marketing slogan. This doesn't need to happen.

Keeping managers and employees focused and on-task requires several things.

- Make sure that they understand what it is they should be focused on. Too often, managers are told to focus on this or that, but if these new activities are in addition to what they were told previously, there is the risk that they try to do everything at the same time. This can be a natural reaction – when you are told to do X, and then told to do Y, and then told to do Z, without any enlightenment about which of these activities has priority over the others, the result can be that you attempt to do them all. The end result is either that nothing gets done, or that what does get done is mediocre at best. Piling on additional activities is okay; just make sure that whomever you pile them onto understands which of the activities takes priority over the others.

- After identifying which activity is the priority to focus on, make it clear how the additional activity connects to the organisational strategy. In many cases I have witnessed, this connection is not made explicit, and the manager minimises the quality and quantity of effort that is put forth.

- Help your managers learn how to prioritise their time. One of the most often made comments of managers is that they don't have enough time to do all the things they are asked to do. In some cases, this may be true, but in many cases, managers do not understand the difference between 'important' and 'urgent' when deciding how best to spend their time.

- Hold regular scheduled reviews with your people to make sure that they are on track with the right activities. The first of these reviews should be used to ensure that there is a common understanding of what 'right' means. The subsequent reviews should be used to check the progress that is being made.

- Ensure that your people have the skills they need to effectively do what needs to be done, on-time, and in-full. In most cases, this doesn't mean telling them to go off to a seminar or a training course – this only takes more time away from being effective. What is usually needed is one-on-one coaching on how to be more effective. Whilst coaching does occupy time, with a competent coach, the time invested pays solid dividends and helps to ensure that your people will be better able to be effective.

Of course, there is another option. You could just do nothing and assume that your people are making the right decisions for the right reasons. But if you choose to do this, you may run the risk that your people will bounce from one task to another, doing all of them poorly, and ending up delivering mediocre performance to your organisation.

## Chart Folly

When the last time you looked at your company's organisational chart? When you did look at it, what did you see? If your company's chart looks like most of them, what you see is something that looks like a pyramid. It might be not perfectly triangular in shape, but none the less, it is a pyramid.

At the top of the pyramid is the big boss. The next row has all the most senior people who the ones who head up the various business functions or units or whatever – these are the people who report directly to the boss. The third level has the people listed to report directly to the functional or business unit heads. And buried in the depths of the pyramid are the people who do the work.

And what do you suppose the purpose of this organisational chart is? Here are your choices: A) to show you where you fit into the organisation; B) to show you who you report to; C) to show you what compensation level you are on; or D) to let you know who are the ones who really run the company. All of these are correct. All this is fine, except for one little thing; most organisational charts have little or no connection to how the work of the company actually gets done.

The purpose of an organisation is to deliver consistently growing financial performance. Yes, I know that most organisational mission statements cleverly omit this point, but the reality is that people start businesses, invest in businesses, and grow businesses to make money. And the way to make money is to deliver performance, regardless of whether the business climate is good or bad. Companies are there to make money. Now if you accept this basic business premise (if you don't, you are probably reading this newsletter in an entirely different universe than the rest of us are in), then it could cause you to wonder why your company is organised like it is.

Now I do accept the point that everyone in an organisation does need to know the hierarchical reporting structure. But I am mystified why more companies do not have an organisational chart that reflects how the work of the company actually gets done.

Think about this for a minute. Wouldn't it make sense to have a chart that shows how decisions are, or should be, made? Wouldn't it make sense to have a chart that shows how various business units should interact with each other to achieve company goals? Wouldn't it make sense to have a chart that shows how business functions like Human Resources, Finance and Training and Development actually support how the people responsible for achieving company goals can actually do so?

There are several reasons that we don't often see organisational charts based on how the work gets done (or should get done). One of these reasons is a throwback to the days of Frederick Taylor, when the bosses told the workers what to do, how to do it, and when to do it. These charts were, and are, all about power and control, and the people whose names are on the highest levels of these charts relish their location and see no viable reason for changing. And still another reason is that most people feel comfortable in seeing the 'order' that these pyramid-looking charts represent with all their nice, crisp, clean horizontal and vertical lines, and charts that show how the work gets done look like interlocking circles. But the question is, 'do they really represent how the work gets done?'

Imagine this scenario: you have been brought into an organisation because you have a needed competence or skill. You are given your company orientation and now you know your pay package; you know where your desk is; and you have the million-page policy manual. You even are told whom you report to and where that department fits into the overall organisational pyramid hierarchy. But because there isn't any chart that shows whom for you to interact with, or how decisions are made, or how the company should operate so you and the rest of the company can help it realise its potential, what are you left to do?

If you are like most new managers, you do what most new managerial hires do; you fall into line and tick the boxes that you are told need to be ticked. This behaviour might be acceptable if you are working for a company with unlimited resources, no competition, no regulatory demands, and an endless stream of revenues. But if your company isn't like that, then you might want to reflect on the need to have the company organised around how the work actually does, or should, get done. Anything else is pure folly in today's business world.

## Brick Walls?

Brick Walls. Two words that are often synonymous with immovable objects. But that is just one perception of what they are. Last week, I listened to the last lecture of Randy Pausch, a professor at Carnegie Mellon University, who recently passed away from pancreatic cancer. In his lecture, Pausch talked about his view of the meaning of brick walls. This was quite timely, as I had recently spoken with a client and in the conversation, I repeatedly heard about all the walls that her company was running up against.

For most business people, the term 'brick wall' denotes an impassable obstruction that can keep you from achieving some goal or target. You see this with statements like *"I am working on the initiative, but can't get past the brick wall of resistance,"* or *"working with the union leadership is about as easy as running into a brick wall,"* or even, *"I was told to go ahead with my plan but no one gave me any resources. It's like hitting a brick wall."* The whole 'brick-wall' concept implies near insurmountable resistance or obstruction. And whilst that is the working definition for many of us, Pausch has a different explanation.

According to Pausch, brick walls are there to sort out the difference between those who are really dedicated to the challenge, and those who are not.

Last week, I spent several hours on the phone with a senior manager who works for one of my clients. She and several of her team members had run into the proverbial brick wall. They had identified an ongoing, fundamentally systemic problem in their organisation and were running out of options to deal with it. Not only was the problem fundamentally systemic, it was also laden with political ramifications for anyone who attempted to resolve it. In the past, several senior managers had pursued a solution to the problem, but the obstacles to fixing it were so solid that they gave up trying, with two of them actually leaving the organisation due to frustration.

In our conversation, I repeatedly questioned how solid the brick wall that they were encountering was. The answer was that it was very solid and they had run out of options to get through it. I then asked, if the problem is that solid, and you cannot find a way to get through it, what will you do? My expectation was that they would do what other managers had done and simply hope that some day the problem would go away by itself. What I heard would have made Pausch very happy…*"James, the fact that this problem is so firmly entrenched in our culture is the reason that we must solve it."* The manager viewed the problem's brick wall not as being insurmountable, but as a signal that it must be solved…and solved now.

Whilst there are many truly solid obstacles in business, often, most of the obstacles we see are there only because we don't make the effort to figure out how to get past them.

You have an initiative that is meeting resistance. *What are you doing to help the resisters see the benefits of the initiative? What are you doing to influence them to at least be open to finding out how it can help the organisation?*

You are trying to work with the union leadership but it isn't working. *What are you doing to first build a relationship with them? What are you doing to bring them into your decision-making process?*

You want to proceed with your plan but can't find the resources you need? *What are you doing to look for alternate resources? What are you doing to see if there is another way to fund your plan?*

Think of what other brick walls you have been running into. Ask yourself these questions. *1) Is this really a brick wall, or is going through it just harder than you thought? 2) Are you using the brick wall as a defence mechanism for not trying as hard as you could? 3) How important will it be to get past this brick wall? 4) How much effort have you really used to break through this barrier to achieve the goal? 5) What else could you do that could either remove the barrier, or help you get around it?*

There is no doubt; running into brick walls is not a fun activity, nor is it highly motivating over time. But if what you want to do is truly important, both to you and to your organisation, it would make sense to either find ways to knock the wall down, or find a way around it.

## Out of Stones?

A subscriber sent me a quote today from an OPEC oil minister and it caught my eye. The quote was, *"The stone age didn't end because of a shortage of stones."* True, so very true. From what I remember from school, the Stone Age ended because people had evolved; they had moved on; they were able to do new things, with new tools, and in new ways. They wanted to change and saw the benefits of changing.

This may explain why many managers are stuck in their own version of the Stone Age. They don't want to change, and don't see any benefit of changing. Apparently, those who do not want to change don't remember the lesson from the actual Stone Age: *those that do not change will not survive.*

Most managers agree that change is about the only constant in business. They also tend to agree that everyone needs to accept that change does happen, and yet many of them are so terrified of changing that you would think they are on some mountain ledge about to fall into the unknown. These people are often the same ones who are oblivious to what is really going on around them. They are the ones who believe that all is well, even when everyone around them is expressing concerns.

They are also the ones who often have two sets of demonstrated behaviours; one in which they say what they think their peers and bosses want to hear, and one when they try to make it look like they are doing what they should do. This is simply an attempt to game the system. This second set of behaviours is usually accompanied by defence mechanisms that often disconnect them from the reality of the situation. The visible evidence of this is typically sinking performance and the degeneration of any sense of effective team decision-making.

Management teams have a choice when they discover that some of their members appear to be living in this Stone Age. They can either do something about it by helping the people accept the reality of the situation they are faced with, or they can negate their explicit and implicit responsibilities to employees, shareholders, and customers by simply closing their eyes to the problem.

In order to convince people of the need to change, there are several things you can do:

1. Make it clear in meetings that being aligned around the acceptance of change is critical. This can be done in the context of identifying the gap between what needs to be done and what is being done.
2. Identify areas where the acceptance of change is not visibly apparent, and the implications on performance of this behaviour. You can see this by looking at cause-and-effect inter-actions of behaviours on performance.
3. Avoid the conversation from taking on a critical finger-pointing tone, whilst at the same time, ensuring that peer evaluation of change readiness will be the norm. The willingness of peers to identify performance gaps and the reasons for them is part of the responsibility of management.
4. Provide coaching support to those who demonstrate a resistance to change. Often, an external coach can provide insights that peers are not able to, and in a way that makes it easier for a manager to accept them.
5. If all these efforts fail to make a difference, ensure that it is clear that a last remaining option is to replace the person who is resistant to changing.

Working to ensure that management teams live and make decisions based on the reality of today's business environment is critical. For those who choose not to live in this reality, the only options are to change...or get out.


## Seeing the Gorilla?

Earlier this year, I was meeting with a management team and to make a point, I showed a video clip of a dozen people tossing a basketball around. When the video clip began, a title appeared on the screen that said, *'count the number of times the ball is passed between the players.'* The video started, and all the senior managers visibly were counting the number of passes. When the video ended, another message appeared on the screen that said, *'How many passes were there?'* As the managers were all shouting out their numbers, another message appeared on the screen. This one said, *'How many of you saw the gorilla?'* The managers were perplexed...until they saw the video again in slow motion, and sure enough, walking right amongst the ball players was a large gorilla walking from right to left across the screen. No one saw the gorilla because they were so focused on counting the number of passes...which is what they were told to look for.

The same dynamic often happens in business. Managers are told to look for certain indicators (metrics) of success, or performance, or revenues, or innovation, or whatever. And in the process of *doing what they are told to do,* they may miss what else is going on. The difference is that in business, what is often missed are the key drivers that impact success, or performance, or revenues, or innovation, or whatever. These key drivers may not be as visible, but they are critical to watch for, and by missing them because they were told to watch for something else, managers can find things out of control very quickly. The challenge is to not only watch for what you are told to watch for, but to also see what else is going on.

The reason is that most indicators that are identified as important are actually outcomes of other things. By solely looking at outcomes, you are doomed to falling into reactive thinking mode in your decision-making.

The best way to 'see more' is to reflect upon the indicators you have been told to watch. The key questions you might want to think about include, *'what actually drives those indicators,'* and *'how are those drivers interrelated?'* By looking at the drivers and their interrelationships, it is possible to avoid the two most common problems with indicator observation.

One problem is that often, managers find that in their drive to do what they are told, they become oblivious to anything else that is important. The other problem is that many managers, in their quest to do what is required, risk being distracted by events that could be deemed to be cool and sexy, as opposed to indicators that are important.

To ensure that your managers are able to recognise the indicators that are truly important (the ones that drive success) as well as the ones they have been told to monitor, there are several things you can do.

1. Identify what indicators your managers have been told to watch.
2. With managerial input, identify what variables drive those indicators. Whilst some of these drivers may come from outside your organisation, the vast majority of them will be internal, and will most probably be a combination of both easily identifiable drivers (headcount, availability of resources, etc) and some that you may not currently measure (organisational culture, ability to use resources wisely, etc).
3. Determine which drivers impact which metrics. This is an important step, for drivers rarely impact only one indicator, but instead create either a positive or negative impact on several of them.
4. Determine what the impact of the drivers is. As an example, the driver 'ability to use resources wisely' typically has a positive impact on 'availability of resources,' whilst 'level of internal competition' can have a negative impact.
5. Identify where the drivers (and indicators that you have been told to watch) fit into the overall dynamics of how work is done in your organisation. This is usually done on a graphical cause-and-effect diagram that, whilst it may look messy, will help create an environment in which managers can make better decisions.

There is no doubt that monitoring key indicators is important in business. But there is equally no doubt that, unless you also look at the key drivers that influence those indicators, the 'gorilla' that you may not see just might sneak up and rain havoc on what you are trying to accomplish.

## The Delegation Conundrum

This is a situation that many senior managers find themselves in: their daily workload is monumental, and they know that unless they do something, they risk falling into the reactive thinking trap that leads to mistakes a potentially massive problems. Their options are usually to either, A) reduce the amount of work they have been tasked with, or, B) delegate some of the workload to others. Truth be told, solution A rarely is really an option, unless your alter ego's name is Clark Kent. And often, solution B is not viable either, usually because they don't believe that some of the people that report to them are competent to handle the challenges effectively. Consequently they slog along, trying to do as much as they can, whilst at the same time, experiencing increasing stress. This usually leads to the same problems of overwork that leads to reactive thinking, which leads to mistakes; the very things they would like to avoid.

I recently spoke with a senior manager who was stuck in the conundrum of wanting to delegate but being concerned that his people could handle the challenge that he could offer them. Whilst I did agree that this is a real conundrum, there was a way out of it for senior managers who really would like to improve the situation.

1. Identify who the people are within a management team who could potentially be the most effective. This in itself can be a tricky proposition, but the only rational way to delegate is to find out who within your team you could expect to deliver the performance you will need. Whilst there can be many ways to determine who you could delegate to, a sound method is to look at how your people think, how they influence others, how they achieve goals, and how they demonstrate leadership. *The purpose of this step is to make a preliminary assessment of*

*whom you think you would be able to delegate responsibilities to.*

2. Hold individual meetings with these people. The purpose of these individual meetings is to find out if your assumptions about their competencies are correct. This is not that difficult to do. Give them (individually) known past challenges that you or your organisation has faced. Ask them what they see as the real underlying issues of the challenge (thinking); how they would have enlisted the support of others to meet the challenge (influencing); how they would have gone about effectively addressing the challenges (achieving); and what signals their efforts would have sent to the organisation regarding the challenge resolution (leading). By listening to how they would have dealt with these past challenges, you can get a better idea of how they would address future challenges. Another benefit of this step is to help you see how your choices differentiate between challenges that are important and those that appear to them to be urgent. Being able to make this distinction – important v. urgent - can be a key to the effective resolution of challenges. *The purpose of this step is to find out how your choices might deal with situations as they arise.*

3. Begin to hold informal meetings with the selected group. This is where the real action is, because you now can give them not only current challenges the organisation is dealing with, but also potential challenges that they might one day have to deal with. The senior managers who do this really well are the ones who introduce scenarios that, on the surface may seem like they would never happen, but as we learnt in the 1970's with the arrival of OPEC, could happen indeed. By giving the group real or hypothetical issues and challenges, you will be able to see who you feel will be able to handle the amount of delegation you are prepared to pass along. *The purpose of this step is to create an environment in which your choices will be able to test their decision-making choices, as well as expand the way they think about challenges.*

4. Begin to delegate some of your responsibilities so you can become more effective in dealing with issues that are important, instead of slogging away on everything.

There is no doubt that in today's business world, managers can't do it all. For them to be effective, they need to be willing and able to delegate some of the responsibilities they have to others. Their ability to distinguish who are the best people to delegate to can be a differentiator between short-term and long-term success. If you choose not to delegate for whatever reason, then it would be good if you actually had super-powers.

## The New Maths

We all know that when you add two and two, the result is four. This is simple maths, and most of us learnt this when we were quite young. Two plus two equals four. Right. It really doesn't matter how you write it (2 + 2 = 4), the answer is still the same. But for some reason, there are managers out there who make decisions as if they believed that when you add 2 plus 2, you could get 5, or 837, or some other equally outrageous and non-sensical answer.

There are ways to deal with this. You could, for example, ban any numbers you don't like. In 1299, the authorities in Florence Italy actually 'banned' the use of zero in mathematics, in a bizarre attempt to justify their own thinking. But trying to change the way people count isn't the answer. And besides, in the world of business, the problem really isn't even a maths problem...it is a problem of how some managers rationalise their own view of reality.

It should be clear to all decision-makers that perceptions have a major impact on the realities that we live in. You can have all the data in the world, you can have signed affidavits that attest to one thing or another, you can even have survey results that identify demonstrated behaviours, but if a manager believes that what he is doing is right, that is what he or she will probably continue to do. These actions are based on several beliefs that, to the person, seem quite logical: *To be successful, one has to make good decisions; I am successful; therefore, I must have been making good decisions.* When faced with this type of logic, it appears to the person that everyone else must be wrong.

When this dynamic – *I am right and everyone else is wrong* - begins to become visible to others, the decision-maker usually does one of several things. Either he slips into denial mode – *what I am doing is right, and there isn't really a problem* – or they begin to exhibit 'pleasing' characteristics in which they agree with everything that is being said to them, but continue to do what they do in the way they have done them in the past. Either of these two behaviours can signal a disconnect between what they believe and what the reality of a situation is.

When confronted with this type of disconnect, there are several things that can be done to try to help the manager understand that his or her perceptions do not match up with reality.

The first thing is to ensure feedback is being provided. There is a caveat to this, however. The feedback being provided should not be aggressive or deemed to be done in a manner that could be perceived by the recipient as attacking. A positive feedback environment is extremely important.

Part of the feedback process should include peer and/or subordinate feedback on demonstrated behaviours. Often this is best done through the use of 'blind-response' surveys or questionnaires. An important part of this is who administers the surveys or questionnaires. It is always best to have a third-party do this, because of the subject is the one who sends them out, there can be the implication that he or she will know who said what. Instead, have the results sent to a neutral person, who can then provide the results to the person getting the feedback. In this way, comments made are usually less influenced by any internal politics.

The second thing you can do is to provide one-on-one coaching for the manager. This usually means bringing in a professional coach. Many times supervisors believe that because of their hierarchical relationship with the person, they should do the coaching. That could be right, but it also assumes that the supervisor is competent to know how to deal with these types of situations, and is equally competent to create that kind of environment. If the subject supervisor is not competent to coach in a positive way, then use someone else. For senior people, this often means utilising the expertise of an external coach. Whilst there will be a cost for this, in most cases, the cost is far less than the cost incurred by aberrant behaviours that lead to mistakes and bigger problems.

Helping a manager who demonstrates that he or she is living a different reality is something that companies need to face. The risk of not addressing this behaviour can be enormous, both in financial and human relations terms, but also in terms of the impact they will have throughout an organisation. By not addressing it at an early stage, the manager will just assume that all is well, and his or her view of their world is acceptable. And it is not.

# The Power of Ladders

During a conversation with a business leader several weeks ago, the subject of decision-making came up. Not decision-making in general; what he was asking about was why one of his managers was making such inappropriate decisions. I said that the Ladder of Inference could provide the answer.

Chris Argyris identified the Ladder of Inference in the 1970's as a way to help understand why people make decisions to do something. According to Argyris, we begin to go up the ladder by 'selecting' (focussing) on some data out of all we can see, hear, observe, understand, etc. We then begin to add meaning to the data that we have selected, and make assumptions on that meaning. We draw conclusions on our assumptions, adopt beliefs about those conclusions, and then take some form of action.

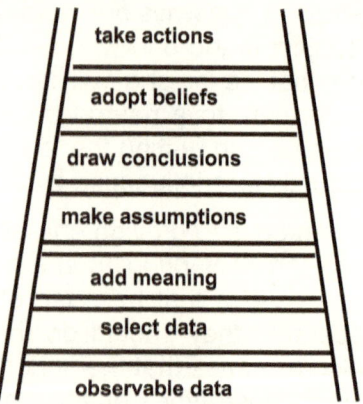

An example of how this works was used recently to explain why commitment was being lost in an organisation.

126

As can be seen, the flow from the observable data up to the actions that the employees are taking follows logical progression. The fact that the company is under pressure could mean that the strategy is not working. A non-functional strategy could mean that the people who put it together weren't the most competent, which could mean that the people that hired them are not competent. Non-competent people do not deserve my commitment and, consequently, I will only put forth the bare minimum of effort. In short, the ladder helps to identify the mental rationale that a decision-maker uses to justify his or her actions.

When you believe that someone may be taking actions based on either incorrect assumptions or on less-than rational thinking, there is something you can do. That is to 'walk' the decision-maker back down his or her ladder. The best way to do this involves asking one basic question. The question is, 'why is (the action chosen) this the best thing to do in this situation?' By beginning with this question, you can help the decision-maker go step by step downward to surface the rationale for what he has chosen to do. The objective of doing this is to help your managers improve their decision-making process by understanding the reasoning behind it.

In the case of the manager making inappropriate decisions, he found by 'walking down his ladder' that he was basing his logic on inappropriate assumptions. Because he had been using assumptions to support his decision-making, his conclusions that reinforced the data were mis-leading and, consequently, his actions were not the most effective.

There could be many reasons to use the Ladder of Inference but perhaps the best reason is that it helps to promote understanding of why people take the actions they take. Whilst going up the ladder takes only an instant, walking someone down the ladder – helping them see the rationale for their decisions – can require some effort. But investing a bit of time in this effort can often make the difference between a highly effective manager and one that needs to be extremely lucky.

I recently became involved in a project to find out if the concerns people feel about some of the challenges facing them can be resolved. This study is quite important because it will get into our mental models about whether the challenges can be resolved or not. There is a crucial point here: the study will not examine *if* the challenges can be resolved, but only if the people *believe* that they can be resolved.

The reason that this point is so important is because our mental models drive our decision-making. If you think that your strategy is crap, then you probably won't put as much effort into making it happen as you would if you believed that the strategy was solid. The same holds true for our leaders. If you think that the leaders of your organisation are not competent to lead you into the future, there is a good possibility that you will not be as committed to them and their leadership as you would if you thought they were competent to lead.

Whilst the study has only recently begun, some of the results are quite startling. Through the use of an online website *(http://hopebubble.ning.com)*, the study initially asked two questions.

1. ***Do you believe that the current crises facing the world can be solved?***
   Study respondents were asked to identify the response that most closely identified their mental model about the question.
   - *yes, we have the capacity to solve the crisis*
   - *we have the capacity but politics will probably get in the way*
   - *no, I think these problems will linger far too long*
2. ***Do you believe that the world's leaders are competent to solve its problems?***
   Again, study respondents were asked to identify their mental models about this question.
   - *yes, our leaders are competent to solve the problems and will do so*
   - *no, our leaders are able to solve the problems but they will let politics get in the way*

Over ½ the study respondents (64%) said that they believed that the capacity to solve the problems is there. But 67% of the study respondents believed that their current leaders were not competent to do so.

The implications of these responses should be of concern to any business manager or senior leader, and in fact, should cause them to reflect on their own situations.

How would your employees respond if they were asked these questions?

- *Do your employees believe that your strategy has potential?*
- *Do your people believe that your company can weather the impact of the current global financial situation?*
- *Do your people believe that your company will  be able to realise its potential?*
- *Do your people believe that the people leading your organisation are competent enough to successfully implement the strategy, or survive the financial crisis, or even ensure that the company will be able to realise its potential?*

Believing that your employee's would answer positively is nice.  But have you actually asked them?  How do you know what they would answer?  What would you do if their answers were not what you would like to hear?  Would you try to find out who said what, or would you try to find ways to demonstrate that you are capable of changing your behaviours so that you would have the support you need to lead your organisation into the future?

Organisational leaders may have all the resources they think they need; they may have solid credentials; they may even have the current backing of their Boards. But if they don't have the commitment and support – *commitment and support are influenced directly to employee's mental models* – of the people who do the work in an organisation, it will be an uphill slog for everyone.

You might like to think that the responses from the ongoing hopebubble study participants may not be representative of your organisation how employees view their situation.  But it is worth considering…what if they are representative?

Business leaders might be wise to examine their demonstrated behaviours…if they really want to create an environment in which their employee's mental models are what they will need to be if their organisation is to succeed.

# The Rucksack Problem

According to Wikipedia, *"The rucksack problem is a problem in combinatorial optimisation. It derives its name from the following maximisation problem of the best choice of essentials that can fit into one bag to be carried on a trip. Given a set of items, each with a weight and a value, determine the number of each item to include in a collection so that the total weight is less than a given limit and the total value is as large as possible."* This is a problem that all decision-makers in organisations face today.

Put yourself in the position of being the key decision-maker in your organisation, something you might already be. You have the responsibility to make choices about all the financial and human resources, all the systems and processes of your organisation. But at the same time, you need to make sure that the choices you make will deliver the best possible performance and at the same time, the highest return on your investments in these assets. In attempting to make your choices, you are pulled by shareholder expectations, analyst's assumptions, competitive pressures, and regulatory demands. In short, the rucksack problem in business is to see how to maximise your return on investment whilst at the same time, being able to effectively manage your efforts. The big question you should be thinking about isn't '*what will you do?*' The big question is, '*how are you going to make the right choices, at the right time, for the right reasons?*'

You could do what is typically done by assigning some sort of value to each of the choice items you have. Then by ranking the items based on the values you have assigned, it may be possible to make some sort of prioritisation. You could do that, but it would be pretty irresponsible. This is because it won't give you what you are really looking for. What will enable you to make the right choices, at the right time, for the right reasons, is to look at the interrelationships between all of your potential choices.

The benefits of looking at the interrelationships between the items instead of looking at the value of specific items can be equated to a good organisational promotion process. Whom would you like to have working for you? Someone who was ranked the highest by his or her MBA programme? Someone who had worked his or her way up through your organisation over the years? Someone who has demonstrated his or her ability to demonstrate sound problem solving?  Or someone who can demonstrate an understanding of theory of sound management practises has acquired the wisdom from actually doing the work, and someone with a proven track record on the job?

By looking at the interrelationships between various choice items, you are able to determine which of these items can provide the best leverage for you to accomplish what needs to be done.  In business, having the best systems and processes, access to adequate resources, and the most competent people is only good if these items can be used effectively together.  This is what leverage is all about.

There are several ways to look at the interrelationships between a group of choices; but the most practical way is to compare them by asking a simple question.

Write the possible choices on a flip-chart, placing them in a somewhat circular arrangement.  Then begin to the question for each pair of choices.  The question is, *'If we use this resource effectively, will it cause the other variable to become effective?'*  The key to this question are the words *'will it cause.'*  A causal relationship is one in which one variable will actually drive another variable.  It is not a relationship of *'if we do this, it **might** help another variable.'*  What you are looking for is a relationship of *'if we do this, it **will** deliver results from another variable.'*

Once you are able to determine which causal relationships can deliver the most benefits, it is easy to see where you should make choices about where to place your efforts for the best return.

In business, each day can present a new 'rucksack problem.'  Regardless of being in good times or in bad times making the right choices about where to place your efforts can be the differentiator to succeeding or failing.  But before you even think of filling your rucksack with effectively appropriate choices, you may want to make sure you are really committed to a journey of success.

# When Only the Annointed Survive

This is a story about missed opportunities, and sadly, it is a story that seems to be permeating many organisations today. The big decision-makers in an organisation make the choice to invest in training and development. They want to capitalise on this investment, so they select their best performers and send them off to a combination intensive learning programme and reward programme. Their rationale is, the intensive learning programme will enable them to do even better than they have in the past, and by having the programme off-site in some trendy holiday spot, the people they send will be rewarded at the same time.

On the surface, you might be thinking that this all sounds good. You combine providing a reward for top performers whilst sending them off to some exotic location and at the same time, helping them learn how to perform even better. It does sound good...on the surface. But by looking below the surface, it is possible to see how this thinking reflects a culture that misses out on opportunities.

In many organisations, the criteria for the selection of 'top performers' to participate in programmes like this is laced with problems. The people that are selected to attend programmes like this are often best described as 'young.' Now to be fair, age really isn't the issue. A mindset that alludes to a belief that longer-term, older employees are not worthy of additional learning opportunities or aren't worthy of being rewarded for past demonstrations of performance is a serious problem.

Another potential problem is the belief that after the programme, the delegates will instantly demonstrate even higher levels of performance. This is a ludicrous concept because many of these programmes are filled with a teaching focus and not a learning focus. Learning takes place through the application of the concepts and theories of what has been presented. And even if delegates believe that they actually have learnt new ways of doing things, the only way these learnings can be demonstrated effectively is through practise. You wouldn't expect someone to go off to a several day programme to learn how to play the violin and then as soon as the programme is over rush out and play with a philharmonic orchestra. The same holds true for delegates who have been chosen to participate in organisational learning programmes. In order for them to effectively demonstrate their new learnings, they need to be able to practise.

The best way to accomplish this is through organised 'practise fields.' A practise field is in reality, an environment in which the learners can test out what they have learnt without any fear that they will make a bad decision, or otherwise muck something up. Practise fields are meant to be safe environments in which learners are able to test out what they have learnt before they find themselves caught up in the day-to-day business world again. A practise field environment is not a one-off opportunity. Organisations that are serious about their people learning should offer classes on an ongoing basis, ensuring that many of the attendees participate long after their learning-reward programme ends. Any organisation that invests in learning programmes and does not enable the participants to practise what they have learnt is missing a huge opportunity to ensure that they will see a positive return on investment in training.

So let's recap. Rewarding top performers with advanced learning programmes can be a good thing, but only if they are open to high performers regardless of age or time in the company. Additionally, the expectation of the delegates is that they will need time and space to practise what they have learnt before there can be a substantial return on investment. All this can be good, but there can also be a downside to these advanced learning programmes. That downside manifests itself in the potential belief that participants are now somehow the 'annointed ones' in an organisation.

Clearly, to be nominated for an advanced learning programme would imply that you are being rewarded for something. But the baggage that can accompany this can be very detrimental. The reason is that often those who participate in these types of programmes are somehow treated differently after their return to the office. Whilst there is no doubt an expectation on the part of management that these participants will be able to demonstrate even higher levels of performance than before, this is often accompanied by them being treated differently than the non-programme participants. This can set up an implicit dual system of further possible rewards and recognition. When this happens, one of the outcomes is that non-programme participants can begin to lose their commitment and their willingness to excel. The end result may be that they become locked into a cycle of not being able to demonstrate the sought after (and rewarded) performance that the company is looking for, and then either chose to leave or are evaluated out of the organisation.

## Robbing Peter to Pay Paul?

Too often, management can become distracted from the implicit challenge that they face. Yes, the explicit challenge is to ensure that the respective organisations that they are responsible for are successful and profitable. But the implicit challenge is to ensure that the decisions they make not only deliver this success next quarter, but in *every* quarter. And to accomplish this, what happens is that they do the equivalent of 'robbing Peter to pay Paul.'

As pressure continues from shareholders and external analysts to 'deliver profits,' some managers fall into the behaviour of making short-term decisions based on reactive thinking. This is really no different from someone who borrows against his or her future salary just to go on a holiday. Eventually, this behaviour catches up to the borrower. And just as it catches up to us as individuals, it will catch up to businesses as well. Eventually, there will be nothing left from future potential earnings to 'borrow' from, and then the end is near. This doesn't need to happen. To avoid it requires two things. A shift in thinking that borrowing from the future is okay, and a clear understanding of what the unintended consequences of these actions are.

Several weeks ago, whilst talking to a senior manager of a large manufacturing company, it became clear that 'robbing Peter to pay Paul' was not only accepted in his organisation, it was rewarded. It was common knowledge that when the sales unit of the company was not '*hitting their numbers*,' the sales managers were told that they had '*better make sure that the targets were achieved, or else.*' The message of 'or else' was a pretty clear signal that their jobs were at risk. So what would you do in that situation? The tendency is to start counting 'possibles' as real sales, or keep discounting until the customer agreed to place an order. Each of these behaviours has major unintended consequences.

Counting future sales as existing sales keeps the cycle of 'robbing Peter to pay Paul' alive and forces sales people to stay locked into this vicious cycle. Deep discounting causes additional shortfalls in financial terms, with the end result being more pressure to produce. Again, reinforcing this very vicious cycle. And the problem does not appear solely in the sales area. Quite often, we have seen production areas under extreme pressure to run at higher than rational levels, just to 'hit the numbers' that have been targeted. In many cases, this results in bypassing required maintenance. It is like driving your car at full speed 24 hours per day, day after day, with the hope that you will get the further down the road than your competitor. But we know that if you do not stop to re-fuel or do prescribed maintenance, the car will simply cease to run at some point, and then your competitor will simply cruise past you.

This is an issue about organisational performance. And if achieving high performance isn't complex enough, in today's business world, you must be able to do continually improve on your performance. Here is the priority hierarchy of performance; A) be able to 'hit the numbers;' B) be able to hit higher and higher numbers; C) be able to demonstrate the ability to higher and higher numbers, consistently. Just being able to do 'A' is simply not good enough anymore, nor is being able to do 'B.' The ability to demonstrate hitting higher and higher number consistently is the real challenge.

Organisations need to ensure that they have in place a solid structure and culture that fosters continual performance improvement, and they need to do it through a clear demonstration of leadership. Traditional management just won't cut it anymore. You can't 'manage' your way out of a structure and culture that propagates 'robbing Peter to pay Paul.'

What is required is a solid grounding in the key elements of sustainable performance improvement. These elements include: 1) a clearly visible and understandable strategic vision for the future; 2) an organisational structure, business processes, and human resource architecture that are in alignment with the vision; 3) support and commitment to the on-going application of technological innovation; and, 4) an organisational culture that accepts and is committed to achieving the vision. The only way that these elements can take hold in an organisation is through clear, committed, visible leadership.

Many organisational decision-makers would say that they do have these elements in place; but the reality is that if they were, the performance-based behaviour of 'robbing Peter to pay Paul' would not occur. This is a greater issue than how best to cut costs; this is a greater issue than just how to get things done; this is an issue about choice. The choice – *your* choice - is, *'do we want our organisations to be able to consistently deliver high performance and realise their potential?'* If the answer is 'yes,' then the management needs to make a choice to that effect. Would implementing this choice be difficult? Perhaps. But the reality is that management is paid to make tough choices, and this decision is far more beneficial over time than just about any other decision that could be made.

## Recognising Your Tipping Point

The tipping point is the term that is often used to explain what will happen if the planet cools enough so that ice keeps moving toward the equator...and reaches approximately 30-degrees latitude as it did millions of years ago When (and if) that happens again, the sea will not be able to absorb enough light to stop the onslaught of ice, and the globe will be completely frozen over. Whilst this prospect is rather chilling (sorry, but the reference is quite appropriate here), the whole tipping point concept is something that business leaders should be conscious of.

In business, the term tipping point could refer to either the point at which a company's downward spiral would be unstoppable. Conversely, it could refer to the point at which the acceptance of organisational change will be unstoppable. Being able to recognise the tipping point before one begins to teeter on it is the subject of this week's newsletter.

There are some obvious tipping points in business; including, having enough financial and human resources, having employees and managers that are able to learn faster than the competition, having innovative products and/or services, and having access to a market that wants and needs whatever your organisation does. And whilst these tipping points are pretty obvious – the tip of the proverbial organisational iceberg – what typically happens is that many of these indicators are measured after the fact. It is easy to see if you run out of financial resources, or even if you don't have enough people to use them. It isn't that difficult to see if your people haven't learnt faster than the competition. It is pretty easy to tell if you have the right mix of products and/or services. It is easy to recognise these facts when you are slipping into business oblivion, but then it is already too late. The real trick is to be able to recognise your slipping point before you find out it is in front of you.

All the previous indicators are easy to see. But because you can only see them after they have occurred, they offer very little leverage if you want to reverse their effects. What is needed is to look for indicators that are not as easy to see. What is not as visible is the level of commitment and support that your employees have for your key decision-makers. Whilst the level of commitment and support may not be as visible as other potential indicators, the leverage that this can provide should not be underestimated.

Commitment and support are direct functions of the mental models of managers and employees. This is not a tangible thing, like being able to physically total up the amount of people or financial resources an organisation has at its disposal. The mental models of managers and employees are an intangible thing; they are difficult to see, and even more difficult to measure…or so many key decision-makers believe.

Mental models in business are impacted by several things: 1) the belief that the organisational strategy makes sense (or not), and will lead the company toward its desired future (or not). 2) the belief that senior decision-makers are truly interested in the input of employees (or not). 3) the belief that the senior team is competent to lead the organisation (or not). You may have access to resources; you may have brilliant people, but if these mental models are not positive, then you may be closer to your tipping point than you might expect. The challenge is to surface those mental models.

Surfacing mental models is only difficult if you try to expose them by direct confrontation. By asking direct questions – 'do you think that we have the right strategy' or 'do you think our senior team is the right one' – may result in politically motivated answers. This is especially true in the case of organisations in which employees do not feel that their input is valued or even wanted. These organisations are typically operated in a command-and-control environment; and offering perspectives that are not in line with the existing management story line can be a risky thing to do.

By surfacing employee's mental models, it is possible to gain critical insights about your organisation's ability to realise its potential, or, the potential that it was about to begin a painful slide downward.

Realising when your organisation is at its tipping point is important. Being able to recognise when it is headed toward its tipping point is crucial.

## Driving Lessons from Mr. Moss

I recently received a note from a client commenting on the opportunity facing key decision-makers in many organisations today. In his note, Richard passed along a quote from an interview years ago with legendary race car driver Stirling Moss. The gist of it was *"When I was younger and I saw something horrible I wanted to stop the car and walk away. I'm older now and nowadays when I see something like that I put my foot down hard because I know everyone else is lifting theirs."* There is a powerful lesson here for decision-makers.

Today, with many organisations stuck in re-trench mode due to the economic conditions that we are living in, there is a tendency to become extremely conservative with business decisions. On the surface, this is only common sense. Whenever markets dry up; whenever customers orders slow down; whenever expenses seem to soar disproportionately; whenever your business prospects appear to be slipping away from you; it does make sense to pull back and become very careful with every pound-euro-dollar that you spend. But this mindset, whist rational in the environment we are in, can also become paralysing.

Paralysed decision-making is usually the result of either A) fear that a decision might go wrong; B) fear of being held accountable for that decision; or C) not knowing what to do. Whilst A and B are closely linked, C stands out as something that, if sorted out, can help avoid the first two fears.

The level of ambiguity in decision-making – not know what to do – can be exceptionally high in the economic situation we are in today. Everyone knows that something must be done to help our organisations survive, but no one seems to be sure what exactly to do. This level can be reduced if decision-makers apply a 'test' to any decision they face. The 'test' is called common sense.

The first element of this 'test' is understanding what you are trying to accomplish through any decision. By having a clear understanding of what you are trying to accomplish, you can begin to work backwards to determine what is the best way to achieve what you want. The element of this test is determining some of the things that could be done. Typically, this involves making a list of all the things that might get you closer to where you want to go. The key to this element is to encourage whomever provides input to not preclude any possible solution. It would not be good to arbitrarily rule out a potential option until it has been tested to see if it could be a good thing.

Next, see which of the potential options would provide the greatest leverage to move you in a positive direction. This is an important point: what you are looking for are the key activities that can provide the most leverage. You are not looking for activities that might be easy, or things you may *think* are best; you are looking for those activities that actually will provide leverage.

With this information, you can begin to develop a plan to move forward. At each point in the planning process, ensure that every identified activity is given the 'common sense' check. What you want to avoid is a plan that looks fabulous on paper, but in reality, implementing it would not represent common sense, and therefore, would not be functional over time.

At this point, you should look to see what some of the potential unintended consequences of using those high leverage activities could be. Often, what appear to be sound activities may carry some serious unintended negative consequences that can negate any gains made. It is also important to identify what contingencies could be used in case you run into resistance or something changes in your plan. Having contingency plans ahead of time – both contingencies that will prevent problems from arising, and contingencies that will mitigate negative effects that may arise – can often be the key to success.

Taking the ambiguity out of any decision process is crucially important if you want your organisation to be able to survive, especially in turbulent times like we are living in today. Let your competitors become paralysed, but you need take advantage of the opportunities that are there.

Winston Churchill summed it up quite well...*"A pessimist sees the difficulty in every opportunity; an optimist sees the opportunity in every difficulty."* This could very well be the time for anyone worth his or her salary to put their foot down hard and do something.

## The Fine Art of Using Tourniquets

Last week I was talking to a good friend of mine who spends most of his time coaching managers in business, and the conversation evolved to why many senior managers of businesses today would be crap doctors. The reason being – and this isn't mean to be funny at all – that many managers of organisations are like an incompetent doctor in a hospital emergency ward. He may know how to recognise the patient's haemorrhaging, but his techniques to stem the bleeding can result in the death of the patient. And this, as you can imagine, would not be a good thing.

The metaphor of *'illness or sickness'* applies well to organisational problems. Let's say you have a company that is 'haemorrhaging' cash at a frightful rate. What would you do? Well most people trained in first aid would tell you to put a tourniquet just above the haemorrhage to stop the bleeding – if you don't, the patient will soon run out of blood and die. This is the same with a business – if you are haemorrhaging cash, you need to stem the flow or you will run out of money. But this is where it gets interesting. Yes, the purpose of the tourniquet is to stop the bleeding, but more importantly, it is to buy some time so that the medical people (managers) can do something more permanent to ensure that blood (cash) doesn't resume pouring out of the patient (company). And this is where things fall apart in business. Too often, when faced with this type of problem, the 'doctors' apply the tourniquet and then go on to the next patient, or in the case of business, the next business problem. And if you have had any first aid training, you might remember that if you leave a tourniquet in place too long, the limb that it is on may develop gangrene. If this happens, the patient can die. And the same goes for businesses – if only quick-fixes (and a tourniquet is a temporary quick-fix) are used, there is a larger risk that the company will wither and die anyway.

All this raises the question, *'why do managers love to use quick-fixes instead of going for more fundamental solutions to new or long-standing problems?'* There are several reasons for this, one being, *'they may not know any better.'* Remember, this is business, and what do shareholders and boards all want? Quick results. You have a problem? Fix it, and fix it now. Profits down? Turn them around before the next quarter's report comes out. Market share eroding? Do something about it immediately. Businesses reward quick fixes, plain and simple.

Go ask a group of managers how they spend their time. I have, and the vast majority of the people I have spoken to say that they spend far more time than they would like fighting 'business fires.' And even scarier is that many of them fight the same fires over and over again. The reason is that they are just applying quick-fix thinking to serious problems. Sure the problem seems to go away – for the time being. But it keeps coming back. This is like putting a tourniquet on a leg wound – the bleeding does stop – but after it stops, telling the patient he can go back to doing what he was doing. As soon as the patient moves about a bit, the wound will open up again and the bleeding returns.

When is the last time you heard conversations in your company about where the company would be in 20 years? Not too often probably. Most conversations are about where the company will be in the next few months or next year. Short-term, quick fix thinking is as destructive as serious competition or lack of resources – it is an example of a clear gap in a company's decision-making ability.

Another reason that managers do a lot of quick fixes is that they are addicted to it, and the reason is they are rewarded for this behaviour. Addiction; you know – if it feels good do it, and the more you do it, the better it feels. Shoot, it feels good to be known as the best 'problem-solver' in the company, doesn't it? *'Got a big problem? Give it to Fred, he can fix anything.'* And because he can and does *'fix them,'* Fred keeps getting promoted; after all, he is good at fixing all those pesky problems. And it apparently doesn't matter that many of them are the same problems over and over again – Fred fixes them so he gets rewarded for his efforts. I am not saying that people shouldn't be rewarded for 'fixing' problems, but I am saying that I think we need to do more rewarding for people who make sure that the company *doesn't have the problems to begin with.* Of course, that doesn't happen too often, because if you don't have the problem, there is nothing to 'fix' is there? And avoiding the onset of problems is harder to see that fixing them. And if you can't be 'seen' doing something, why bother when the rewards go to those who do the visible stuff?

Using a quick fix in business is like using a tourniquet - you have to understand the consequences are of your actions. Sure the tourniquet stops the bleeding, but if you don't do something when the immediate problem is over, either the bleeding will resume or the patient can die. Applying a quick fix solution in business is fine, as long as you then do something to make sure the problem doesn't come back again. And before you use the quick fix, you had better be pretty sure that something else even worse than the original problem doesn't happen because of what you do.

## The Return of the Mad Hatter?

Staying ahead of the competition is important, and one of the ways companies do this is to ensure that their managers and employees have the right skills and competencies – the right abilities to get their respective jobs done effectively. Although there are some different views on what is a skill and what is a competency, there seems to be no disagreement that managers and employees need them. And whilst it is clear that appropriate competencies are certainly important, for some reason, the whole competency issue has appears to have gotten way out of control in some organisations. Recently, there was a request for proposals for leadership training for an organisation in England. And typically, the organisation, in their request documents, listed the competencies that they are looking for, organisational level by level. The list is quite typical: each employee at each organisational level, the request for proposals stated, will need somewhere in the vicinity of twelve competencies (each one articulated in the request), and each specific competency will have a multiplicity of descriptors. Reading the list(s) was like being the central character in Lewis Carroll's book about Alice.  Has the business world gone mad?

I will be the first to admit that when organisations realise that some of their people are just not equipped to manage or lead, as they should be, the natural tendency is to go out and see what other organisations have for management or leadership competencies. Fine.  But where things begin to run amuck is when the 'researchers' of 'the appropriate' competencies start to take some of the competencies from one organisation, and some from another, and some from still another, and slam them all together in a bouillabaisse of competency soup.  Suddenly, the effort to compile the list of competencies becomes the goal and not the improvement of managers to manage and leaders to lead.  I know of a company where this is exactly what occurred – the list became so unwieldy that there was no way that employees would be able to be accountable for real improvement.  What happened was that everyone was so busy ticking off the boxes, that they lost the plot of why something needed to change.

I have worked with another company in the UK where they had begun to go this direction – assembling the longest competency list in the western world to prove that they were serious – when luckily; people came to their senses.  Instead of a huge, complicated, convoluted, diabolically unwieldy competencies and descriptors, they came up with four competencies that they felt were important. And then they figured out how to know if their managers were exhibiting movement toward them.  And guess what?  The initial feedback was that the 'system' (don't you just love it when something becomes a 'system' in a company?) was way too simple to work.  An interesting reaction, as that was the point of doing it that way.  As soon as 'systems' and 'processes' become too complicated, the complexity of them just create opportunities for managers and employees to 'game the system' and avoid the possibility of being held accountable.  The effort instead becomes an exercise in 'box ticking' instead of becoming better managers and leaders.  The senior management, however, stuck to their position that 'simple was better,' and achieving high levels of the four competencies became the goal of all managers and employees. The best part was that the four competencies were the same at all organisational levels. And here is why.

When it really comes down to it, there are only four things that either make or break a company. How people 'think' about situations, opportunities, challenges, and risks. How they 'influence' others to buy into initiatives, to get behind and support the companies goals, and to build alignment supporting the company's mission and vision. How they 'achieve' the company's goals and targets so they actually are hit, how they get the work done, and how they do their jobs more effectively. And lastly, how they demonstrate real 'leadership' so that the people who report to them become committed to where the company is going. This issue of 'leading' is not just one for the most senior people in a company. At every level in an organization, employees look to someone who will show them a path to follow, to provide the guidance so they can grow, and to create an environment in which they can be successful. This happens in the boardroom and it happens for the third-shift cleaners.

Just four competencies that work in any organisation, and are the things that really make a difference. So guess what? Some of the feedback was that these four competencies were 'too generic' and could apply to any organisation. Well no kidding – so that makes them bad? No, that makes them appropriate. Remember, the big issue is how to get the company – through its people – to actually perform better. And what better way than to improve the way that managers and employees think, influence, achieve, and lead? Anything else would just be 'Mad Hatter thinking.'

## Do You Really Want the Shirt?

I am not the world's greatest sports fan, but I do remember what it was like to go to a football match and sit in the stands with friends watching all the action on the pitch. And you know something? Every time I have done this, I have noticed something happening near me. The people I was with would tend to watch the match and then proffer advise on how the players should have played. Bad kick, poor ball handling, sloppy footwork…the list goes on an on. And the same thing happens in the office. We sit on the sidelines and then make comments about other people's actions. Poor deployment, bad meeting facilitation, sloppy workmanship...and on and on. So what is it that causes people to make observations about the actions of others, especially in the case of work, instead of offering to assist? Is it better to just sit on the sidelines and snipe away at our peers? Do we for some reason, like to see others become relegated to the scrap heap of apparent incompetents?

Sitting on the sidelines can be great fun, and clearly it is safer than being in the midst of the action, but in the realm of business, it is something that some might consider to reflect a lack of commitment to success. In organisations, just as in any team play, the only way success happens is when everyone is in the game. Now it is clear that 'being in the game' for some people may mean out on the pitch, for some it might be keeping the team fit, for some it might be selling tickets, and for some it might be cheering from the stadium. Regardless, each of these people 'is in the game.' We all need to recognise that real success doesn't occur when some people become so risk-adverse that they would rather just sit and wait it out until they know what side to cheer for. That represents politics in the workplace to the n'th degree. And when type of environment is around you, none of us will win over time.

Winning in business means not only 'hitting the numbers,' but it also means that everyone *wanting* to participate in the journey toward success. It means that everyone needs to *see* the desired *end goal* and do whatever they can to achieve it. It means that just sitting on the sidelines should not be allowed.

Think of the last time you were in a 'meeting before the real meeting.' You know, these are the meetings that take place over coffee where people discuss what they think will happen in the real meeting. It is those pre-meeting meetings where you can get an idea of what kind of meeting participant they will be.

Some people go to meetings as 'prisoners.' You know – a prisoner is someone who is attending the meeting because they have been told to be there. They have other things they would like to, or should do; but their boss has said they need to go, so they go...and they sit on the sidelines. Some people are there as 'vacationers.' A vacationer is someone who attends the meeting because it is better than doing what they really should or could be doing. So they sit on the sidelines. Some people go as 'sophisticates.' A 'sophisticate' is someone who believes that they know more than anyone else in the meeting. They could do the facilitation better, they could make a better presentation, or they could have drawn on better data. They think they know it all, and they sit on the sidelines. And then there are 'explorers.' An 'explorer' is someone who may know something about a topic, or may know nothing about it at all, but in either case, are keen to learn as much as they can. 'Explorers' are rarely found sitting on the sidelines – they want to become involved, to participate, to learn and share, because that is what exploring is all about.

These four categories of people do not exhibit these characteristics because they have them in their DNA. They exhibit these characteristics because of their ability to make choices. We all have the ability to decide which type of employee we will be. Whilst we have many things to do, when requested to attend a meeting, we can make the conscious choice to take it as an opportunity to learn something. We can decide that though we think that attending the meeting is better than doing our 'day job responsibilities,' what we learn in the meeting just might help us do our day job better and easier. We can decide that, though we may be pretty smart about many things, being in the meeting *and* actively participating may help others learn what we know. These decisions are all part of learning and sharing...the key to being an explorer.

I am not advocating everyone necessarily being on the organisational pitch at the same time. That would be mass chaos – can you imagine everyone at Old Trafford all piling onto the pitch because they want to play? Not a pretty sight. But I am advocating that everyone who has something to contribute, should do so in the most appropriate way. Just sitting back on the sidelines doesn't even deserve the team shirt.

## Compliance or Commitment?

If there is something that senior managers don't like to talk about, it is their ability (or inability) to get people onboard with their strategic plans. This issue is hidden in a shadow of semantics, with the essence of the topic being, what exactly does 'onboard' mean?

The word onboard is a historical reference to getting people on a ship before a journey. But this is where the problem lies: are the people 'onboard' because they have been told that they need to be, or are they 'onboard' because they think that his journey is sound and worthwhile?

For many managers and employees, getting onboard with strategic initiatives, or even change initiatives, means that they are following the company line that was set forth by the lads in the top jobs. They do this because they are told that this is what needs to be done. But do they believe it? This is where the distinction between *compliance* and *commitment* lies.

If you get your people onboard because they have been told to be onboard – compliance – they will not put forth the efforts that you need from them. Compliant people rarely do any more than exactly what they have been told to do, and this means you will not get any more than the bare minimum from them. And to make it even worse, you will have to police the people to make sure that they even do that.

However, if you can get them committed to your strategic direction; i.e. they are onboard because they *want to be* onboard and *see the benefits* from moving in this direction – you will find that they will provide the fabled 110% that will be needed if you are to be able to really achieve the strategic goals and targets.

Here is where the real question lies. How can senior management gain *commitment* from their managers and employees? Too often, the methods used to gain commitment can be summarised by the adjectives *weak, ineffective, and demeaning.* No wonder companies rely on compliance to drive initiatives. This need not be the case.

Commitment to just about anything is put forth because people *want* it. They see the big picture; they see the benefits of it; they see how they fit into it; and they see how their efforts can contribute to its success.

Internal marketing efforts are good vehicles to put clarity around what the big picture is, and what its benefits are. But internal marketing usually falls short on helping managers and employees see how they fit into the big picture, and fall even further short on helping them see how their efforts can make a difference. Yes, slick, four-colour brochures and a deluge of emails can attempt to address the questions, but the reality is that the people driving these efforts (senior management) need to get out of the office and start talking with, and listening to, their people. The key words here to remember are, "talking with" and "listening to." Progress will not be made if employees sense that they are being 'talked at.' They want to know that their contributions are valued, and talking 'at' them sends the wrong signal. Talking 'with' them sends the right signal, as does listening to them.

Now if you are a senior manager of a company that has thousands of employees, this might seem a bit daunting. You don't need to listen and talk to everyone; but you do need to find out who the key influencers in your company are, and sit down with them. Being a key influencer has little to do with hierarchical status, but more to do with the strength of the internal network of the person (or people) and the level of trust and respect they have from those in the network.

Find out who the people in your organisation are that the managers and employees respect and listen to. Seek them out and talk with them, but even more importantly, *listen to them.* If you can understand their concerns about what you want to accomplish, there is a good chance that you can get them to see why it is so important, and how they can help make it real. The worst thing that can happen is that you will not be able to get them onboard, so listen them closely; the best thing is that you just might learn something about how to do it better next time.

At the end of the day, it is all about getting things done…and by far, it is easier to get things done working with people who are committed rather than it is with people who are compliant.

## Hearing the Hum?

Did you hear the 'hum'? The 'hum', as reported recently on the news several years ago (and according to the Wikipedia website) is, "*a generic name for a series of phenomena involving a persistent and invasive low-frequency humming noise not audible to all people. Hums have been reported all over the world, especially in Europe. …its source and nature are hard to localise.*" When I first read the story in the news, I assumed that the reporter was referring the millions of refrigerators in the world that all seem to emit some low-level sound signalling the compressor hard at work; but then I realised I had heard it in business for many years.

In business, the "hum" can take on different characteristics. But most often, the hum manifests itself in off-line conversations that rarely fit with stated organisational values. There is no doubt that off-line conversations are a fact of business – always have been, and always will be. But the question to be asked relates to how managers are using these conversations.

In some organisations, the off-line 'hum' relates to getting people onboard for specific initiatives and/or budgetary concerns. This is almost understandable. Initiatives and budget concerns are a natural thing to assume that people are talking about. But what is a problem is when the conversations begin to stray into the area of internal politics or the relative competence of peers. These conversations can add little value to an organisational strategy and, in fact, do nothing other than distract managers and employees from the task at hand.

The very fact that the 'hum' is there becomes an organisational undiscussable, and that in itself is a reason to address it. The best way to reduce, and eventually eliminate it, is to openly talk about it. This means when management meetings take place, the 'hum' should be put on as an agenda item.

If you choose to put the 'hum' on the agenda of your meeting, here are some of the things that might happen.
1. Some participants will assume you have lost the plot and are reading too many science-fiction novels.
2. Some participants will deny that they have ever heard the 'hum,' and consequently believe it isn't there.
3. Some participants will not want to talk about it because it represents issues and challenges in the organisation that are currently undiscussable.

But the good news is that, after explaining what the 'hum' is in business, you people should want to talk about it. This is because they can (hopefully) see the destructive nature of having this take place whilst organisations are under increasing pressure to deliver consistently increasing performance. The question is, *how can you actually get people to talk about things that are currently undiscussable?'* The best way is to address them head-on.

One of the problems about openly talking about undiscussables is that the list of them is often far longer than you would expect (or like to admit). Several years ago, I was working with a senior management team of a service organisation and it became clear that there were several undiscussables that needed to be talked about so the team could move forward. Within minutes, the list of potential items to discuss completely filled a flip-chart.

To figure out how to deal with this, you simply need to look at your undiscussable list and see which issues have the greatest impact on the organisation's ability to realise its potential, or in this case, the issues that are creating the most problems in this area. Get those out in the open first. If you don't deal with these, the rest of the list won't make any difference anyway, and will relegate you to remain a second-rate organisation that will not be able to achieve what it needs to achieve.

And for those of you that don't actually currently hear the 'hum,' be careful not to believe it is not there. Just because we don't see or hear something, it doesn't mean it isn't there. Often, the 'hum' resides just below the surface, and because of this, it may only be recognised when you are actually listening for it. It would be nice to believe that we shouldn't have to put any effort into listening for the 'hum' because it isn't there, but that rarely is the case.

The 'hum' is real. The 'hum' is there...and it is not the office refrigerator. You just need to listen for it...and then decide if you care about your organisation enough to get rid of it.

## A Good Cat?

In the late 1970's, Deng Xiaoping of China is reported to have said, *"It doesn't matter if a cat is black or tabby; if it catches mice, it is a good cat."* What he was referring to, according to reports at the time, was that he really didn't care if Chinese farms were Party-run communes, or privately held...as long as they produced enough food to feed the people. This message is something that some senior company managers should think about.

Most organisations have sets of policies and procedures. It might be safe to assume, the larger the business, the greater number of policies and procedures there are. There is a good reason for this – organisational populations need some basis for understanding the rules that govern what a business does, and how it does it. However, in many organisations, the policies and procedures become metaphorical handcuffs, causing otherwise creative and innovative employees to become cautious or even worse, not creative and innovative when they are faced with challenges.

Policies and procedures are necessary, but should not become restrictive in the way they are applied. And whilst the application of policies and procedures can be one problem, an even greater problem can be that the people who developed them often treat them as 'their baby' and will resist any challenges to them.

Too often, conversations about whether or not policies and procedures are being followed become sidetracked by defensive attitudes on the part of those who wrote them. This is usually due to the fact that they do not want to look as if they have not done the job they were told to do. The belief, mis-guided or not, is that if it appears that they have not done what needs to be done, then they may be perceived as not competent. This, as we know, can lead to not having a job.

Regardless of the reason why conversations can become defensive, the real question might be, if the policies and procedures aren't being followed, how were they developed? One answer might be that those people who put them together are often not the ones who are bound by them. I heard a case-in-point several years ago when I was speaking at a university. The planners had designed a well laid-out campus, with large amounts of green-space between buildings, and very smart looking walk paths connecting them. It didn't take long to notice that students were not following the walk paths, but instead, cutting across some of the green spaces diagonally to reach different buildings. The planners responded to the despoiling of the grass by putting up signs and small fencing, which soon escalated to bigger signs and a taller fence, which then escalated to more restrictive messages. Eventually, common sense prevailed, and grounds-people simply put gravel onto the now well-worn path and campus life continued. There is a strong lesson here.

On paper, the design of walk-paths around the green space made sense, but life does not happen on paper. People who come up with rules, which in most organisations manifest themselves as policies and procedures, need to do several things before they try to institutionalise them.

1. See if the new policies and/or procedures reflect common sense. If they aren't common sense, they probably won't be followed.
2. Look at what some of the unintended consequences of new policies or procedures are before they are implemented. There are always unintended consequences of decisions, and if you don't identify them before implementation, fixing the resultant mess will only make things worse than it is now.
3. Talk to the people who will be impacted by the rules to see what you might have missed. Alternative perspectives are always important to determine, and often, those most impacted by decisions will be able to see what you may have missed.
4. Develop a contingency plan in case the policies or procedures are consistently circumvented. Some employees will always try to game the system. Make sure you are prepared to deal with this.
5. Explain how the policies and procedures will be good for the company, and for the employees. Making the connection between decisions and daily work is always key if you want employees to buy in to them.

Policies and procedures are important to have in organisations, but of even greater importance is having the willingness and ability to get things done. If your policies and procedures are too restrictive (or just plain stupid) things won't get done, then what will you do?

## Those "E" Words

According to Wikipedia, *"Efficacy is the capacity to produce an effect. Efficacy measures this capacity under ideal conditions. It is these conditions that distinguish efficacy from the related concept of effectiveness, which relates to change under real-life conditions."* Efficacy and effectiveness. And then there is the other E word, efficiency. For most people, efficiency is all about accomplishing things quicker, with less effort, and in most cases, for less money.

Efficacy, effectiveness, and efficiency. In business, we use these three words; but the one we use the most is efficiency.

The fact that efficiency is the E word most often used could be due to several factors, with the one that makes most sense being that efficiency is the easiest to recognise. The outcomes that are most often tracked for efficiency are like the tip of an iceberg. They are easy to see and easy to measure; and because of this, we tend to look for efficiency as a metric that is worth measuring. But the reality is that looking to make things more efficient provides the lowest leverage to ensure that an organisation can realise its potential.

Effectiveness, or more appropriately, striving to become more effective, provides far greater leverage in the context of business. Effectiveness is all about decision-making and understanding. Effectiveness is all about knowing what is the right thing to do, for the right reasons, and at the right time. If we make decisions that are more effective; i.e. decisions that can actually accomplish what needs to be accomplished; typically what accompanies them are gains in efficiency. If we make decisions that are more effective, things will be accomplished in less time, because there will be less need to fall into reactive thinking mode. Decisions that are more effective require less effort to implement because contingencies are thought out and ready if they are needed. Decisions that are more effective cost less because parameters are understood. Becoming more effective is more powerful than becoming more efficient.

Granted, the results of becoming more effective can be more difficult to measure. But this is only the case if the people making decisions look for metrics through a myopic, short-term lens. Looking for the easy to see, easy to measure can drive decision-makers into the efficiency-is-everything trap. Organisational decision-makers, who want to both see short-term gains *and keep them,* need to shift their thinking to look at effectiveness as the key metric to look at.

And that leaves us with the third E word, efficacy. That definition said that *'efficacy is the capacity to produce an effect.'* This could provide the highest leverage of all the three E words in business. This is because efficacy involves individual and collective choice, and choice is the key word.

Managers and employees have the ability to make the conscious choice whether to be committed. They also have the ability to make the conscious choice to use that commitment to be effective in how they do what they do. But it is senior management who have the ability to make the conscious choice to ensure that their people have the resources and learning opportunities that they need to truly be effective. Without these resources and learning opportunities, any commitment on the part of employees and managers will never be realised. And yet, it is senior management that often are the ones that complain about employee commitment, effectiveness, and efficiency.

This does raise the question, "whose responsibility is employee commitment, effectiveness, and efficiency?" I know some managers who think that commitment, effectiveness and efficiency are the responsibility of employees, but the bottom-line reality is that they are largely the responsibility of management.

It is management that sets organisational direction and, therefore, has the responsibility for ensuring that all employees understand the direction, the reasons for it, and a rationale for how it will get there. It is management that controls expenditures for training and development that enable employees to learn how to become more effective. The same holds true for efficiency; without investment in training and development, the chances that employees will be able to become more efficient are slim.

In short, if management wants to raise the level of efficacy in their organisations, they need to take the first step and create an environment in which it can happen. It is only management that can make 'real-life' and 'ideal' conditions the same.

## It's Never Too Late

There is a line in The Gate House, a book by Nelson DeMille that, whilst part of a conversation between two of the novel's characters, could have been a key message in a book on sage advice for business decision-makers. The line is, *"It's too late to change the past, but never too late to change the future."*

Many managers in organisations today seem to be stuck in the past, and this can mean constantly reliving past successes or horrors. There is no doubt that organisational decision-makers do have the opportunity to learn from the past, but the reality is that the past is exactly what it is...the past.

The annals of business history are littered with stories about once great companies that are either out of business, or on the veritable precipice about to fall into it. And whilst the number of now defunct companies is huge (and growing), the list of companies in which managers are living in the past is probably greater by a massive multiple.

History has taught us that learning from the past is important. Many decision-makers have fallen into the trap of trying to re-invent the wheel for just about everything they do. This is often due to the fact that in their headlong rush to reduce costs, they have made so many experienced people redundant that they are faced with a loss of organisational memory – knowing what works and what doesn't work because they have experienced it in the past. Because of this loss, they often find themselves trying to do things that will just be a waste of time, effort, and resources.

There are other organisations where key managers are still re-living previous episodes of organisational achievements; i.e. *'remember when we used to be....'* and, *'in the past, we were the ones that...'* This too can result in mis-placed time, efforts, and resources (not to mention being eaten alive by the competition) because people become too focused on the past and lose sight of what needs to be done for the future.

What organisational decision-makers need to do is learn from the past, but not allow themselves to be trapped in it. In order to do this, it is important to have a clear picture of where an organisation is going.

Most organisations do claim to have that visionary picture for the future, but often, what is missing are the elements of it that allow managers and employees to really make the connection between what they do, and the desired future. Typically, the elements that are visible are the 'tip-of-the-iceberg' dimensions of what the company wants to become. These can include what percentage of market-share it wants, or what level of revenues or profits, or even what their competitive status is; i.e. 'biggest in the industry.' These are important elements to have visible, but the chances that they will be realised are slim unless the other elements are visible as well.

The elements that are often missing include; A) what types of policies and procedures will be needed in the future, B) what kinds of demonstrated behaviours on the part of management will be needed, and C) what mental models will managers and employees need to have to achieve the needed levels of commitment and motivation that will be required so desired future can become reality. Unless these elements are clearly identified and made visible to all managers and employees, they will continue to work and think in the same way they have in the past.

In addition, any communication about the desired future vision needs to be accompanied by a clear, rational explanation of why this vision for the future is critical, and how the organisation will get there. These elements are key in order to help managers and employees make the connection between the desired future and their day-to-day activities and demonstrated behaviours. If they cannot make this connection, communication about the future vision will take on the appearance of just more internal P.R. and be forgotten in less time than it took to produce it.

All this does take effort. Identifying all the key elements of a desired future can be painful, but only if the organisational decision-makers haven't taken the time in the past to think like this. But that is what this is all about…making the effort to change the future. If they aren't willing to put in the effort, then it will be clear evidence to managers and employees that the future really isn't that important.

## Bending Spaghetti

Were you aware that if you hold a piece of dry spaghetti in two hands, with one end in each, and then begin to bend it, it will never break into two pieces? I wasn't sure if this was true or not until I had exhausted a package of the pasta myself. Every time I bent the spaghetti, it broke into three or more pieces. Actually, it didn't really just break – it shattered sending bits all over the kitchen. I went online to see why this happens, but then realised that the same thing happens metaphorically in business. We often try to accomplish something, but our expected outcome is quite unpredictable.

Two professors at the University of Paris discovered the behaviour of spaghetti. What they found was that, as the spaghetti reaches its limits of flexibility, *'waves travel along the length just after the initial break. These waves trigger an 'avalanche' of new breakages, causing the stick to fragment.'* It is the same basic dynamic in business.

Decision-makers who come up with organisational initiatives often come up with plans that on look terrific on paper. They look at what needs to be done, put together what they believe is a comprehensive plan to make it happen, get everyone to sign off on it, and then un-leash it onto a company population. In most cases, the people who come up with the implementation plans are not idiots, but equally in many cases, the plans do not go as they were supposed to. The reason is that they don't understand what happens when you try to bend spaghetti.

Unless decision-makers, regardless of how smart they are at their day-jobs, look at two things, their initiative implementations can be at risk. The two often-missing things are; 1) What the implications are of this initiative on organisational culture, and, 2) What the unintended consequences are that will surface when the plan is implemented.

To understand the first point, one needs to look at the demonstrated behaviours of senior management. Do senior managers demonstrate the values that they tell everyone they need to operate within? Will the new initiative fall into line with the values? Will senior management be visibly involved in the real work of the initiative implementation? Will senior management provide the time and resources needed to ensure that the initiative can actually be implemented on time and in full? If the answers to any of these questions are 'no' or 'not sure,' it would appear that there is little understanding of the second point.

Most organisations that are serious about improving their manager's ability to make better decisions typically offer, either internally or externally, training programmes in managerial skills. The intent of these programmes is fine. The problem is that better decisions are rarely the outcome of good intentions alone.

In order for managers to learn how to make better decisions, they not only need to improve their level of skills; they also need to have a better grasp on the impact of their decision-making processes. There is logic behind this statement.

- In decision-making that impacts people, there are no absolute 'right' answers, only answers that are better than others at any given point in time.
- The potential effectiveness of business decisions relies heavily on the fact that the decisions need to be clearly understood by those who are expected to carry them out.
- The people on the receiving end of business decisions determine the potential effectiveness of them based on their own mental models of the decision-maker(s) and the decisions themselves.
- Therefore, the ability to implement a decision is heavily influenced by the impact it will have on those who are expected to do something with it.

Too often, decisions are mis-interpreted; the rationale behind them is not understood; and, they run counter to the existing mental models at play in an organisation. When any or all of this happens, the chances you have for having an effective decision implementation process is slim, at best.

Managers need to have the opportunity to learn the *impact of their decisions* on an organisational population, and senior management needs to create the environment in which this can happen. Without this learning, the risk that decisions and actions will fracture an organisational culture is high, and the mess you are left with when the shock waves filter through the organisation will be worse than what happens when you try to break spaghetti.

## Position Determines Perspective

No doubt about it, position determines perspective. Clearly, this statement can be taken two ways. Position can mean the level you hold within the organisation you work for, or it can mean how you look at what is going on around you in your organisation. But regardless of which meaning you would like to think of, position does determine perspective. Here are several examples.

Example 1: You are a senior manager in your organisation, and you, because of your work schedule, rarely have time to spend with anyone other than your peer senior managers. Your phone log shows incoming and outgoing calls to your direct reports and other members of your senior team. You have lunch with your peers. You have coffee with your peers. You have meetings with your peers. The employees you have under you really can't possibly understand what you are up against, so you talk to those in the same situation. Your beliefs and assumptions begin to be in alignment with those of your peers. You become insulated from the day-to-day activities of your employees.

*Your perspective becomes skewed and narrow because you are not able to connect with the people who do the work in the company.*

Example 2: You are a front-line worker, and because of the explicit and implicit communications structure, are not able to talk directly with the head of your business unit. You are not able to see how your efforts fit into the bigger picture because no one takes the time to explain it. You begin to lose motivation because no one takes the time to show the company's appreciation for all that you do to hit goals and targets; goals and targets that seem arbitrary because no one takes the time to explain why they are important.

*Your perspective becomes slanted to believe that your efforts are not valued.*

Example 3: You are a mid-manager in a business unit that seems to be under constant pressure to deliver higher performance. Because of the past results your unit has shown, your budget requests are not supported. The given rationale being that the company needs to invest more in the areas that have been achieving or surpassing goals and targets so that they can continue to realise their potential. Over time, you find it harder and harder to achieve the goals and targets that are set for you because you don't have the resources you need to meet them.

*Your perspective becomes jaded because you begin to feel that no matter what you do, or how much effort you put forth, it won't make any difference.*

What all these examples have in common are the fact that the perspectives of the subjects change over time, and the changes carry some potentially dire ramifications.

Perspectives that become skewed and narrow because you are not able to connect with employees who do the real work of the company (example 1) result in further isolation from what is really going on in an organisation. People who experience this tend to become more and more disconnected from the reality of what goes on and what is needed to make things better.

When your perspective causes you to believe that your efforts are not valued (example 2), your level of motivation and commitment begin to slip. With less and less motivation and commitment, you are less likely to voluntarily become involved in what could be critical organisational initiatives.

When your perspective leads you to believe that no matter what you do, it won't make any difference (example 3), any efforts you put forth to help the company will be reduced, either in amount, or in effectiveness.

What is most interesting (in a very depressing way) is the fact that the evolving perspectives that take place (as in example 1) often result in the perspectives that are seen in examples 2 and 3.

The good news is that senior management, because of its hierarchical position, has the ability to prevent all these perspectives from occurring. The best way to do this is to include managerial behaviours in performance appraisals. One of the most important behaviours to evaluate is how in touch managers are with the reality of the people who do the day-to-day work of the company.

The benefits of doing this are numerous, and include the avoidance of the perspectives found in examples 2 and 3. And who knows, those managers might actually learn something at the same time.

# Churchill's Truth

Winston Churchill said something years ago that rings true today in business. He was quoted saying, *"courage is what it takes to listen."* So very true.

Most managers I have met in my work are good at giving direction and some other presumed managerial-type duties. But it is a far less percentage that are good at listening. The fact that it doesn't happen as often as it should is one thing; the reason for not taking the time to listen is problematic. Not listening can occur for one of several reasons, including; they think that their employees don't have anything valuable to contribute, they believe that they don't have the time to listen, or that they are afraid of what they will hear.

Listening is one of those 'soft-skill' things that often get little attention or effort in company training programmes. Most programmes have a slew of courses like "making effective presentations," and "communicating effectively," but these are all about talking *at* people. What organisations need to do is help their people learn how to listen to people.

Listening to people has two main dimensions: hearing the words that they say, and understanding what could be behind those words. Often what happens, someone might be saying something to you, and before they are even able to finish what they are talking about, we begin to formulate our own response. This often occurs when we are receiving feedback.

You may have experienced this scenario. You are called into your boss's office and he begins to give you feedback on the last presentation you made that didn't go well. Do you;

A) Try to explain that the other people in the room weren't paying attention?
B) Try to explain how your IT people had messed up your presentation slides?
C) Wait until your boss is done talking and then say, *"This is what I am hearing you say,"* and then paraphrase what he has said.

If you do either A or B (or anything other than C), you have fallen into defence-mode thinking and probably will not even be able to understand the real message that your boss is trying to communicate. Receiving feedback but thinking defensively sends the signal that you really are not interested in the feedback, or in improving your communication skills.

In communications, there are two key elements: what is said (or written), and what is heard (and understood). The gap between what is said and what is heard can often be monumental, and it is this gap that can result in serious problems. If you are on the 'providing' side of the communications equation, it is your responsibility to ensure that what you say is what people hear. If you are on the 'receiving' side of the communications equation, it is your responsibility to ensure that what you hear is what is being said. But it doesn't end there – the 'hearing' part of the communications equation isn't just about the words that are spoken; it is also about understanding what is behind those words.

We have all experienced examples of, when having a conversation with someone, almost before you are even finished talking, the listener is already responding. This might be fine if the conversation was taking place on a quiz show on television where the quickest answer wins. But in business, it signals that the listener really isn't listening at all, and instead, formulating a response that will either refute what has been said, or attempt to put forth a different perspective.

By ensuring the listener really understands what has been communicated is the only way to ensure that information is not mis-interpreted or not completely understood. All it takes to avoid this potentially devastating problem is wait until the speaker is done talking, and then begin with, *'this is what I am hearing you say,'* followed by your summary of the message. This question is very powerful. It will help to avoid confusion, mis-understandings, and inappropriate mental models from forming.

All this may seem to slow down the communications process, but in reality, because it can eliminate mis-understandings, mis-direction, and confusion, it acts to speed up effective communications.

Winston Churchill was spot on...listening does take courage. It takes the courage to ensure that what you hear is actually what is being communicated. It takes the courage to ensure that your messages are received in the way you have sent them. Actually, taking the time to listen is nothing more than common sense truth.

# The Magic Square of Leadership

Do you know what a 'magic square' is? It is a matrix with the same number of squares both vertically and horizontally, each filled with numbers. Regardless of which direction you count – up, down, or diagonally - the total is always the same amount.

| 4 | 14 | 15 | 1 |
|---|---|---|---|
| 9 | 7 | 6 | 12 |
| 5 | 11 | 10 | 8 |
| 16 | 2 | 3 | 13 |

And what, you might be wondering, does this have to do with leadership? The answer is… everything.

In today's business lexicon, there are two terms that are often (and incorrectly) used interchangeably – management and leadership. As a good friend told me, management is *'the science of achieving agreed results through the efficient use of resources".* That is all about keeping things under control. Leadership, on the other hand, is *"the art of persuading people that things can be changed for the better".* That is all about creating an environment in which managers and employees can realise their potential. There is a huge difference, and this is where the magic square comes into play.

The Magic Square can be a metaphor for what both management and leadership actually do. Management, or importantly *the demonstration of management skills,* would be applicable to making sure all the numbers (horizontally, vertically, and diagonally) actually do add up to the right number. Leadership – *the effective demonstration of leadership skills* - however, would be applicable to ensuring that managers and employees would know how to make the puzzle, and for what reasons.

Whilst some might say that this may be a semantic distinction between management and leadership, but there is a difference. The difference can be seen in the results that an organisation delivers. Both management and leadership can deliver high performance. Often, they can both deliver high performance consistently over time. But without clear demonstrations of leadership, managerial skills can only ensure that the results are delivered. In many cases, this means through specific directives about what to do in any given situation. By implication, management, being all about control, needs to have people around making sure the goals and targets are achieved.

By having clear demonstrations of effective leadership, managers and employees are able to *see and understand* what needs to be done and why it is important. The need for mass-amounts of people checking up on everyone else is diminished, or in many cases, eliminated. One indicator of which environment you may work in can be found by looking at the types of learning opportunities that are available to you.

If the process of learning that your organisation uses reflects *single-loop learning (learning what to do),* you are probably in a management mind-set organisational environment. But if you are in an organisation that focuses on *double-loop learning (learning what to do and why that is important to you and the organisation),* then you are probably working in an environment that believes that effective leadership is the path forward.

There are other indicators of a leadership environment that are equally important. Do your senior people, in the quest for answers, realise that questions and how they are asked are crucially important? Do your senior team have a common view of the organisational vision, and talk about it as the context for decisions? Does your senior team clearly exhibit the same behaviours that they expect from you? Do you understand how your day-to-day activities – regardless of what your hierarchical position - contribute to the overall success of the company?

We should all ask ourselves these questions. None of these questions can be answered by traditional data, but instead the answers represent our individual and collective mental models. If some of the answers you receive are in the negative, then it might be beneficial to find out what is behind the mental models. Are they based on mis-directed assumptions and beliefs that have no real substance? Is it because that is what the employees have come to believe based on what they have seen?

Like the Magic Square, discovering the answers can be fascinating. But knowing how they are derived is where the benefits lie...and magic has nothing to do with it.

## The Rectilinear Trap

**rec·ti·lin·e·ar** , *an adjective.* \,rek-tə- li-nē-ər\
*definition:* moving in or forming a straight line.

In business, especially when putting together a strategy, there seems to be a belief that the line from where your organization is now to where it wants to be in the future should be a nice, easy to follow rectilinear line. Apparently the strategy guys who believe this either have never really had to implement a strategy, or still think that Santa Claus comes down the chimney on Christmas Eve.

Here is what most strategic plans would like us to think. Your organisation is currently at a place I will call "X." Your plan says you are going to "Z." Along the way, you will find milestones or indicators that you are making progress. I will call these "Y." There could be a lot of "Y's." If you follow the 'plan,' you will arrive at "Z" in accordance to the timeline set out in the strategy. Right.

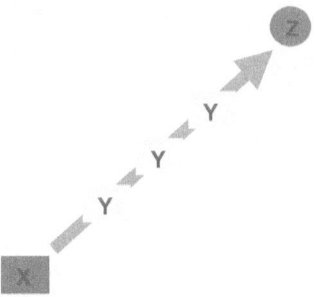

The reality is that implementing a strategy rarely allows for rectilinear thinking to work out. What most times happens is that you begin at "X" and do head toward "Z," but along the way, whilst you are keeping your eyes out so you can see the various "Y's" along the way, you get side-tracked.

The reasons you get sidetracked usually are because you become distracted by a plethora of real or imagined challenges, opportunities, or competitive pressures. When it is apparent that the very nice straight-line path has been lost, usually one of two things happens: either you end up pounding ahead at full-speed to get back on the path and find those elusive "Y's" (but may not even know where they are now), or you begin to think differently. Thinking differently is the only way to find your way forward, but sadly, it might be too late. The best thing is to think differently *before* you begin the implementation process.

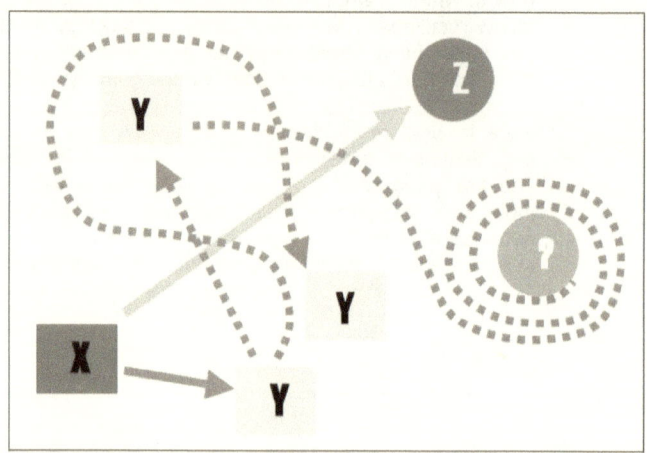

Thinking differently means that it is important to:
1. Identify *what else could happen* when you implement the strategy before it does. This isn't all that difficult, but it does require that you listen to what other managers and employees think could go wrong. Once you have a list (if it is a short list, you need to listen more closely), then develop a set of things you can do to offset potential problems. The identification of contingencies should identify both what can be done to mitigate the effects of problems as well as (hopefully) prevent them from having negative effects on your efforts.
2. Be prepared to use a logical rationale for why you will be undertaking the strategic direction that has been selected. Too often, implementation problems occur because not everyone involved really understands either the plan itself, or the rational behind it (or both). By using either inductive or deductive reasoning as the logic behind the reasons for the strategy, it will be easier to ensure that everyone knows what they need to do, and why.

3. Help your people make the connection between their day-to-day activities and the strategy.  If managers and employees are not able to see how their activities are connected to where the organisation is going, and why it is going there, the risk is high that a strategic plan will become just another company initiative that is someone else's responsibility.
4. Prioritise the milestones or indicators into two groups.  These groups should identify which ones are critical to see, and which ones would be nice to see.  Without this prioritisation, it is possible for managers and employees to lose sight of what is really important.

Rectilinear thinking is a good thing, but only when what you are attempting to do is simple, and does not have the potential for problems.  Implementing a strategy is neither of them.  The only way to have a chance of actually being able to accomplish what a strategy sets out to do, on-time and in-full, is to think differently.

## Filling the Gaps

Here is how communications usually work in business.  Step 1: Senior management makes some big decision, and they know that they need to make sure their people understand what is going to happen.  Step 2: The internal communications people are called in to craft a press release or a speech for the masses.  Step 3: The information is passed along though the various internal communications vehicles that most large companies have.  Step 4: The management team cascades information about the decision in meetings.    Step 5: Everyone sits back and congratulates themselves on a job well done.  Sadly, that often isn't the way it really happens.

What really happens is that often, in the case of printed communications, the 'message' raises more questions than it answers.  In the case of verbal communications, the 'message' sort of evolves a bit from person to person.  The end result is that in many situations I have seen, the targets of the communications – managers and employees – have gaps in understanding that need to be filled.  And because managers and employees are human, they tend to fill these gaps themselves with assumptions and conclusions that are incorrect.

In today's business world, it is difficult to see why senior managers are not more concerned about this. The risks associated with managers and employees taking inappropriate (or blatantly incorrect) actions because they have filled the gaps in information can be devastating to an organisation.

In order to reduce or eliminate the perceived need of managers and employees to fill the gaps they see and feel in communications, there are several things you can do.

1. Communications should tell a story. Think about what the story is you need your people to know. This is a far different question than determining what data they need; think about what the story is. In most cases, it would make sense to ensure that all business communications is in the context of where an organisation is going. Tell the story and show how it will impact the organisation's ability to achieve its vision.

2. Before you issue the communication, regardless if you do it verbally or in printed form, test it out. Explain it (or share it) with a small group of people from various parts of your organisation to see if it tells the story you want it to tell. It is important to realise that, whilst you are not looking to hear there is a problem with your planned communications, it is better to find out about it before you actually let it out to the greater population. Take the time to find out if your planned communication will answer more questions than it creates.

3. Ensure that as part of your communication process, you enable and encourage feedback so you can answer any questions that may arise. This can be a bit tricky, as simply asking for feedback may not be enough. In the case of verbally communicated messages, you do have the option of checking to make sure that what you have said matches up with what was heard. To do this, ask whomever you are speaking with what parts of the message will make the greatest impact on what they do. In this way, you are creating a space for a response and have the chance to clarify any points that are unclear. Written communications are a bit harder to elicit feedback or questions, but it is important to at least identify a way for readers to ask for clarification.

4. In all forms of communication, always remember that what

you say or write isn't as important as what the listener hears. What recipients of communication interpret as your message will either help them understand what you are doing and why, or cause them to fill in the blanks on their own. It is your responsibility as the one with the message to make sure that those you are targeting with it understand what you are saying. Simply relying on listeners to hear what you are saying isn't enough. Your message, your responsibility. Ensure that the people you are targeting are able to understand it.

In business, there are only two types of information; good news and bad news. More and more senior managers are finally understanding that the only real bad news is when their people 'don't know' what is going on or why. The challenge is to make sure that this doesn't happen, because if it does, your people will fill in the gaps themselves, and that rarely is a good thing.

## Carrots and Sticks

There often comes a time when senior managers believe that they are left with only two options: carrots and sticks. According to the Wikipedia definition; carrots and sticks refers to, "*Carrot and stick (also "carrot or stick") is an idiom that refers to a policy of offering a combination of rewards and punishment to induce behavior.*

Rewards in business seem to be more plentiful than punishments. Managers and employees are offered bonuses and/or promotions for demonstrating above average performance. All that is fine. But sometimes, managers and employees that demonstrate performance or behaviours that are not in line with what is needed or expected are shifted from one position to another. For some reason, this action is supposed to eliminate a real or looming problem. The reality is that in most cases, it is just a reactive myopic solution to a fundamental problem within the organisation. Do these decision-makers who take this route (usually senior managers) really believe that this will provide a fundamentally sustainable solution, or do they think that this 'quick-fix' will be enough to change the performance or behaviours of the person?

There is no doubt that in some cases, working in a new environment can be enough to stimulate more effective results, but in most situations, all this does is to prolong the agony by trying to avoid the inevitable.

Managers or employees who do not demonstrate the performance or behaviours that are sought after need to be put on notice that what they are doing, or how they are doing it, is not acceptable. If the problem stems from a lack of knowledge of what do to, these employees need to be provided with opportunities to improve. This usually requires some aspect of helping them learn how to perform better, or why it is important to them and the company. But if it is not a skill issue, or an issue of understanding, that only leaves a *willingness* to demonstrate performance or behaviours to deal with. The way to address this is not through simply shifting the people from one place to another within an organisation.

Patterns of poor performance or behaviours need to be documented, with the people who are demonstrating them put on notice. If that doesn't result in the needed shift, these people need to be given the opportunity to demonstrate poor performance or behaviours for some other company. In plain talk, that means they need to be sacked.

Over the years, I have met some senior managers who struggle with this. Sacking someone isn't fun to do, but the reality is that in either a good economy or bad, non-performance or behaviours that do not match with stated organisational values should not be viewed as acceptable.

Leaving managers and employees who demonstrate poor performance or behaviours in an organisation has two effects: It will not allow a company to realise its potential, and it acts as a signal to other employees that there is no reason to try to excel. This can be even more devastating over time. Why should they? If those who demonstrate poor performance or behaviours are not punished, why should anyone else put forth any extra effort?

Enough is enough: managers and employees who do 'go that extra mile' for their supervisors (or the company as a whole) do need to be rewarded. It really doesn't matter if the reward is in the form of a promotion or a bonus, but they need to be rewarded for ongoing exemplary efforts.

Those managers and employees who do the opposite over time need to be sent away. Period. And for those readers who are now thinking that it can be extremely expensive to get rid of some managers or employees, they need to look at the reality of the situation. Leaving managers and employees who demonstrate poor performance or behaviours in place in an organisation – even if their position is shifted to another area – will only exacerbate an already bad situation and will send the wrong signals to everyone else. The resultant impact on culture and therefore performance, will make the cost of sacking them pale in comparison.

It certainly is understandable that some senior managers become frustrated and feel that they are left with only two options at times. Using carrots and sticks are viable options at that point, but they should only be considered when you are not afraid to use the stick when it is needed.

## What is the Big Deal with Mental Models?

Well, mental models are a big deal. Mental models are the way that people sort out how to understand the environment in which they live and work. They can provide predictive and explanatory reasons for why people act in the way that they do. Being able to understand manager and employee's mental models about the organisations they work for, and the work that they do, can be extremely powerful in working to improve performance. That is the good news.

The 'not so good news' is that our mental models are constantly evolving, and quite often, they do not necessarily represent the reality of a given situation. Instead, mental models represent 'what we *think* the situation is.'

Here are a few examples of mental models that belong to some managers that were interviewed recently.

- *'Our management team is not taking us in the right direction.'*
- *'My subordinate is just not up to the challenge.'*
- *'My department always gets short-changed at budget time.'*
- *'This is the best company in the world.'*

There are two things that these statements have in common: none of them represent facts, only what people may believe; and, these beliefs can and will impact individual and collective performance.

Statement one, *'Our management team is not taking us in the right direction,'* is a mental model of a person that believes that his managers are probably not the right ones to lead the organisation into the future. If you believed that, would you be willing to put forth extra effort to help the management team achieve their goals? Probably not.

Statement two, *'My subordinate is just not up to the challenge'* is a mental model of a manager who believes that the employee is not willing or competent to do what is expected of him or her. And because of that, you (as the manager) probably won't give him (or her) the chance to prove your mental model is not right. And if this is the case, do you think that he (or she) will ever be able to perform up to your expectations and realise his (or her) potential in the company? Probably not.

Statement three, *'My department always gets short-changed at budget time'* is a mental model of a person that believes he might be under additional stress and pressure to deliver results because others in the company are treated differently. If this were you, would you be willing to continually strive for increased performance under the belief that you aren't being given the resources you need to deliver it? Probably not.

Statement four, *'This is the best company in the world'* represents a mental model of someone who likes his job, likes the company, and apparently likes the way the company is being managed. Does this sound like someone who you want working for you and with you? Probably yes.

So lets look at the four statements again. A potential outcome from statements one, two and three is that employees who have one or more of those beliefs will not be your best performers. Secondly, if they have any of those beliefs, there is a high risk that they will develop a 'bunker mentality' – 'just trying to survive by doing the bare minimum and not willing to put forth additional effort.' And this risk is like a contagious virus in an organisation that can spread to others.

The last statement, however, represents a mental model that is very positive. This is the type of employee that you want to have in your company. Someone who likes what he sees, and most probably will be willing to do whatever it takes to help the company achieve its goals.

So, a logical question might be, 'how can we help people shift their mental models about the company and its management?' First, we need to remember that mental models are not necessarily based on facts, but on 'what people think is going on.' This means that you need to help people 'see' a better picture than they currently see. You need to help them reframe their mental models about where the company is going, how it will get there, and who is going to lead the way. This is done through open, honest, and trustworthy communications.

Second, it can be very beneficial to talk openly in meetings about the fact that we all have mental models and their potential impact on organisational performance. Think about when new initiatives are announced in those meetings. A lot of 'head-bobbing' goes on – people giving their visible approval to what is being announced, but then later, at the *'other'* meeting at the coffee machine, what they *really* think about it comes out. Give them the time and opportunity to say what they *really* think in a safe environment where their input is valued. Knowing the reality of existing mental models prior to starting an initiative is better than not knowing and ending up with a problem.

Mental models are not just some 'soft' issue that can be overlooked. They are very real and the way they are acted out can make the difference between a highly motivated, committed workforce that will demonstrate high performance, and one that will never realise its potential. Take the time to understand them...take the time to learn from them. They can make a real difference, both for you and for your organisation.

## The Dark Side of Alignment

Every January, when a New Year rolls around, one might assume that what all senior managers have wished for would be to have greater alignment around the initiatives that they propose. You know – alignment; complete and unwavering support for proposed initiatives on the part of managers and employees. Alignment - no dissention, no whinging, just complete and unwavering support. That kind of alignment begins at the senior manager team level, and whilst it does seem like it would be a good thing, there is a very dark side to achieving it. That 'dark side' occurs when groupthink begins to take over.

The term 'groupthink' has been used to describe what happens when a team or group of people are trying to reduce the risk of conflict and instead reach consensus without *critically testing, analysing, and evaluating ideas.*' When this occurs, independent thinking can be lost in the rush to achieve group agreement, often regardless of the validity of an opposing view.

Typically groupthink surfaces when a team is under high levels of directive leadership; has a high level of homogeneity of team members social backgrounds and ideology; or is isolated from outside sources of information or analysis.

According to Irving Janis, a researcher who has done extensive work on the topic of groupthink, some of the symptoms of groupthink occurring include:

- *Illusions of invulnerability* creating excessive optimism and encouraging risk taking.
- *Rationalizing warnings* that might challenge the group's assumptions.
- *Unquestioned belief* in the morality of the group, causing members to ignore the consequences of their actions.
- *Stereotyping* those who are opposed to the group as weak, biased, or spiteful.
- *Direct pressure* to conform placed on any member who questions the group, couched in terms of "disloyalty".
- *Self-censorship* of ideas that deviate from the apparent group consensus.
- *Illusions of unanimity* among group members, where silence is viewed as agreement.
- *Mind guards* — self-appointed members who shield the group from dissenting information.

Senior managers, when asked if they believe that groupthink could be occurring in their teams, often begin to become highly defensive, which only reinforces the potential for groupthink to take place.

The effects of groupthink can be devastating, and include the potential for incomplete or not-thorough understanding of the challenge at hand, a failure to properly and effectively understand risks associated with an initiative, and a failure to identify and consider contingency plans. The result is ineffective, or more appropriately, irresponsibly defective decision-making.

Having said that, not making decisions in a timely manner – in the quest to make sure everyone's voices can be heard - can be equally irresponsible and result in stagnation of a management team's ability to drive an organisation. Clearly, there must be a balance in how alignment is found in organisational decision-making.

When your team has been charged with making a decision, you should, according to Jarvis;

- Ensure that the view(s) of the most senior managers are not expressed before team members have had an opportunity to give their perspectives on the validity of the potential decision
- Assign at least one person of the team to act as 'devil's advocate' during discussions (with the role changing every meeting)
- Ensure that internal and external experts in the given field be invited to share what they know
- For large-scale decisions, have an independent group within the organisation explore various options available

Having alignment when making key decisions is important without a doubt. But as has been seen in the media, just having everyone agree that the decision is a good one doesn't make it a good one. And unless you want to wake up one day and find yourself in a situation like we have seen in the past (the Bay of Pigs invasion, the banking fiasco, or some of the other ill-advised decisions we have all read about in the news), then you had better make sure that the alignment you achieve is based on sound, data-based, effective decision-making…and not on the fact that It may seem like a good idea at the time.

# Wishing for Oprah?

A few days ago, I received a call from a manager who was caught in a real dilemma. She told me that she has been struggling dealing with one of the members of her team and didn't know what to do. In her words, *'he is pretty smart, but he isn't fitting in with the rest of the team and seems to think he is above all the rules and policies that our team has subscribed to.'* Okay, that can happen. I pressed her to see what options she thought she had to deal with the situation. *'I am afraid to discipline him or even confront him because I think it may cause disruption with the rest of the team.'* Right. This was beginning to sound like the manager really was caught in a dilemma, but not the one she saw looming in front of her.

Being a good manager means several things. Typically, this list includes; building alignment in your team around what needs to be done and why, getting things done on time and in full, and maximising the return on investment of resources that your team uses. It also includes making tough decisions when they need to be made. I don't think I have ever seen in a managerial job description anything about being all warm and cuddly like Oprah.

Being a good manager does rely on the ability to demonstrate a sound mix of both hard technical skills and soft skills, but it does not mean that you should let one or more people in your team think and act as if they *were* the team.

Managerial decision-making is full of choices. The manager who rang me can, if she chooses, use this situation as an opportunity to build a highly effective team. She can also let her situation be the pre-cursor to the complete demise of all that she has worked for. Assuming most people in her situation would like to use the situation as an opportunity, here are some things she could do.

1. First, document the behaviours that are being demonstrated by the person who is not acting in accordance with organisational values or directives. This is extremely important and should always be done. Do not record hearsay or speculation, only what behaviours have actually been demonstrated.

2. Consider using the Ladder of Inference to help understand what is causing the situation. Using the ladder is a good way to

understand why people react in the way they do to certain situations. In the case of the phone call I received, it is entirely possible that the team member's behaviours are a result of the manager's behaviours.

3. With that information, meet with the team member and again use the ladder to help him see the impact of his behaviours on the rest of the team. Part of this conversation should include what options the manager is left with if the behaviours do not change.

Find out what you, as the manager, can do to help the person change his behaviours. This is a good thing to do for two reasons. This helps shift the burden of the conversation from blame to growth, and it is entirely possible that something you are doing, or how you are doing it, could be contributing to the problem.

4. In the next team meeting, surface the issue of individual and collective organisational responsibility. Don't lecture the team about responsibilities, ask them for input as to what they see their responsibilities are. Often, this means you may need to have them describe what they actually do in the organisation. These descriptions should not include job descriptions, but instead focus on what they perceive that they actually do to help the organisation achieve its goals. This can surface many misconceptions about what managers really do to create a positive environment for employees.

Also in the team meeting, raise the subject of team undiscussables. Almost every group of two or more people have some things that, whilst they may be problematic, no one is willing to talk about. If things that are perceived to be undiscussable are not addressed, they could become major issues that negatively impact a team's ability to be effective. If needed, drive the conversation along the lines of cause-and-effect to show what can happen if undiscussables are left to bubble away under the surface. Make addressing at least one undiscussable a set agenda item for each subsequent team meeting.

If all else fails, the manager who rang me still does have two options left. One option is to fulfil her managerial responsibility to build a performing team and get rid of the problematic person. The other option is sort of a long shot, but she could call Oprah and ask for a big hug.

# Talking Rubbish

We have all experienced this in business. And whilst I am not sure if business decision-makers have learnt this 'skill' from politicians (who have refined this to a science), it is clear that many managers have become well recognised for talking rubbish. This is how it can happen; and just to clarify, being recognised for talking rubbish is not a good thing.

Historically, we have become used to politicians talking rubbish. We have all seen this; you ask a politician a question, and the answer you receive has so little to do with your question that you would assume they didn't even hear you – assuming they answer at all. Becoming used to people talking rubbish it doesn't mean we like it, of course. And sadly, it seems that more and more, talking rubbish has filtered its way into the land of business.

Talking rubbish can appear in several ways:

1. Trying to convince your peers and/or direct reports that you know more than you do. This typically occurs when you are asked tough questions and your responses either aren't appropriate, or so far out of line that it is apparent that you are well over your depth. This is quite evident when some senior businessperson is asked to explain why his or her company's performance has slipped. In many cases, you would think that the question the person heard must have no connection to what the answer is. Seriously talking rubbish.
2. Telling your direct reports how to deliver performance when you don't have a clue yourself. This often happens when you really don't have a clue how work gets done in your organisation. Your direct reports will listen closely to what you say, but in the back of their minds they will be thinking "what an idiot. He has no idea what he is talking about," with the end result being a loss of respect and commitment. Not a good thing.
3. Espousing behaviours that are in alignment with organisational values when you do not exhibit these behaviours yourself. This is the classic 'do as I say and not as I do' situation and typically results in loss of commitment to whatever you attempt to get your people to do in the future.

It is the last example that is the most destructive in an organisation, and here is why.

- Your boss interacts or makes decisions in a way that does not match up with organisational values.

- You see this as 'he doesn't walk the talk' behaviour

- You make the assumption that he thinks he (or she) is 'above' the rules.

- You come to the conclusion that a boss who doesn't walk the talk is not someone worthy of your respect

- You arrive at the belief that people who are not worth respecting are not worth being committed to follow

- You become de-motivated, and begin to think that this is not the company to work for

- You either settle into delivering a malaise of mediocre performance with the hope of not being sacked, or decide to leave the company

Clearly, this is not what one would want to have happen in an organisation, especially if you are the one whose behaviours have been causing the problems. The situation, however, is that most people who have been recognised as talking rubbish don't believe it themselves. Instead, they often believe that what they are doing, and how they are doing it is exactly what needs to be done. This set of beliefs often leads them to think they are surrounded by incompetents or chronically poor performers. This might actually be the case, but unless they are open to actually considering that it is their demonstrated behaviours that might be causing the problem, they will never know for sure.

The only way to see if your people think (even a little bit) that you might be talking rubbish is to get some feedback. But here is where this can become difficult. If you are talking rubbish, there is a good chance that you wouldn't believe direct feedback anyway. So you have to look for indirect feedback.

Ask for someone who doesn't work for you and has no vested interest in you or your position to solicit feedback on the perceptions of those you speak with, talk to, and/or report to you. There are only a few really important questions to get answers to.

A) Do your people think you are competent to lead them?

B) Do your people believe that you demonstrate appropriate leadership for your position in the organisation?

C) Do your people believe that you 'walk the talk?'

If the answers to any of these questions are 'no,' then you may want to consider getting some help adjusting your demonstrated behaviours...or get your CV in order because if you don't change, you should be sacked.

## Over-Used and Abused

*"Lessons will be learnt."* Yes, it is the phrase that we all have heard over and over again..."*lessons will be learnt.*" Your company doesn't get the results it wants, so management reports to employees and shareholders that whilst the results weren't as anticipated, "lessons will be learnt." Right. So if you have heard this statement, the next time it comes wafting out of some senior managers mouth, you may want to ask yourself two questions, *"if lessons will be learnt, then when?"* and *"If we are learning lessons, then why do we seem to re-live these situations over and over again?"* The answer is, of course, that lessons clearly haven't been learnt. And in many organisations, they won't be.

To understand why, you first need to put some clarity on who will actually be doing the learning. First, organisations don't learn. We banter around the expression 'organisational learning,' but organisations don't learn – people learn. People have the ability to learn what to do, how to do it, and why it needs to be done. The outcome of learning is shown through demonstrated behaviours. These behaviours could be shown in how managers interact with each other and with employees; they can be shown in performance related outcomes; and they can be shown in organisational climate studies. But the bottom line is that organisations don't learn, people learn. And if learning isn't taking place, in most cases, it isn't because the people are stupid. It is because there are organisational structures in place that do not support learning.

Years ago, the author of The Fifth Discipline, Peter Senge, said that the speed in which people learn is probably the strongest organisational differentiator in business today. This statement is still valid, but if an organisation does not have a culture and structure that supports and nurtures learning, it will not take place.

If you want to see an improvement in the way things are done in your organisation, you might want to first explore what structures are in place that support learning. The structures that will make the most difference include A) the mental models about learning on the part of management and employees are in place; and B) how much budget money – in both good times and bad – is committed to support learning. These structures should take the form of the following:

1. Genuine support from senior management for creating learning opportunities. The word 'support' doesn't mean that they *say* they support learning; it means that they stress that learning is important, and that they create enough time and space for employees to enrol in some type of learning activity.
2. Making demonstrated applications of learning an integral part of performance appraisals. If learning is not explicitly made part of performance appraisals, then employees will not take the need to learn seriously. This should not imply that simply taking courses is enough – what should be part of the appraisal process are the demonstrated applications of learning.
3. Senior managers need to visibly participate in company-run learning activities. Whilst most organisations stress the development of courses for the greatest number of employees, clearly there are some courses that would apply to senior people as well. For off-site courses that senior people participate in, they need to ensure that others in the organisation are aware that even senior managers are learning as well.
4. Human Resources, or whoever is responsible in your organisation for training and development need to make sure that their principle focus is on learning, and not on just offering courses. Too often, the metrics used to measure effectiveness of training becomes a 'tick-the-box' activity that just shows how many people sat through some programme. The only metrics that are important are, A) How many people have been able to demonstrate real learning? and, B) What is the difference for the organisation's effectiveness have the programmes made?

The whole thing about learning lessons is important, but the questions asked by managers and employees are valid. If learning truly is taking place, it does follow that problems should not be recurring over time.

Whilst is should be clear that dealing recurring problems over and over again will result in additional, non-planned costs; it also needs to be recognised that the biggest cost will be the impact that not learning has on an organisational population. Senior management needs to get their act together and either demonstrate a real effort to learn lessons, or stop talking about it. These are the only two options there are.

## Doing Your Job

We have all experienced things in business that are frustrating. It might be the fact that senior managers do not seem to respond quickly enough to competitive pressures. It might be the fact that we don't receive what we believe to be a fair performance evaluation. It might even be the fact that we aren't given the resources we need to effectively meet expectations. But the one that frustrates me the most is when it is clear that another manager has been repeatedly demonstrating behaviours that are not in alignment with organisational values...and nothing is done about it. Frustrated is just a mild adjective compared to what others have said when they see this happening.

Here are a couple of scenarios that may ring true to you. Your organisation has a 'code-of-conduct' that all managers and employees should follow, but a manager continually skirts them and displays behaviours that are clearly opposite. Mid-managers habitually state that they are committed to the strategy, but then do whatever they can to obstruct its implementation. You see a manager use his or her position as a vehicle for personal gain. The lack of repercussions when you see these scenarios sends a very bad signal to the rest of the employees.

If you talk to some senior managers, the list of reasons for not doing something about these people is about as long as the Amazon River. But the reality is that penalising or sacking these people are a clear responsibilities of management. If nothing is visibly done, then the senior managers should face the same options. Here is why.

- Organisational values are put together in order to provide a framework for managers and employees to use in their decision-making about what to do, and how to do it.
- Delaying or avoiding penalising or sacking repeated violators of organisational values sends a signal that the values are not important.
- Organisational values that are perceived to not be important will not be followed.
- When organisational values are not followed, an organisation runs the risk of diminishing the authority of all senior management decisions.
- If senior management decisions are not perceived to be valid, there is no possible way for an organisation to achieve its goals, targets, and realise its potential.

This logic makes it clear that senior managers need to demonstrate behaviours that are in line with what they expect from other managers and employees. If they don't, they should be disciplined or sacked. The question is why this sometimes doesn't happen. When pressed, managers often state one of these reasons why:

- *It is very expensive to terminate an employee.* Guess what? It is even more expensive to keep an employee that isn't demonstrating appropriate performance behaviours. The reality is that letting these people continue to flaunt rules and values sends two signals to the rest of the employees: 1) the rules and values are not important, and 2) management is not strong enough to do what they should be doing. In either case, management's authority, both explicit and implicit, will be diminished, and lead to continued and additional behavioural problems. This will lead to reduced productivity and increased costs.
- *We haven't done a proper job of documenting behaviours that are not in alignment with organisational rules and values.* Okay, so whose problem is that? And even worse, what does that say about the competence of management to do what they are paid to do? Documenting both good and inappropriate performance behaviours is part of a manager's job. If you aren't doing that, you shouldn't be in a managerial position. And again, the signals that this excuse sends are all negative and can be very detrimental to the climate of your organisation.

- *The person has been put on notice and will most probably now adapt his (or her) behaviours.* Right. It would be nice to believe that having a quiet word will make a difference, but repeated demonstrated patterns of behaviour that are not in line with expectations typically will not change easily, if at all.
- *I don't like to fire employees.* Well, get over it. There is no doubt that getting rid of managers or employees who do not demonstrate appropriate behaviours isn't fun to do, but it is part of the job. Creating an environment in which managers and employees can realise their performance potential is a key to long-term organisational success. Keeping that environment viable for all managers and employees is your responsibility.

In management, there are only two options: either you fulfil your managerial responsibilities or you don't. One of them is to make sure that either your people demonstrate appropriate behaviours or you do something about it. If, after documented warnings, they continue to act in a way that does not match with your company's values, you need to do your job get rid of them, and better sooner than later. If you don't, your boss needs to get rid of you.

## Michelin Expectations

One of the things about going to a Michelin-starred restaurant is that your expectations are quite high. Actually, exceedingly high. And in most cases, these expectations are met and, in some cases, exceeded. That is what the whole Michelin star thing is about – a way to designate set your expectations around which restaurants serve exceedingly well-prepared food. But some times, you go to a highly rated restaurant, and the service or the food doesn't meet your expectations. There are similarities in the world of business.

Two areas in business where expectations often create problems include high performing employees and the implementation of initiatives.

The problem of high performing employees occurs when there is an expectation that once an employee has been designated as 'high performer,' they will consistently exhibit the same levels of performance. I have no doubt that, if someone makes the conscious choice to be a high performer, they will most likely always try to deliver at the same level. But sometimes their ability to deliver can be hampered by either mis-aligned expectations, or decisions that will make that level almost impossible. In order to ensure that your expectations can be met, there are several things you can do.

1. When delegating responsibilities, be realistic. Most organisations believe in 'stretch' goals, and on the surface, having goals that will cause an employee to achieve higher levels of performance that you typically see. This is a good thing. But it can turn bad when the amount of 'stretch' that is requested is beyond any imaginable scope. Use some common sense when setting stretch goals so that they are not deemed to be unreasonable. Unreachable stretch goals will only result in employees losing motivation or commitment to management's ability to make decisions.
2. Make sure that when you assign someone to lead the implementation of a new initiative that they have the resources they need to deliver it on-time and in-full. One of the principle reasons that managers and employees do not deliver the level of performance that is anticipated is because they are not given access to either the resources they need or to the time to do it. In some cases, this is because the people planning the activity don't have a clue what resources will actually be required, or how much time it will take. In other cases, it is because the planners just assume that whomever makes the assignment will ensure that the time and resource requirements will be provided. In either case, the end result is that the performance that is expected is not delivered. Whilst one might think that this shouldn't be a reflection on the person (or persons) charged with delivering on the expectations, it often is; and the person (or persons) who were once thought of as high performers is no longer given the rewards and typically accompany high performance.
3. Reward high performers for the performance they deliver. People respond to rewards, and the research has shown that whilst money is typically thought of when the term 'reward' is mentioned, one of the greatest rewards that can be given is recognition. Make sure that your high performers realise that

you and your organisation appreciate and value their contributions.
4. Learn to manage the expectation of others. This is an area where many of us fall short. We easily banter about our ability to deliver upon someone else's expectations, but are not as good when it is time to put those expectations in some form of context. Your supervisor gives you a new assignment and tells you when it needs to be completed. Will you really be able to meet those expectations with the resources and time you are given? Your CEO talks openly about his or her vision for the future, and why it is important. Do you also hear that the vision is actually a moving target and what is really needed is movement in this direction, or do you hear that 'we just need to get there?' In order to manage expectations effectively means we all need to be willing to ask, and respond to questions about them. This is key so we have clarity around what the expectations are, when they need to be met, and what else might happen as you achieve them.

The only thing more important than setting expectations is managing them. Because if you don't manage expectations effectively, what you will end up with is an environment filled with discontent, malaise, and a belief that you are not competent to lead...and if that happens, no one will follow.

## Quantum Mechanics for Business

Have you ever wondered why it can be so bloody difficult for an organisation to realise its potential? The answer might be found in Quantum Mechanics. According to an on-line dictionary, Quantum Mechanics is all about *"the set of scientific principles describing the behavior of energy and matter on the atomic and sub-atomic scale. Much like the universe on the large and very vast scale (i.e., general relativity), so the universe on the small scale (i.e., quantum mechanics) does not neatly conform to the rules of classical physics. As such, it presents a set of rules that is counterintuitive and difficult to understand for the human mind, as humans are accustomed to the world on a scale dominated by classical physics."* Okay. By now you are probably thinking, *'What is he going on about,'* or *'how does any of this apply to business performance?*' The connection is as real as the paper (or computer screen) you are reading this on.

To explain the connection, I will give you some reference points. Organisations could be compared to business universes. They often are relatively large and, in the case of global organisations, have large scales that they operate in. You and I (and all other individual employees) operate on a very small scale. And whilst overall business performance can be quite predictable, it is the demonstrated actions and behaviours that stem from our mental models that can play havoc with what organisational performance is expected. This dynamic – individual behaviours based on pre-existing mental models – can explain several things in the business world. These things include 1) the ability of an organisation to achieve its strategic goals; 2) the willingness of an organisational population to accept and be committed to moving toward a company vision; and 3) why specific population groups in an organisational structure seem to be obstacles to both items 1 and 2.

The reasons for these are that many organisations have employees who, on the surface, appear to be acting in a way that is not what is expected. This behavioural gap, regardless of whether it is real or perceived, is typically due to one or more issues. These include:
- The employees do not understand what expectations are.
- The employees do not see the connection between their day-to-day activities and long-term organisational success.
- The employees believe that they should not have to behave in the way they are told (typically based on company values) because they do not see their superiors demonstrating the same sought-after behaviours.
- The employees are incompetent.

Ensuring that an organisation can realise its potential, and all that includes, is the responsibility of senior management. Part of their responsibilities, besides the obvious ones around hitting business targets, include creating an environment in which employees *can* reach their potential, both individually and collectively.

If employees do not have a clear understanding of what expectations are, it is management's job to provide that clarity. If employees do not see the connection between day-to-day activities and long-term organisational success, it is management job to help them make that connection. If employees are not behaving congruently with values because they don't see their bosses doing the same, it is the job of management to act as a role model. And if employees are incompetent, it is the job of management to either ensure that they receive the learning opportunities they need, or find someplace else for them to work.

In some organisations, management seems to view things differently, and sees only the reasons for low employee performance to be due to the problems caused by the employees. This sets up a culture of blame and dis-satisfaction on both sides, which will do nothing to improve performance.

Businesses function much like Quantum Mechanics, on a set of principles. The most obvious one is *you have to take in more money than you spend.* The less obvious one is that *employees will only perform if they understand what to do, why to do it, have the right skills, and believe that their efforts will make a difference.*

If that last principle is not visible and real in your organisation, then your company's performance will be much the way Quantum Mechanics appear to many people – well confusing and not very easy to make sense of.

## Crucial for Whom?

This is an often-asked question in business today, especially by those who are told such enlightening statements as, *'you have to reschedule everything, next week will be crucial.'* Right. As if every other week isn't crucial. Unfortunately, due to both the shifts in the way we do business today, and the ability of managers to make effective decisions, the word 'crucial' has lost much of its meaning.

Explicitly, crucial in business terms denotes something that is urgent, critical, and massively important and it needs to be dealt with. Implicitly, however, it usually means that something has run amuck and to complicate things further, someone has managed to forget to deal with it in the right way, at the right time, and for the right reasons. And because of this, it has become 'crucial.' Unfortunately, because so many people call 'crucial' meetings that people are 'requested' to attend (the word 'requested' is used with tongue firmly pressed to cheek), that the usual work doesn't get done on time or well, and then it too becomes 'crucial.' See a negative reinforcing loop here?

There should be a clear difference between things that are important, and things that are urgent, but because of the pattern of behaviour that has been mentioned, the lines have become blurred, and all things seem to becoming crucial. This, in a word, is lunacy.

The word crucial has two different interpretations. Crucial can mean *things that need to be done that are critical if an organisation is to be able to become more effective and move toward its desired future.* This meaning makes all the sense in the world, but the other meaning – the one that seems to be the definition in common use – is, *things that need to be done because somebody didn't do something right, or forgot to do something.* The problem lies in the fact that quite often, what hasn't been done well, or hasn't been done at all, may not even to be important at all in the big scheme of things that are important. The real issue for organisations today is the ability of planners and senior management to distinguish which things are really important. This ability – the ability to effectively prioritise – is sadly lacking today, and because of it, managers and employees alike find themselves scurrying around, panicking to try to respond to all these 'crucial' demands that prevent them from helping their organisations realise their potential.

Prioritising what should be worked on is not all the difficult, but when done well, it quite often plays havoc with what some people believe are intuitively correct to focus on. Several years ago, I was looking at an organisational strategy at the request of the CEO and what I found was amazing. The company had developed a comprehensive list of over 200 things that needed to be done to ensure that their strategy would work. But luckily, they realised that there was no way that their managers and employees would be able to do all 200 and do their traditional day-jobs. That was the good news. The bad news was that the method selected to identify the list of priorities was based on what several managers' *thought* was the *most* important. But even then, the list of activities that needed to be focused on had over 25 items on it.

It was suggested to the CEO that the only way to make substantial progress was to identify the vital few activities that would provide the greatest leverage for making the strategy happen, and to do it with a prioritisation tool. The CEO, a bit frustrated by what he perceived to be a lack of progress, agreed. The short-list of 25 items was arranged on a flip chart in a circle and the relationships between all of them were tested.

Testing relationships means asking the question, 'if we do item 1 effectively, will it cause item 2 to occur? If we do item 2 well, will it cause item 1 to occur?' This process was used to test the relationships between all the items on the flip chart and what resulted was a list of 3 things, that when done well, would result in most of the rest of the items to be resolved. This method, using a tool called an Interrelationship Digraph, did several things. First, it removed all the ambiguity about trying to figure out where to apply precious resources and time; second, it identified which items of the short-list would provide the greatest leverage; third, it caused managers to re-think their mental models about what is really important; and fourth, it began to remove the need for thinking that everything is 'crucial.' The key was to ensure that managers and employees would be able to focus their efforts on the vital few things that really need to get done, and by using a prioritisation tool, they were able to determine what those things were.

The next time that someone tells you that you need to stop doing what you are doing to do 'crucial' things, you may want to ask two questions. 1) Why is this meeting 'crucial?' and, 2) How will this 'crucial' meeting help us achieve our organisational goals more effectively? At the end of the day, the only thing that should be considered crucial in any organisation is that the company can realise its potential. And sadly, in today's culture of 'everything is crucial,' this just won't happen unless we change the way we prioritise what we do.


## Organisational Mandarins

The "Mandarins" are a group a people who have a very important job in the government, and who are sometimes considered to be too powerful and often masters of less-than-clear language. It is no accident that Great Britain's Whitehall officials are known as

Mandarins. Their language is often as hard to understand as anything spoken in Beijing.

According to an on-line reference, *"The key to appreciating traditional Mandarin is understanding the often complex sentence structure. This allows exponents to leave readers with a clear sense of what is being said even though a literal analysis of the text would allow the author to deny ever having suggested such a thing."* Often, what we hear is *"I could be completely wrong, but..."* What the speaker really means is more like *"I know far more than you but you should already know that."*

The Mandarins of the business world often think of themselves as the organisational elite, which is an interesting perception, as the view of most organisational populations is that they are rarely deserving of trust. This is because the prevailing belief is that most 'Mandarins' do not have a sound grasp on how the work of the company actually gets done, but are quick to criticise when things don't go as planned.

There is no doubt that organisations today need a population of smart, experienced people who know how things really get done. There is also no doubt that without this wisdom, companies waste time and resources on continually being forced to re-invent 'the wheel' each time a new opportunity or crisis erupts. But what they do not need are a group of people who think they are smarter than they really are. The fact that in many organisations, there is the perception that there are people who exhibit mandarin-like behaviours often slips into the category of 'undiscussables.' This isn't too surprising, as if confronted with this belief, anyone who does exhibit these behaviours would simply business-speak the conversation into a new direction anyway.

If your organisation does have a group of managers who believe that they should be considered "Mandarins," there is something you can do.

1. As with all organisational undiscussables, the first thing to do is begin to openly talk about the fact that some employees perceive that there are company mandarins. The discussion doesn't need to focus on who they are, but instead, focus on what the impact and ramifications will be on the organisation and its ability to consistently deliver superior performance for its customers and shareholders. Part of this should focus on *'what*

*will happen to organisational morale"* if mandarin-like behaviour would be allowed to continue. The best way to do this is to have the team – group – meeting attendees (pick which ever one is most appropriate) identify the cause-and-effect relationships that revolve around these behaviours.

2. The managers who are exhibiting mandarin-like behaviours need to be brought in for one-on-one meetings so that they can see the impact of their behaviours on the organisation. A logical outcome of these conversations would be the typically expected, *"no, that's not me" and "I don't act like that"* and of course, *"why would you even think I do that?"* The answers to these questions are normally, *"These are the behaviours that your peers or subordinates see."* These reactions are usually made in a very defensive manner which is based on the mental model like *"who are you to even accuse me of anything?"* In most cases, these conversations end up with a recommendation to arrange coaching for those whose behaviours are problematic, or do not believe their behaviours are a problem at all. Coaching people who exhibit these behaviours can work, but only if the person admits that he or she might actually be doing them.

3. Use the tried-and-true method of carrot and stick. The best way to do this is to connect mandarin-like behaviours to a performance appraisal process. This would mean that managers or employees who exhibit those behaviours are 'marked down' on their performance appraisal. This can only be done if steps 1 and 2 have been done, and if these behaviours have been brought to the attention of those who exhibit them.

Managers or employees who have wisdom earned over time can be a good thing for an organisation. But when this earned wisdom manifests itself in mandarin-like behaviours, any potential value is diminished rapidly and can result in more problems than it is worth.

## Hayflick's Phases

Leonard Hayflick figured something out 50 years ago that has had an impact on our ability to learn why cells grow. Hayflick, in 1961, demonstrated that a population of normal human fetal cells in a cell culture divide between 40 and 60 times. His work showed that human cells go through three basic growth phases. These phases are typical of what happens to managers and employees of an organisation who are experiencing positive growth as well.

Hayflick described the first phase as a time when cells were created. This was followed by a time of cell proliferation—or as Hayflick called it, the time of "luxuriant growth." After so many months of doubling, eventually the cells reach what is called the "phase three phenomenon," where cell growth is diminished and eventually stopped altogether. The same thing happens when managers and employees find themselves in a positive work environment. Phase one is when a new leader comes onboard and begins to make positive changes. Phase two is when everyone is excited and becomes committed to the new leadership. And phase three is when malaise begins to set in. Although these three phases may apply to cell growth, they do not necessarily need to follow the same path in organisations.

The first two phases in organisations are great, and many of us have experienced them. These are the phases that internal marketing people love to write about. But we hardly ever hear about what can happen next.

It is the third stage that can be problematic, and in many organisations, could be equated to a creeping cancer that can negate many of the gains made in the first two phases. There are several things you can do to continue gained momentum and avoid the onset of malaise that signals the onset of phase three.

First, it is crucially important to realise that organisational performance is both directly and indirectly a function of the mindsets and perceptions of managers and employees. Our mindsets heavily influence our willingness to buy-in to organisational initiatives and accept organisational change. In order to leverage this ability and willingness, the first thing that needs to be done is make it perfectly clear not only what is going to change, but why it is going to change. It is also key to ensure that you are open to how these changes will impact the day-to-day work lives of the managers and employees who will be affected. By doing this, you are able to remove any ambiguity that may reside in the minds of those affected. If you don't do this, these 'gaps' in understanding will be filled in by the people themselves, and the result is rarely good. *Be open about what will happen and why.*

Second, identify key influencers in the organisation, and use them to help spread the word. This is one area where things often go wrong, usually because senior management may confuse the term 'key influencers,' and simply assume that they are senior managers. In most organisations, the key influencers appear in all organisational levels, and are the ones that others look up to for their demonstrated leadership abilities and are held in high respect. Identify who your key influencers are and brief them before the changes are unveiled to the overall organisational population. *Use the key influencers in your organisation to help spread the word.*

Third, and of critical importance, is the need to build and sustain momentum. What has been seen is that initiatives are begun with a flourish, and are accompanied by both explicit and implicit promise of change. If, however, the 'promise' seems to become lost due to what could be other important business issues or distractions, then managers and employees begin to assume that this was just another pile of internal P.R. crap. The problem is typically that this is a reflection on poor planning on the part of those who were attempting to drive the initiative. Building and sustaining momentum is a direct function of managing expectations. The key lesson here is to not promise anything that can be delivered. It should be no surprise that managers and employees will become disenchanted if they believe that initial excitement and promise will slowly sink back into business as usual. *Build and work to sustain momentum.*

The onset of malaise on the part of managers and employees that equate to Hayflick's phase three can be avoided, but only if you do something about it before it appears. Because when it does begin to appear, it is too late.

## Having It All

Even though the days of Frederick Taylor are long gone, there still is confusion about the linkage between personal and organisational performance, and learning. Confusion might be a mild adjective to use, as companies from all sectors still are not making the connection. The evidence appears all over the place: performance slips and cost cutting ensues. Cost cutting typically means areas where easy reductions are identified and targeted, and in most organisations, that means anything to do with learning.

Just to clarify, there is a distinction between teaching and learning. Many mid-to-large sized organisations do have training departments that produce vast arrays of offerings designed to help improve the skills of managers and employees. But when you look closely at many of these offerings, they are more about teaching than learning. This can be seen when you examine the metrics used by these departments to justify their budgets. Typical metrics often include *the number of courses, the number of attendees,* and, *participant feedback.* All these are nice, but let's look back at the purpose of doing the training. If you ask training departments, they will say that their intent is to *'help improve the skills of managers and employees.'* A fine goal, but then it might be appropriate to ask why having a lot of courses, or funnelling a lot of people through them, or asking how much participants liked the course, are important metrics. The only metric that is important is *'as a result of the training, what will you do differently.'* Again, if the intent is to give people more skills, the measure should be *'will you be able to use these skills?'*

Now there are some people that would say that learning to become more effective isn't as important as achieving performance. There is no doubt that performance is important. I would take the position that performance, and achieving it, is critical for long-term organisational success. But at the same time, if you look at the issue systemically, if you aren't willing to invest in managers and employees ability to become more effective, the only other method available is to have them work harder. This may work in the short-term, but it is not a sustainable solution and will, over time, result in de-motivation, stress, mistakes, and a reduction in commitment to organisational directives. Accordingly, by supporting learning – and supporting means ongoing budgetary support as well as verbal support – increases the capacity of managers and employees to be effective, which will enable them to work better together, be more highly motivated, make fewer mistakes, and become more committed to an organisation and where it is going. The cause-and-effect relationship between learning and performance is clear.

The real question isn't what to do in order to improve performance; the question is how to best improve performance. The answer is to incorporate learning into performance improvement efforts.

The challenge isn't to make a choice between performance and learning; the real challenge is to find ways to use learning to enhance performance. Too often, the reality of this challenge is lost because of the confusion between training and learning. The solution can be found in two areas.

First, make sure that your 'training' efforts are measured by how much managers and employees actually learn. The term 'learn' means that your people are now able to apply what they have learnt and this application can be measured in terms of improved performance. Second, ensure that your meetings incorporate the application of learning in their agendas. This really isn't that difficult, but it does require a shift in mindset from 'training and learning' are different than performance to 'learning is the way to improve performance.' In order to do this, performance related agenda items need to include looking at the cause and effect relationship between actions and results.

In addition, the agenda items should look at the impact of managerial behaviours on performance. The relationship between manager's demonstrated behaviours and the resultant performance is unmistakeably clear. Managers whose 'managerial style' is more focused solely on 'hitting the numbers' instead of providing clear inspirational leadership rarely are able to sustainable performance results over time.

The opportunities to shift performance abound. Whether it is specific training sessions, usual management meetings, or even team-building retreats, combining learning with performance discussions is the most rational way there is to ensure that what the company wants and needs - performance - can be consistently delivered.

The connection between performance and learning becomes even clearer when you put it into the context of return on investment. Making investments in creating an environment in which managers and employees actually learn is the best way to improve performance. The old adage could be wrong: in the case of performance and learning, you can have your cake and eat it too.

Reaping What We Sow

There has been quite a bit of scientific research that has been going on about mirror neurons. In case you aren't up to speed on this research, the essence is that *"A **mirror neuron** is a neuron that fires both when an animal acts and when the animal observes the same action performed by another. Thus, the neuron "mirrors" the behaviour of the other, as though the observer were itself acting."* If you are a manager in a company that has evidenced low levels of alignment, or behaviours that don't match up with organisational values, you may want to read on.

In order to understand how this can impact an organisational climate, it is important to look first at some of the beliefs and assumptions that the research has surfaced. One of them is that we learn empathically when we are young children. We learn to walk not because our parents draw stick figures on a flip chart explaining the theory behind how walking actually occurs. Equally, we don't learn to walk by having our parents run us through a series of PowerPoint slides instructing us in the benefit of walking. We learn to walk because as children, we see everyone else walking. We learn the language that surrounds us as children. If your parents and friends speak Spanish, you will learn Spanish. If they are German, or French, or English that is the language you will learn. We learn to associate our behaviours with those that we see.

This learning process extends to other living beings as well. Species of birds that flock learn from each other. In "The Living Company," Arie de Geus told the story of how UK milk bottles used to not have a top on them. Birds had easy access to the rich cream that would settle on the top of each bottle when they were delivered to homes. In the 1950's, milk bottlers figured out that by placing a thin aluminium cover on the bottles, birds would be prevented from doing so. But de Geus goes on to explain that the titmouse, a flocking bird, figured out how to peck their way through the aluminium cover, and soon the titmouse population throughout the UK had learned this behaviour. Robins however, a non-flocking bird, never seemed to pass along this learning. So how does all this apply to organisational behaviours?

There are several ways that the impact of mirror neurons can effect your organisation, and most of them are connected to management actions.    If your senior management team demonstrates behaviours that you wish other managers and employees to demonstrate, these behaviours will most likely begin to filter down through the organisation.    This doesn't involve an onslaught of lectures or pleas to comply.    All that is needed is a clear demonstration of the behaviours that you want others to replicate.

Of course, if senior managers demonstrate behaviours that do not match up with company values, or exhibit behaviours that are at odds with a company culture, other managers and employees may begin to emulate those.  This is especially true for the subordinates of those managers who demonstrate behaviours that are at odds with values and/or culture.

The issue becomes more problematic if those managers who are exhibiting behaviours at odds with values or culture are not seen to be disciplined, or dismissed.  If you are working for someone who is behaving in this way and is not disciplined, your own logical thinking process may look like this.
- *my boss demonstrates behaviours that don't match our values*
- *my boss is successful*
- *you don't need to demonstrate value-driven behaviours to be successful*
- *therefore, I do not need demonstrate value-driven behaviours either*

For those senior managers who have been striving to build a values-driven organisational culture, this can be a serious problem. In order to avoid this from occurring, there are a couple of things that you can do.

1. Clearly act as a role model for the behaviours that you wish others to emulate.  If you do not demonstrate the behaviours you seek from others, there is no reason to expect that they will.
2. If you are aware that you have managers who demonstrate inappropriate behaviour, explain to them the impact of what they are doing.  If that doesn't shift their behaviours, use your performance appraisal process to negatively impact their bonus or position status.

The research on mirror neurons may appear to be solely for the scientific community to digest, but it does help explain why some organisations perform in the way they do.  We learn from each other; the challenge for management is to choose what they want us to learn.

## What Is Your Achillies Heel?

The story of Achillies is pretty well known. Achilles, thought to be virtually invincible, was struck down when an arrow struck him in his heel. The term 'Achilles heel' has become synonymous with a previously unknown weakness. All businesses have their own Achilles heels, and like the Achilles in the Greek legend, they are thought to be inconsequential...until they potentially lead to the demise of the company.

Recently, I became aware of a growing service organisation that has its own Achilles heel. The problem, as with many companies, is that management doesn't recognise it as a problem.

The subject organisation is relatively young, and led by two highly visionary founders. They repeatedly speak about what the future could hold for their organisation and its employees. And whilst his message is powerful and inspirational, the reality for employees is that the founders are living in their own little dream worlds. Some of their key messages include being recognised by clients for brilliant work so that their company will be able to grow to become a serious competitive threat. But what the employees are seeing (and feeling) is completely different.

After conversations, it became apparent that there were three major themes at play that capture the mental models of employees. The themes were:
- *"What mirror are they using?"*
- *"We thought silos were only for farms"*
- *"You get what you pay for"*

### What mirror are they using?
This theme related to the belief that the senior management of the company (including the two founders of the organisation) seem to have a completely different view of their own competence and abilities to lead. Whilst employees interviewed acknowledged that

the founders were smart enough to begin the company and grow it to its current size, there was a pervasive belief that the gap between what they see as a potential future and what the employees see is insurmountable. This gap in beliefs is typically due to either lack of communication, or lack of ability to lead. In either case, the perception of a gap between the founders view of future reality and that of the employees will only lead to disenchantment, a decline in employee morale, and a lessening in employee commitment to company initiatives and direction. Senior managers always need to ensure that employees both see and understand their future vision. And equally important is the fact that employees need to understand how the company will get there.

## We thought silos were only for farms.

This theme was typical for an organisation in which management makes it clear that collective team decision-making and efforts is the only way to achieve company goals, and yet has put in place structures in which departments and teams are implicitly not permitted to work together. Sending mixed signals to employees – we need to work in teams to succeed, but then not fostering an environment to do this – will only lead to frustration and a belief that management does not walk the talk and is not competent to lead.

## You get what you pay for.

This theme title is pretty self-explanatory, and relates to the level of commitment that employees are willing to put forth. Management to be sustainably successful, especially in an espoused team environment, should be visibly interested in employee input. This 'interest' should include actively soliciting input as well as being open to listening to what employees want to contribute. If employees perceive that this 'interest' is only superficial or non-existent, the employees will lose any incentive to try to make an organisation more effective or a better place to work. This breeds an environment of malaise, which will only result in a decline in performance.

These three themes are evidence that the Achilles heel for this organisation is the level of leadership that the founders are currently demonstrating. Over and over again during interviews, employees made the message clear: *"These guys are nice, but they are blind to the reality of what is going on in the company."* The attempts by the founders to show that they are concerned have been perceived as a feeble attempt to placate them with lip service, when in reality, nothing has been seen to change. It is apparent that their current level of success will be short-lived unless something changes.

All organisations have their own Achilles heel of one sort or another. In many organisations, such as the one in this issue, the Achilles heel is an undiscussable, but it is there. The solution is to recognise that all organisations have them; to talk about what yours are; and then do something to ensure that your company doesn't end up like Achilles.

## An Egg Solution

Being faced with fundamentally complex and recurring problems is something that seems to occur more and more in business today. And whilst it would be nice to believe that we are becoming better at solving them, often, we become trapped in our own mental models about what is, or is not, possible. A good example of how these mental models can inhibit our thinking occurred almost 600 years ago.

Filippo Brunelleschi was one of the foremost architects during the Italian Renaissance. In 1418, Brunelleschi and Lorenzo Ghiberti were given a challenge to come up with a design for a dome for the Santa Maria del Fiore cathedral. Because the challenge had design parameters, with one of them being that the finished dome would be larger than any had been built to that date, there was no doubt that the winner of the design challenge would only increase his reputation as architect. What is fascinating is that, whilst Brunelleschi did win, and is remembered for the dome, it is not because of his design. He is remembered for how he came up with a solution to the challenge.

The story is that both men were asked to present their designs to a merchants guild to decide whose design was the best. They were told to make an egg stand upright on a piece of marble to show that they could make a functional dome. What Brunelleschi did was take the egg and give one end of it a blow on the flat piece of marble, allowing it to stand perfectly upright without any supports.

If Brunelleschi was a manager in any of the myriad of companies suffering through some serious problems today, he would undoubtedly be recognised as the company hero. Probably for good reason; after all, he is the one who figured out how to solve the problem. But in today's business world, our thinking can become inhibited when even trying to understand what the problem is that we are facing. When we don't understand the real problem, one of several things happen: We begin a disastrous downhill spiral that typically ends with the demise of our company; We struggle to the point of exhaustion, hoping that with some luck, someone will figure out an answer; or, we tend to look to our own company hero. This last option is both good news and bad news. If you are one of those company hero-types, you are certainly in a good position in regards to job security (the good news for you). But, overall, this is very bad news for the company. Here is why.

When we are facing really tough problems (which seem to be an almost everyday occurrence in some organisations), we have a choice. We can either default to our company hero to come in and save the day, or, we can increase our capacity to solve problems. Each of these options will have a positive impact on fundamental recurring problems. But relying on a hero to come and 'save the day' is only a temporary, quick-fix answer, and not a sustainable solution.

This is clearly a choice, and either option will tend to have a positive impact on those pesky problems. However, if the choice taken is to become reliant on our 'hero,' it will breed an addiction to the belief that problem solving is something each of us don't really need to worry about. After all, we do have that problem solving hero who can fix anything.

This dynamic means that, as our addiction to "it isn't my problem" grows, the chances that we will ever see the need to even contemplate our problem solving capacity will drift away. This may be acceptable to some organisations, but what happens when the company hero hits a roadblock that even he or she can't get past?

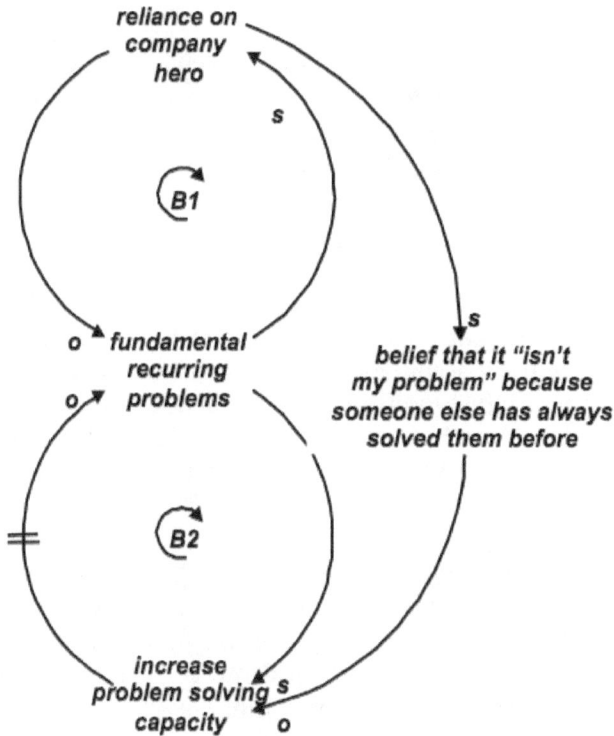

Or what happens when he or she decides to move on to bigger challenges with your competitors? Suddenly your options aren't all that great. You could look around for another hero (a pretty short-term fix), or you could do what you should have done to begin with, which is increase your problem solving capacity. This is assuming that it isn't too late to do that.

Most companies today would love to have someone as clever or brilliant or whatever, as Brunelleschi. Someone who can see a solution to a problem that no one else seems to be able to see. Sadly, not all organisational problems are solved as easy as smashing an egg on a piece of marbel.

# The "A" Word

The "A" word is, of course, accountability. And whilst this seems like a relatively straightforward topic, it can be mis-applied in many situations by managers. I was talking to a manager recently and asked him to define accountability for me. He said, *"My boss is holding me accountable."* I understood what he meant, but that wasn't a real definition.

I decided to Google 'accountability' and my computer came up with 43.200.000 potential links. That wasn't too helpful, so I instead asked a group of employees of a mid-sized company what they thought accountability was all about. What they told me wasn't a real definition either, but instead a listing of examples of what it was like when there wasn't accountability in the managerial ranks that were their bosses.

*"We get put on some project team that everyone knows is understaffed and under-budgeted. When we don't hit the milestones we get a bollocking, but the manager in charge of the project gets away with just making excuses. Where is the accountability there?"* And then there was this comment. *"We have all these company values about respect and accountability and the more senior the manager is, the more they don't follow the values. And because they are the bosses, they seem to think it is okay. It isn't, and my whole department is pretty cranked about it."* Apparently, they didn't seem too happy about the way the accountability issue is handled in their organisation.

These two examples – dodging accountability through using excuses, and the application of double standards – should make resolving the entire accountability issue a high priority in companies. But for one reason or another, it lurks just below the surface of visibility and has, in many organisations, become an undiscussable. The reality is that the entire accountability issue is often caught up in a structural tension dynamic.

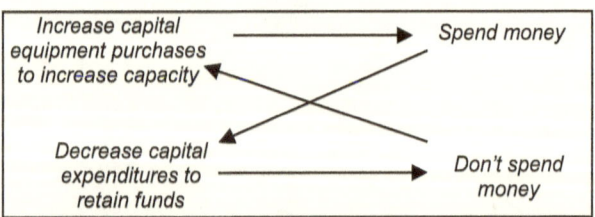

Structural tension occurs when you have two needs that can be fulfilled with opposite actions. Typically, structural tension occurs when the two opposing solutions related to spending or not spending money. But structural tension also occurs due to accountability issues.

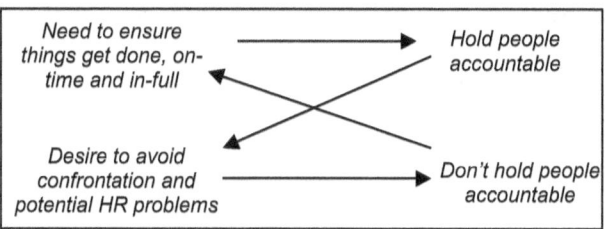

There is very little argument about the need to get things done in business. The 'agreement' gap often occurs when trying to figure out how to do that in the best way. One school of thought says they best way to get things done is to simply hold managers and employees accountable for their actions. But there is another train of thought that says if you really try to hold people accountable, you will risk having HR problems and personnel confrontations. The people who subscribe to this belief believe that holding people accountable is not the best way to get things done. This structural tension – hold people accountable or not hold people accountable – can only be resolved in one of two ways. Either mandate it or have it become part of the organisational culture.

If you decide to mandate accountability, you will need to have it become part of the stated policies and procedures that all employees know about. But because organisations are comprised of humans, you will also probably require either a group of people to police this 'accountability rule,' or just assume the entire organisational population will turn into informers. There is another downside to the mandated solution. Policies and procedures are good to have in companies, but if you have been working in an organisation for more than a week or two, you already know that the next thing after having mandated rules is the onset of gaming the system. Now you will need people to police the people that are policing the accountability issue. Not a good idea.

The other way to ensure that things get done is to have a set of organisational values that managers and employees alike subscribe to. By shifting the issue of accountability from a corporate mandate to *"the way that business is conducted"* value, the need to police it diminishes greatly. Of course, like all other leadership issues, the only way that this can work is if senior managers make the conscious choice to demonstrate that they are willing to be held accountable first…and always.

This could lead you to define accountability as *"what leaders are willing to be held to."* Nice definition.

## When Things Are Not as They Seem

I loved it when I was living in London. It is a wonderful city, but there are a few things that can be a bit disconcerting to visitors whom have never been there before. One of them surfaces if you are trying to ask for directions, and relates to the pronunciation of certain words. A good example is Grosvenor, as in Grosvenor Square or Grosvenor Place. From the way the word is spelt, you could assume that it is pronounced GROS-VEN-OR, but in reality, it is pronounced GROVE-NER. Another example is Beauchamp,

as in Beauchamp Place. Again, from the way it is spelt, you would think that Beauchamp should be pronounced BOW-SHAMP, but it is really pronounced BEE-CHAM. Chiswick is actually CHIZ-ICK. Worcester is in reality WOO-STER. Leicester is LES-TER. Berkeley is BAR-KLEE. This difference between the way we think things are or how they appear, and the way they really are extends to things well beyond street signs in England.

In business, there can often be a mis-understanding or confusion between how things appear, and what they really are.

An often seen scenario is a meeting in which the boss says something, and then follows it with, *"are there any questions?"* The room goes silent as no one wishes to look as if he or she doesn't understand, and all that is seen are gently bobbing heads signifying to the boss that everyone is in agreement. Now to be fair, it could be that everyone actually does understand, and they truly are in agreement. But what are the implications if some of the people do not understand both the message and its implications? What happens if some of the people mis-interpret the message and then go off and proceed with actions that could be detrimental to the company? It really doesn't matter if you think that this doesn't happen often in your company. What does matter is *what if it does?*

In order to avoid this type of risk, there are several things you can do. If you are the one who is trying to make a point, you can ask to see if everyone really does understand. The key here is to consider *how* you ask the question. You don't want to ask it in a way that will cause everyone to feel that you believe they are idiots. You want to ask the question in a way that shows that you are just making sure that your communications are being heard.

This can be done with a short introduction, such as, *"As this is a very critical issue, I just want to make sure that we are all understanding the same thing. Can someone please tell me what I just said?"* This technique gives you the opportunity to make sure that your message is clear, and if it isn't, the opportunity to make it clear. If you are one of the recipients of the message, it is a chance to validate in your own mind that what you heard is what was meant to be heard.

If you are one of the people who the boss is speaking to and you want to make sure you 'get the message' without appearing to be stupid, what you can do is ask for clarification. Again, the challenge here *how* to ask the question. An often-used method that does work begins with *"this is what I am hearing you say,"* followed by what you believe the speaker said. By doing this, you are giving the speaker the opportunity to clarify what he or she said, and at the same time, showing you are concerned about doing the right things for the right reasons.

I have sat in many management meetings in which both scenarios have taken place. The level of overall effectiveness and team performance in the groups that actually do check to make sure that everyone understands is far higher than in the meetings where everyone simply assumes that they are all on the same page. In many cases, these assumptions could be correct, but the risk that they could be incorrect should outweigh any concerns about asking for clarification. If you think you will look bad by asking for clarification, how do you think you will look if you get something wrong because you didn't ask?


## The Influencing Challenge

It has been said that there are two ways to do something; the hard way and the easy way. This could be paraphrased for how people in organisations can be influenced; there is a blatant, in your face way, and a way that is more subtle. In both cases, the ultimate objective is to cause people to demonstrate behaviours that they otherwise may not do.

A subtle way to influence people is through 'priming.' Priming is a term that references how it is possible to influence decision-making by exposing people to subtle environmental changes. The examples include wine merchants who are able to increase their sales of French wines by playing French music in the store, and selling more German wine when they play German music. The studies have also shown that we tend to eat more at a buffet if the plates we are given are larger; and the greater the ceiling height in a room, the greater the creative thinking. Okay, so this whole priming thing – conditioning people to behave in a certain way based on the environment - can make a difference in the way people think.

There is another way of influencing that is at the other end of the spectrum. There was an experiment with 5 monkeys that shows this. The 5 monkeys were kept in a cage with a ladder. Some bananas were kept on the top of the ladder. Whenever one of the monkeys would climb the ladder to get the bananas, all the monkeys were sprayed with ice-cold water. Soon, the monkeys begin to police each other, and would prevent any other monkey from climbing the ladder. Eventually, the cold water was turned off, but the monkeys kept policing themselves. Then, one monkey was removed, and another monkey put in it's place. Sure, the monkey didn't know about the forbidden bananas, so when it tried to get the banana, the other monkeys would stop him. Soon, the new monkey started policing the other monkeys too. Eventually, one by one all the monkeys were replaced in the group, but the monkeys kept policing themselves, even though none of the original monkeys were there and the reason for policing themselves was not existent.

These two ways to influence people – clearly ways that are at opposite ends of an influencing spectrum – the subtle way and the 'in your face' ways to influence. Whilst there is no singular right way to cause people to demonstrate different behaviours, it does seem that the more subtle approach is more suitable in today's business climate. Here is how you can use this approach to improve demonstrated managerial behaviours.

First, forget that influencing skills have anything to do with organisational hierarchy. Quite often, the people who are the most effective at influencing do not hold hierarchical positions. Next, find something you need to influence people about.

Let's say you are working in a company where you are desperate to increase the levels of cooperation and respect. You could (A) have large posters printed that say in big bold letters, *"Working collaboratively is a good thing. Let's all do it."* B) send out an email stating that non-collaborative efforts will result in immediate termination. C) make bonus payments for demonstrated collaboration efforts. Or, you could (D), just find pockets in your organisation where collaboration is working and then ask those people why they are doing it.

Option A, whilst probably a good way to decorate some hallways, rarely accomplishes anything other than the employees taking the attitude of *'it's just more management propaganda,'* and *'why don't they stop wasting money on signs like that and make investments in our people and equipment.'* Obviously, not a great option. Option B is also not that great an option, as threats rarely work and typically only cause resistors to dig in deeper. Option C, whilst on the surface looks interesting, is also a poor choice. Rewarding people for the behaviours that they should be already demonstrating will only result in gaming the reward system, and raise expectations for extra rewards for everything. Option D, however, makes quite a bit of sense.

By finding out why the people who are working collaboratively do so, you should be able to learn how to help other managers and employees see the benefits of doing it. Of course, part of this discovery process may surface things like the story about the monkeys, but that is okay if you can learn how to avoid having that happen in the future. The real challenge is to remember that influencing is not about changing people's mindsets. Influencing is all about creating an environment in which they can successfully adapt their beliefs and assumptions.

## Un Capricho?

A few days ago, I received a phone call from a company I had been asked to work with several years ago. I turned down the opportunity at the time, but would receive calls occasionally since then. The call was "interesting," and it went more or less like this...

*CALLER: Do you remember when you were advising us, you helped us put together the plan for our ABC (not its real name) project? Well, the implementation process began according to plan, but after about 4 months, things started slipping.*

*JBR: What do you mean by 'slipping?'*

*CALLER: We started to miss our milestone dates for some of the elements of the plan. And because of this, the entire implementation is beginning to fall apart. Can you give me some hints about what we can do?*

*JBR: What part of the plan are you seeing the slipping taking place, and why do you think this slippage is taking place?*

*CALLER: Actually, there isn't just one place. We seem to be losing traction in many areas, but mainly in the areas where our managers were leading the project elements themselves. As for why this is happening, all my managers are saying is that their teams don't have the right people on them. We thought about changing the team members, but this will slow things down too far.*

*JBR: If I was there now, and I walked around and talked to some of the team members, what would they say? Would they say that your managers are providing sufficient leadership to drive the project?*

*CALLER: James, right about now, I don't care how they get the project done, as long as we get back on our timelines. We have too much at stake to miss this thing. As for having sufficient levels of leadership, right about now, leading is a capricho until we get back on steam with the initiative.*

The call did go on for a while, but it appeared that my message wasn't the one the CEO was looking for. When I had met with this potential client several years earlier, it was pretty apparent that even then, demonstrating leadership was considered to be a capricho (a luxury or extravagance). This problem is not one that exclusively resided in this CEO's mind.

The whole issue about leadership is one of choice. Leadership isn't a job description, nor is it a set of characteristics that someone may or my not have. Leadership is seen through a series of clearly demonstrated actions that match with organisational values, and each of us has the ability to choose to do them or not do them.

For the person who rang me to declare that demonstrating leadership was a luxury shows pretty clearly that he is missing the point. He was confusing 'what' needed to be done, with 'how' was the best way to do it. As this newsletter has stated over the past seven years, there are two ways to accomplish things in business. One way is to drive performance through hard-core management. This is the often seen take-no-prisoners approach that does deliver results. But the impact on an organisational culture is pretty dire, and requires an entire team of metaphorical policemen with metaphorical whips to keep everyone in line and on task.

The other way is to drive performance through demonstrated leadership, where the most important job is to create an environment in which 1) managers and employees know what is important, and why it is so; 2) managers and employees clearly understand how their contributions help the organisation and its customers; and 3) managers and employees understand the impact of their own individual and collective behaviours.

This doesn't mean the objective is to create an all warm-and-fuzzy workplace where everyone hugs and sings Kumbaya all day. It does mean the objective is to create an environment in which high performance gets delivered because everyone knows how important it is. And if you are one of the bosses, it also means that you still have to make tough decisions.

If you have managers who are not demonstrating the behaviours that fit in with the environment you are trying to create, then you need to sack them. Not one day, not some day. They need to be sacked now, because if they aren't, the rest of the organisation will begin to believe that all the value-based demonstrated leadership is just lip service. And if that happens, then sustainable high performance will be a dream, and you keeping your job will be a capricho.

## The Easy Part is the Glasses

It happened again last week. I had been talking to the MD of an organisation that was, as he said, '*stuck.*' He was going on about all the problems his company had and when I enquired as to what he was doing to resolve them, he kept falling into, '*well, in the past when we had major problems, we used to...*' Well guess what? There are a lot of things I used to do too, but in today's business world, either you get on top of things or you spend the rest of your life reliving the past – after all, it will make great filler when you fill out your bankruptcy papers.

Living in the past is nice. We all have memories of how we did this or that in business, but the business world today has evolved a bit further and, because the transaction time has compressed to just about nothing with all the technology we are addicted to, there just isn't time to dilly-dally around when you should be moving forward.

The other thing the MD said was that his manager's were having problems getting their employees to change fast enough. This can be a challenge, but my experience is that, whilst many managers are good at pushing for change, they really don't have a sound grasp about what it is like to *be at the coalface of the changes.*

I have always found it pretty amazing that those that are in management quite often just assume that employees should be able to deal with all the changes that organisations go through. Yes, managers have to deal with change as well, but for some reason, many managers still assume that because they manage to survive the changes they go through, the rest of the employees shouldn't have a problem surviving as well. This could be a fair mental model, after all, being a manager quite often isn't that much fun. However, if you are a senior manager, and really want to get a sense of what everyone else in the organisation is up against, the next time you have a senior management meeting, try this out.

Have the senior managers stand up and pair off. It doesn't matter who pairs up with whom, just get them to pick someone else in the group and stand with them. Next, have each pair face each other and then have the pairs of people turn around so they are back to back so they can't see their 'partner.' And then tell them to change something about their appearance. Actually, tell them to change three things about their appearance. They can undo their ties, they can muss up their hair, they can take their glasses off (assuming they wear glasses), they can pull their shirts out, they can do any three things that will change their own appearance. When they have done this, have them turn back so they face each other. Next, have them identify the three things their partners had changed about their appearance.

After they have all experienced this for a bit, tell them to once again turn away from each other and change three more things. No, they shouldn't just change things back to the way they were; but change three more things about their appearance. Then have them turn around and identify their partner's changes again. (In most cases, the changes are identifiable, and the pairs of people are beginning to have a bit of fun playing this apparent silly game.

But now, have them do it all once again. Yes, turn away from each other and change three more things. By now, you will begin to find that they are not having quite as much fun, usually because they think they are running out of things that they think they can change. If you have to do it a fourth time, do it. And if you have a real sadistic thread in your body, force them to do it a fifth time. What do you think you will find?

The managers will be struggling to both deal with this exercise of constant change, and the ability to keep changing can begin to make the game not fun anymore. And if this isn't enough, there doesn't seem to be any rationale for asking for all these changes. This, quite often, is the reaction of employees to change efforts, and it shows just what those employees are up against. Employees feel that they are the brunt of most change initiatives. They feel that just when management gets through with one change initiative, another one comes along, quite often before the previous one has really reached completion.

Will light bulbs go on in the heads of senior management? Perhaps, but perhaps not. It really doesn't make a difference...what you have done is given them the opportunity to experience what everyone else in the organisation experiences, and if they don't learn from that, well, ... well, that is another whole issue.

Employees undergoing change within an organisation need to understand why all the changes that they are faced with are taking place. They need to have an understanding of what the changes will bring, and most importantly, they need to know that the changes will make things better. Organisational change is not just a cute game that we can see an end to.

## When "Obvious" and "Best" Can Be Different

We hear so much lately about why it is so important for managers to use their intuition when making decisions. There are books, articles, and quite a few testimonials about managers who *just knew* what to do; and have shown sterling results because of their intuition. All this is fine, but if these guys are so sharp, why haven't they managed to buy lotto tickets on the *right* day?

Intuitive decision-making is fine, but it usually only works when managers have consummate amounts of luck, and also been able to explore *counter-intuitive* options.

Several years ago, I was invited to participate in a strategic planning session for a large unionised organisation. The planning group was good – not only were there 'management planners' in the group; the organisation had also expanded the group to include key union officials, direct and indirect customers, key suppliers, and community representatives. The group, with a facilitator, had been working through a series of potential goals and targets to focus their employees on, but the cohesiveness of the group that had been present for several meetings began to fall apart when it became time to select the central focal point of the plan.

Of the fifteen or so options, several did seem quite logical. The organisation was in need of massive investments in technology, and some of the planning group lobbied long and hard for that as the key goal should be *improve utilisation of new technology*. The organisation, located over several sites, each with its own management team, was complex and its processes had many overlaps. Some of the planning group were quite intent on *improving processes and systems* becoming the big goal. And there were even a small group of members who had their hearts set on *delivering improved customer service* as the main goal. All of these clearly were important and really quite obvious. And as with many planning groups, it began to appear that if one goal were selected over another one, some of the participants would not be that committed to its implementation. So instead of letting the session degenerate into political infighting, the facilitator decided to take the group to an unknown territory for them: he took them into the land of *counter-intuitive decision-making*.

The fifteen or so potential goals were written on sticky-notes and arranged in a large circle on several flip-chart sheets that had been taped together to form a wall of paper.

He then began to ask the same questions over and over again. Pointing to the sticky-note at the top of the circle, he said, *'if we focus on this goal, and get it, will it cause this to be achieved as well?* (pointing to the next sticky-note in clock-wise direction). He then asked the same question referencing the top sticky-note and the next one around the circle; and the next one, and the next one.

Each time, the planning group would either respond with, *'yes, the top one will cause the other one to be achieved,'* or the opposite. He would then draw an arrow pointing from the one that would *cause* the effect to the one that would be achieved. Once in a while, the group would respond collectively that neither sticky-note goal would cause the other one to be achieved, so he would not indicate any *causal* relationship. After asking for the group to examine all the potential causal relationships around the circle, using the top one as the starting point, he did the same using the second sticky-note as the beginning; and then the third sticky-note, and the fourth and so on, until he had checked every possible relationship.

Eventually, the completed picture looked like a huge plate of pasta, with arrow-headed lines interwoven all over the circle. Then he had someone from the group simply count up the number of arrows going out and in for each stick-note – arrows going *out* indicated that a sticky-note represented a high leverage driver, and arrows going in indicated *outcomes* of the drivers. The end result was something that was quite disconcerting to the group. The *favourite* choices all suddenly looked to be *outcomes* of the more effective, driving goals. It was a simple thing to just count up the out and in arrows, with the sticky-note with the most out arrows representing the goal that would make the greatest impact for the organisation. The goal that had the greatest influence on all the other goals contained the words, *'improve the decision-making process.'*

The result was very counter-intuitive. The previously *logical* choices were all outcomes of an improved decision-making process, and light bulbs throughout the group began to click on. Had they stayed with one of the previously favourite choices, they perhaps would have been able to accomplish something, but the potential of the organisation would not have been realised. Sometimes the *obvious* is not the best; and exploring counter-intuitive thinking can surface the best way to go.

## Range Anxiety

A good friend who is heavily involved in the auto conversion industry was recently on a radio programme speaking about some problems with electric cars. The big subject of the conversation revolved around range anxiety; the concern about the distance your electric vehicle will go before running out of power. Range anxiety. Having this concern does seem appropriate when speaking about electric vehicles. It should be a concern when talking about business.

In the world of business, range anxiety can refer to several things; including, the length of time an organisation can sustain high performance, and the length of time a senior leader can remain in his (or her) job.

The length of time an organisation can sustain high performance is a direct function of several variables. I say *several* variables, but the one that has the most dramatic impact relates to the second item. This variable is all about the ability of senior people to clearly demonstrate leadership.

There is no doubt that the tip-of-the- performance iceberg is populated by such variables as profitability, market share, competitive threats, and resource availability. But these tip-of-the-iceberg variables are only good if you want to measure what has already taken place. If you want to find out how you will do in the future, you need to look below the tip-of-the-performance iceberg and look to the structures that drive performance behaviours over time. These variables include; the level of alignment and commitment to goals and initiatives; the breadth and depth of organisational values; the ability and willingness to innovate; and the impact of demonstrated leadership.

The reason that I said earlier that the key variable of range anxiety is the ability of senior people to clearly demonstrate leadership is that it is this variable that drives the level of alignment and commitment to goals and initiatives; the breadth and depth of organisational values; and the ability and willingness to innovate. Without clearly demonstrated leadership, other variables begin to slip away and cannot be sustained. And if these variables are not sustainable, high performance over time will not happen.

It should be obvious that one of the biggest impediments to clearly demonstrated leadership is a lack of one or more of the competencies of *thinking, influencing,* and *achieving.* It may not be as obvious that another big impediment is the short-term view often taken by external analysts and/or shareholders.

Typically, this is how it all works. A CEO is brought in because it is believed that he or she has the requisite talents to deliver sustainable high performance. This person typically has been chosen because of a clear track record in a similar situation, or in the case of a new company, the belief that the person's past work history is compatible with what is needed. The person begins the job with incredible support, and is able to operate with managerial and shareholder support. But over time, some cracks in the support foundation begin to appear and over time, some of the CEO's decisions begin to be questioned. At this point, it doesn't take long for the disenchantment to set in and a search for a replacement CEO is begun.

In many cases, the onset of disenchantment is perhaps warranted. But in other situations, the disenchantment is a direct function of creep of internal politics, and a demand for instant gratification on the part of shareholders. Either way, the dynamics that are put into place almost ensure that the next person to fill the CEO position will be doomed as well.

There is a strong message here, and it is one that should be learnt by the people who make the decisions regarding the hiring of senior people. The message is:
- High performance can only be sustained in an environment in which managers and employees want to make it happen
- Managers and employees will only be willing to achieve sustainable high performance in an environment in which they believe their actions are valued
- Creating an environment in which managers and employees feel valued takes time and clear demonstrations of leadership
- Giving organisational leadership the space and time to create a high performance environment requires a long-view on the part of shareholders and analysts.

This message is clear: range anxiety doesn't add any value to an organisation. If you want to add value by consistently achieving high performance, let your leaders create an environment in which it *can* happen.

# Is Alchemy a Managemeent Competence?

You remember alchemy, don't you? According to most reference books, alchemy has to do with changing lead into gold, or trying to. Over the years, alchemy, or the pursuit of it, has been connected with making something out of nothing. And now, it is apparent that in some companies, alchemy has become a management competence. Some might know the competence as 'managing with smoke and mirrors' or 'being so busy stirring things up that accountability can never take hold;' but the bottom line is the same thing – there are managers out there today who just don't get it – and then blame everyone else for their lack of ability to know what to do.

I recently was at a company in which the senior management team has developed the alchemy competency to a high degree. There I was, brought in to review how the company's senior team was making its decisions; good company – not the biggest, but over 500 people; spotty growth pattern, but almost a 20 year history; and company morale sliding downhill. After talking to some employees, I observed the senior in action for several hours. I was mystified how they had managed to survive for as long as they had before all the mid-managers quit.

Several things were going on in rarefied air of this senior management team. First, the head of the company had this pattern of behaviour in which he would hire internal consultants for specific tasks. These hires were not slouches – as a matter of fact, most of them had been pretty smart, but over a period of time – usually a year or two – they would be relegated to the scrap heap of worthless people who should be sacked. And by then, he had become enamoured with a new concept and hired someone else. The next most senior person had a pattern of behaviour in which he would keep making explicit and implicit structural changes in the mid-management that no one seemed to know what was expected of them. A nice technique – keep stirring the pot and you will never have time to see what you have made, much less, let the changes have a chance to take hold and realise their potential. And the next most senior person had a pattern of behaviour that resembled sort of a Jekyll and Hyde personality shift. For one week, he was your best friend, supporting whatever you thought was the right thing to do; and the next week, was all over you like an invasion force, taking no prisoners. The only thing that they seemed to have in common was an innate ability to expect that for their efforts, they would see consistently high performance. If this isn't the practise of alchemy in the workplace, nothing is.

And where do you suppose that I found out all this? From employees and the senior managers themselves. Talk about a political environment. In a group, you would have thought that they all had the same secret handshake, but as soon as you talked to them separately, they unleashed barrage after barrage on each other. Senior management team? Not even close. How about senior management collective was more like it. Nice place to work? Not even close again.

What these senior people seemed to not understand was that keeping things changing constantly does not create an environment for success. When I inquired why they kept everything up in the air all the time, the response I received was that they didn't feel that their employees were up to the challenge all the time. This is no different than that a parent who, deep in his heart, truly wants his children to grow up to be good citizens, good parents, and good partners. But in the process of growing up, most children begin to 'test' their own decision-making abilities. Parents are then faced with the dilemma: do we tell our children which decisions they make are wrong or do we support them, with the expectation that they will learn from mistakes? If we don't let our children make their own mistakes, how will they ever learn? It is the same with a business: if senior managers don't trust their employees to do what is best, employees will begin to not even make decisions; because if they do, they will expect that their 'collective Dads' (senior management) will criticise them constantly. Not exactly a motivator, is it?

Back to the guys in the head offices. These three top managers are at the fabled 'fork in the road.' If they continue to demonstrate the same behaviours over time, they will continue to get spotty results; they will continue to have employee morale issues; they will continue to go through supporting managers faster than water through a sieve. And more over, their behaviours are putting the company at risk. I can't tell you how many employees I spoke to were seriously thinking about moving on, but the number in percentage terms was staggering. Apparently that is okay with the senior team, after all, they seem to think they can make something from nothing...and at the rate they are going, that is what they will have to work with.

# He's a Bird; He's a Plane...No, Wait...He's Invisible

Whilst it is pretty clear that not all managers can make good leaders, the whole question about 'what is a good manager' looms large on the minds of most senior teams as they look to create more depth and breadth to the company's ranks. It is a fair question...'what are the characteristics of a good manager?' Clearly, a good manager is one who gets the job done – that is a given. But the larger question should be, 'what behaviours do our managers demonstrate?'

Several years ago, I was asked by a CEO to do some work with a quite senior person whose behaviours kept getting in the way of him getting the job done. He was good, very good actually, but he had this tendency to irritate almost all the people who worked for him. As his job responsibilities took him all over Europe, he had this tendency to fly from one city to another, day after day. And in each city, he would meet with 'his people' to monitor their progress in achieving goals. Okay, so on the surface, this sounds pretty good – a very focused manager who worked his tail off to make sure the job got done, but that is where the good news ends. I went with him on several of these trips to see what was going on, and was amazed at his stamina...and his blindness to what the unintended consequences of his behaviour were. Upon his arrival in a city, he would immediately be taken to the office where his local team was working and ask for a progress report. Then he would go on to berate his people for either not achieving the goals that had been set for them, or for not exceeding them by enough. Next would be a lecture on what would happen to them if his team didn't improve, and improve fast. Then it was off to the airport to fly to the next meeting. It was then that I understood why he was known as a 'seagull manager' – fly in, drop bad news all over the team, fly out.

In a fast-paced, ever changing business environment, making sure employees have the right guidance can be critical. There are many companies where this challenge is causing problems. The one that comes to my mind is in the UK. The company is caught in the proverbial catch-22 situation: you have to take the time to get the decisions right, whist at the same time, you can't afford to stop to even take a breath to think about what to do next. And this environment is playing havoc with some of the manager's relationships with staff. One manager that I met a while ago had so many balls in the air that it became almost impossible to juggle them successfully. He would rush from one problem to another, barely getting any of them sorted out. And this behaviour percolated down through his teams; with the outcome being that the signal was that it was 'okay' to flit about from one problem to another, with problem resolution being desirable, but rarely expected. Racing from one problem to another, a 'Concorde manager' if there ever was one.

Last year, I was in a meeting with a direct report of the CEO of a global company. His responsibilities included creating a positive work environment for all the employees of the massive company. His plans appeared to be sound, but later I found out that there were some serious undercurrents that would prevent him from accomplishing what he had been charged to do. On subsequent visits to some of the sites where his company had personnel, I enquired as to 'how things were going.' When the consistent response was 'not well,' I asked how the employees were able to communicate this upward. 'To whom?' was again a consistent response. So I would say, 'well can't you tell Mr. So-and-So?' And guess what? I have yet to find anyone in the front lines of this company who have ever heard of this person, much less the fact that the company has a person doing this type of work. Here is a senior manager who is charged with dealing with all the people issues that plague companies today, and it is as if he doesn't even exist – the 'invisible manager.' It does seem a bit strange to expect him to gain the trust of the employees if he isn't out there making contact with the employees, doesn't it?

In all of these examples, we find managers who are working their tails off, with the best of intent, but missing the point of what managing is all about. In the case of the 'seagull manager,' telling your employees that they are worthless *and then not helping them to do better* is pretty lame; and it fosters lame results. The 'Concorde manager' is so busy buzzing from one problem to another, he will never see resolutions to the problems, and this behaviour only sends the message that 'doing a lot in a mediocre way is better than doing something right.' And for the 'invisible manager,' not 'being visible' is a sure sign that the responsibilities that he had are not really important after all; and breeds the feeling of 'no one cares about us in the home office.'

All of these managers needed to do only one thing to 'change the game.' And that one thing was to look in a mirror and understand some of the unintended consequences of their behaviours. Then, it is just a choice – a choice to be a good manager (and potentially a good leader), or keep telling yourself that you are important and you know better. *(It helps if you don't have any mirrors around when you do this.)*

## Recycling Old Masters?

Have you ever wondered what happens to the 'old masters' of business? You know, the retired CEO-types who evolve from hard-core management tycoons into the guru's of business that we all, for some reason, pay enormous amounts of money to listen to. What is it that makes these guys so attractive that they command serious fees for telling their stories and spreading their business gospels? Is it that we think that what worked for them will work for us in our corporate situations? Is it that what we perceive to be business wisdom is seriously lacking in today's business climate? Or is it that we think that just by hanging out with them, we will become one of them?

I can remember not that many years ago when Dr. Deming went on the speaking circuit. He regaled us with stories of common sense techniques to improve our business. Well worth the price of admission most believed. Then there was the likes of Peter Senge – who brought us a peaceful understanding of the need to look at our organisations systemically; Stephen Covey – who we paid good money to learn how to become more effective; Tom Peters – who paced back and forth on a stage haranguing us about why our businesses were in the muck; Jack Welch – who tells us how he did what he did at General Electric; and just about every other business leader who has managed to retire without being indicted from some crime, or has just come out with a new book. We even have football coaches speaking about how their success can be translated into business. What is it that causes us to be willing to go listen?

Some might say that these guys (and the speaking circuit is certainly filled with retired business types today) tell us something that we can't get any other way. Fair enough, but many of them preach a message of *common sense* in decision-making. What? We have forgotten common sense? Well maybe, and maybe, going off to hear some guru is a good way to get it back into our heads. But I fear that paying to hear someone like Jack Welch or any of the others generates the same result as buying their books does – the books look great on your office bookshelf, but what are you learning from reading it? When we go to a seminar and listen to some expert (or just someone who believes that not being sacked makes him an expert), do we actually do things differently when we get back to the office?

It is even more interesting wondering how these guys (some of them have been on the business speaking circuit so long they make the Rolling Stones look young whilst on tour) keep current with what is going on in business today. Do they, through their individual consulting businesses (and I am sure they all hire themselves out at some pretty steep day-rates to impart their wisdom), keep abreast with current trends, the changing landscape of the business world, and the ever-evolving issues that keep managers awake at night? Or are they just telling the same old story over and over and over again?

There is an additional risk in *learning* from the old masters of business. Many of them are telling really important stories about how they did this or that in the company where they used to work. They do make great stories, but too many attendees seem to think that because Mr. So-and-So was able to pull it off in his company, they can do the same in theirs. As a very wise man once told me, *'in your dreams.'*

Because Mr. Welch did what he did at G-E, does this mean that he could do it again at some other company? Maybe, but the reality is that in most cases, tremendous business success is a function of using common sense, *and being in the right place at the right time.* We all *heard* Dr. Deming's message of continuous improvement because we were ready to hear it. A lot of us *heard* Jack Welch's message of six-sigma because we were ready to hear it. And at the time, both of these messages seemed so new, but were they really? Are we so locked into hearing about *new* things that we neglect really understanding the common sense of how to get from point A to point B? I have sat in on senior management meetings where the CEO will say that he just read a new business book and that he is buying copies for all his key managers so they can start doing whatever the book talks about. But rarely do I hear CEO's talk about creating environments in which common sense in business decision-making will be rewarded. Perhaps we have forgotten what common sense in business really is?

One could argue that some business themes are timeless and chocker with common sense: how to make better decisions, how to turn a failing business around, and even how to create an environment in which a company can realise its potential. And I suppose that a expert-type guru could tell that story repeatedly; but some of the guys out there are preaching what they believe to be *the new way*, a way that explained even further in their just-published book I imagine. This, I find, is a bit like sending your overweight, obsessively rude, drooling drinking buddy to New Bond Street everytime styles change. No matter what he buys, it won't do anything other than result in a well dressed overweight, obsessively rude, drooling drinking buddy. For managers to run off to hear the *latest thing in business* before they get in touch with common sense is about as rational.

The next time you have the opportunity to attend a speech by some business expert-guru-whiz-bang, think about what you really want to get from the talk. And then think about what you will do differently if you hear it. If investing in hearing business wisdom (or just some new theory about how to apply a little understood technique to double your production levels in the factory) is important to you, then you need to be prepared to do something differently with that message. If not, the only thing that probably will be changing is the bank balance of the speaker.

## The Illusion of "Doing the Right Thing"

I have been noticing lately that quite a few companies are doing the right thing...or so they think. With all the consultancies running about preaching 'the cure' for business ills; with all the business books prescribing remedy courses that appear to have a cook-book approach; it is no wonder that many managers feel confident that they are doing what they need to do to achieve sustainable results. But there is a lingering problem. Why is it that in so many cases, efforts to improve processes and systems seem to wilt as fast as a flower in the desert when the work is done? Could it be that management is under a false illusion that they have done everything that they need to do? I think so.

There are more cases in point for this than there are members of Parliament. Example 1: a large UK-based manufacturing company recently went through a significant programme to *tighten-up* their systems and processes. They brought in a competent group of consultants who, to be fair, did do a good job. But when the project was completed and the consultants departed, the gains began to slip away like the tide in Cornwall. Management couldn't understand what had happened. They contacted the consultants, who, sensing opportunity, came rushing back to do some *tweaking*. Within a couple of weeks, things were back to where management thought they should be; only to find that after the consultants departed again, things began to slip again.

Example 2: one of the energy giants who decided to take the opportunity of seemingly never-ending profits to join the lemming-like drive to become *lean*. After a series of workshops with high-powered, credible speakers who spoke the gospel of improvement, management was happy, and convinced that they had done the right thing. Within a month, the decision-making processes had begun to slide back to the way they were before, and if it weren't for the struggle to spend some of the gusher of profits that they were encountering, someone in a posh office might have said something. Example 3: an American service organisation that wanted to eliminate all the duplication in efforts decided to follow the path worshiped by six-sigma devotees. They sent people out to six-sigma seminars, bought books on the subject for all their managers, and brought in one of the most well renowned six-sigma consultancies. Everyone got the message, and through a Herculean effort, managed to identify massive savings through the reduction in variation in what they did. It only took the company less than six months to see the variation creep back. So what is going on here? Why are many of the gains that are achieved in these case examples lost over time (and a short time at that)?

Each of these companies forgot two key challenges. First, all the efforts that management makes to improve whatever they want to improve will fall by the wayside over time if the mid-managers and front-line employees don't see management changing too. Employees are not stupid. They can see when management is just acting out change as if they were in some business-oriented Punch and Judy puppet show. Demonstrating commitment to change is more than just sending out emails pledging 'a new way' and appearing at site-based forums to spread the word.

Second, quite a few companies out there have pretty solid management teams. Just look at the results that they are achieving. But a lesser amount of them have solid, inspirational leadership to fire the troops up, and keep them fired up. The ability to inspire employees to achieve greatness does not automatically come when someone gets that big desk and a Blackberry. Inspirational leadership is something that not everyone has, or can achieve. But it is something that can make or break an improvement effort; and without a doubt, it is one of the key things that can sustain the gains from the effort. Inspirational leadership is all about creating environments in which organisations can realise their potential.

All this brings us to the next element of illusion. It was announced this week that the Board of BT (in all their wisdom), has decided to ensure that several of their key senior people stay on the job; and they decided to do this by incentivising them with massive salary and bonus structures. How nice. Is this really the right way to keep good people? Sure, money does talk, but it does seem a bit odd to pour out cash incentives to some senior people, whilst at the same time, working desperately to keep costs down. Yes, it does seem that it is getting harder and harder to keep good talent onboard, but it also seems rather ironic that the Boards that are more than willing to spend, spend, spend to keep the senior guys in their offices are the same group of people who whinge like crazy when the employees (the ones that do the actual work) try to get a minute fraction of a rise in pay. Is the BT Board rewarding these senior types for being great managers or great leaders who inspire the employees to achieve greatness by creating environments where the company can realise its potential? Are these Boards enabling the senior guys to realise *their* potential, or just bribing them to stay?

Creating, nurturing and sustaining environments that allow organisations to realise their potential is the most important thing that a leader (or a Board) can do. Yes, making sure that the troops 'hit those numbers' is important, but anyone who can be a tough manager can do that. But hitting the numbers is not as good as ensuring that the company can realise its potential. Think about this: what if the financial targets that are sought after are just a partial view of what could be achieved? Which would you, as a shareholder, like to see? But management as a whole will never be able to marshal the employees to realise their potential unless they can connect with the people and inspire them to do so. This isn't the same as building the Bridge Over the River Kwai because this is what you have been told to do; this is more like climbing Mt. Everest, because you *want* to.

Simply deciding to go down the process improvement road, or the lean manufacturing highway, or the six-sigma motorway, or the bribery autobahn isn't enough. Demonstrating inspirational leadership and personal commitment to the journey is what the employees will either see, or not see. And that is what will determine how far down the road you will get without being sucked backwards again by the big Hoover of complacency.

## Leave the Gun, Take the Cannoli

In one of the Godfather-series movies, there is a line where Clemenza says,*"leave the gun, take the cannoli."* Clemenza provided clear, concise directions to Rocco, leaving no ambiguity of what should be done. Sadly, many managers in organisations today do the same. We have all been in meetings where a manager, when asked for more clarity, often responds with "you know what to do," or, "I think it is obvious what we expect you to do." The end result is that the one who is (supposedly) receiving clear directions is left up to his or her assumptions of what should be done. There is, of course, a way to ensure you are doing the right thing, and that way is to ask. But here is where a problem can arise.

By asking – "Sorry, but I still am not clear on what you want me to do" – it is entirely possible (and probable in many organisational structures), that your boss will begin to think you are not the right person for the job, that you are not smart enough to be on the team, or not worthy of advancement. This can lead to you not even having a job, much less the one you did have.

If you want to make sure you are doing what your boss wants you to do, you do need to ask for clarification, but in a positive way. One way that works well is to say, "Okay, here is what I am hearing you say." By repeating what you have heard, you are doing two things. First, you are demonstrating that you are listening and paying attention to what your boss perceives in "clear directions." Second, you are demonstrating that you want to make sure that you do the right thing. There are additional benefits from asking the question in this way. If you believe that you don't have the time required to do the task/lead the initiative/whatever, you can then follow up with, "Okay, good. Can you also tell me where this task/initiative/whatever fits in with our other priorities, so I can know which task/initiative/whatever I can adjust in my priorities of responsibilities?" By asking this follow-up question, it shows that you are conscious of the bigger picture and that you don't want to be spending valuable time on something that suddenly may not be as important.

Now have no doubt, your boss may not have the answers to your questions, and because of this, he or she may become a bit frustrated by your lack of blind obedience. But if that is the case, your ability to succeed over time in a company where blind obedience is more important than doing the right things for the right reasons will be pretty slim.

## Flushing Yourself Down the Drain

Everyonce in a while, a story comes along about an organisation whose management decision-making process is simply too chaotic to believe. I first heard about the organisation a few months ago, and since then, the reports of incompetence have only grown.

The organisation is international, but whilst that can make decision-making a bit complex at times, in this case, that is not where the problems lie. The problem issues are ideal for an MBA case-study programme.

**Issue 1: Organisational Vision.** Senior management has been either ineffective in sharing a corporate vision, or simply haven't worked on out yet. This one is pretty simple to understand and, consequently, do something about if management wanted to. The simply truth is that if an organisation doesn't have a clear, understandable vision of where it wants to be in the medium term (3-5 years), it will be pretty difficult to ensure that managers and employees will be able to implement decisions that will enable it to get there. This is, of course, because they won't know where "there" is.

There was a study done multiple years ago to test the importance of a clear vision. At a workshop, a participant population was divided into three equal sized groups. The groups were sent to separate areas of the room, each area having a large table. Each group was supplied with a facilitator who explained the exercise; to put together a jigsaw puzzle with the time recorded by the facilitators. Part of the challenge was that whilst all groups were given the same puzzle, in Group A, all 15 members were able to see the cover of the jig saw puzzle box. The cover of the jigsaw puzzle box has a picture of what the completed puzzle would look like. In Group B, only one person was given access to a picture of the completed puzzle. In Group C, no one was given access to the picture of the completed puzzle. Every five minutes after the exercise began, the three groups were told to stop so that the facilitators would be able to identify progress to that point; i.e. how many puzzle pieces had been correctly put together. After thirty minutes, the exercise was stopped. Group A, the group in which everyone had a picture of what the completed puzzle would look like, had managed to put together 90% of their puzzle. Group B, the group where only one person had seen what the completed puzzle would look like, was less than 50% finished. Group C, the group where no one knew what the picture of the completed puzzle would be, barely had any pieces correctly assembled.

A picture of an organisational vision is not different than the picture of a completed jigsaw puzzle; if you don't know what you are trying to achieve, it will be virtually impossible to make progress in achieving it.

### Issue 2: Setting Up Managers for Failure
The dynamic looks and acts like this. There are two employees under a manager's supervision. They both have been working for the same manager in the same department for quite some time, and when pressure to improve performance increases he looks to both employees to see how they are doing. Employee 'A' has been performing well, but not as good as employee 'B.' What does the manager do? What would you, as their manager, do? You probably would begin to supervise employee 'A' lot more than in the past. And in the process of doing that, the 'supervision' can evolve into 'second-guessing' and then a reduction in the number of decisions that employee 'A' is even *allowed* to take.

On a departmental scale, the dynamic shows up when two different business units are competing for resources. Business unit 'Y' has been successful in the past, whilst business unit 'Z' has not been delivering the performance that it is charged with delivering. You are the budgetary decision-maker who has to sort out which of these business units can receive the resources it is asking for – what do you do?

In the case of the subject organisation, the dynamic takes on a third appearance. A new manager is hired and immediately begins to demonstrate his competence and ability to deliver on goals and targets. The senior manager recognises the new manager's abilities to deliver and begins to push more responsibilities his way. The new guy takes on the challenges and in the process, sees the scope of his job take on a broader spectrum.

The senior manager continues to load on additional responsibilities, and with them, new priorities. Over time, the number of additional "priorities" have become broader and broader. However, the new guy has not been provided with additional budget for hiring support, nor has he been provide with any additional compensation. And then one day, the new guy receives a phone call from the senior manager who rips into him for not "staying focused" on his initial priorities, the one's he was hired to deliver.

In all three of these examples, the organisation is creating an environment in which managers will fail over time. When senior management see managers with an inability to consistently deliver performance, they will replace them. The reality is that this is how the new manager had been hired. The dynamic – hire new talent, but have them attempt to function in a doomed to fail environment, and then replace them – is a fundamentally systemic reinforcing dynamic, and over time, will spell doom for the organisation itself.

**Issue 3: Hierarchy Rigidity.** There is no doubt that organisations need some form of hierarchy. All population structures have some form of hierarchy, and whilst, as in the book Animal Farm by George Orwell, it is nice to think that everyone should be treated equally, the reality is that "some animals are more equal than others."

Hierarchical problems occur when managers are put in hierarchical positions for the wrong reasons, and/or without the skills and competencies to be good at what they do (or should do).

Typically there is an expectation that a hierarchical manager will coach or mentor those managers who work for him or her. This expectation is based on an assumption that the one who is higher in a hierarchy because he or she has better skills and competencies and the best way to increase the overall competence of an organisation is to have the more senior people share what they have learnt with those who work for them. On paper, this seems like a pretty good system. On paper.

The reality is that often, managers are put into hierarchical positions for the wrong reasons. An example might be that someone is put in a hierarchical position because he or she related to the most senior people, or because of a merger or acquisition. The reasons are not important. What is important is that managers who have managers and employees reporting to him or her are competent to manage, to lead, and to coach or mentor others. If they are not, the organisation itself will suffer.

**Issue 4: The Apparent Lack of Testing of Decisions.** Testing decisions is not a complex thing. In most organisations, someone makes a decision (or perhaps a team makes a decision) and then someone is instructed to go off and implement the decision. This really is pretty simple: make a decision and then implement it. Where this fails miserably is that sometimes, decisions are not good ones and when implemented, the decision can have disastrous outcomes.

By testing decisions before they are implemented, it is possible to avoid the negative impacts of poor decisions. This process is not exactly rocket science, but for some reason, company's struggle to do it. Here is how decision testing works.

- *Someone makes a decision.*
- *Before the decision is implemented, someone asks what the unintended consequences of the decision could be.*

That's the process - the *entire* process. Make a decision, and then, before trying to implement it, think about what else might happen when you implement the decision. To be fair, when testing decisions before implementing, sometimes the *"what else might happen"* can be good, or even great news. But in most situations, the *"what else might happen"* is something that wasn't thought of and that means not good.

In the subject organisation, the *"what else might happen"* also can include *"how will people react to our decision."* The descriptor

232

"people" can include internal managers and/or employees, but it can also include customers or suppliers. An example surfaced when a decision was made, and that decision – something that would negatively impact their distributors – was not communicated to the distributors that it would impact. Not only was the decision not communicated to the distributors, their input was not even solicited in the decision making process. The problems that surfaced soon after the decision was implemented began to almost immediately cause problems for management and in this case, those problems not only surfaced in the organisations bottom line, the problems also resulted in a lack of trust in management itself. This became apparent in a Ladder of Inference example.

The ladder example was used to identify the beliefs and assumptions of the distributor team upon finding out what the organisation had done.

When the decision had become visible, key people in the distributor organisation began to add meaning to that decision. In this case, the meaning that they attached to it was that there was a secret agenda going on in the organisation they distributed for. This meaning led to the assumption that the decision could be the first of multiple decisions that could hurt the distributor.

The conclusion drawn was that the subject organisation didn't care about the fact that the two organisations had worked together for a long time and were willing to sacrifice that working relationships. This conclusion led to a belief that the subject company – the one they had worked with for years – now could not be trusted. Because of this belief, they began to watch for other indicators that the organisation could not be trusted, and eventually, looked for an alternate organisation to distribute for.

Organisational vision, setting up managers to fail, hierarchy rigidity, and the lack of testing of decisions; four separate, but inter-connected elements that can devastate an organisations abiltiy to succeed and be sustainable.  The question is, if you were the most senior person in this organisation, or on the Board of Directors, would you think that its prospects were good?  If your answer is anything other than "*no,*" you are not part of the problem... *you* are the one flushing the organisation down the proverbial drain.

# Index

# About the Author

*James B Rieley is an advisor to CEO's and senior leadership teams both in Europe and the Americas. He holds an earned Ph.D. in Organisational Effectiveness, and was the CEO of a successful manufacturing company for over 20 years. Soon after selling his company in 1987, he began to advise CEO's and senior leadership teams from all sectors on how to make more effective decisions.*

*He is the author of multiple books and papers on realising personal and collective organsiational potential. He has written more than 350 weekly articles for a subscription business service, as well as a weekly column for the Daily Telegraph in London.*

*Rieley is a British citizen who currently lives in the British Virgin Islands, and can be reached at jbrieley@rieley.com*